D0917143

1 - 1 - 87

HQ
798
D8.5

Dyhouse, Carol.

Girls growing up in late
Victorian and Edwardian
England.

NORMANDALE
COMMUNITY COLLEGE
9700 France Avenue South
Bloomington, MN 55431-4399

DEMCO

GIRLS GROWING UP
IN LATE
VICTORIAN AND
EDWARDIAN
ENGLAND

STUDIES IN SOCIAL HISTORY

Editor: HAROLD PERKIN

Professor of Social History, University of Lancaster

Assistant Editor: ERIC J. EVANS

Lecturer in History, University of Lancaster

—◇—

For a list of books in the series see back endpaper

7572343

HQ
798
D8.5

GIRLS GROWING UP IN LATE VICTORIAN AND EDWARDIAN ENGLAND

DISCARDED

Carol Dyhouse

Department of Education
University of Sussex

NORMANDALE COMMUNITY COLLEGE
9700 FRANCE AVENUE SOUTH
BLOOMINGTON, MN 55431-4399

MR 01 '84

Routledge & Kegan Paul
London, Boston and Henley

First published in 1981
by Routledge & Kegan Paul Ltd
39 Store Street,
London WC1E 7DD,
9 Park Street,
Boston, Mass. 02108, USA
and Broadway House,
Newtown Road,
Henley-on-Thames,
Oxon RG9 1EN

Set in Press Roman by
Columns, Reading
and printed in Great Britain by
Redwood Burn Ltd
Trowbridge

© Carol Dyhouse, 1981

No part of this book may be reproduced in
any form without permission from the
publisher, except for the quotation of brief
passages in criticism

Library of Congress Cataloging in Publication Data

Dyhouse, Carol, 1948-
Girls Growing up in late Victorian and
Edwardian England

(Studies in social history)
Includes bibliographical references and index
1. Adolescent girls – Great Britain –
History – 19th century. 2. Adolescent girls –
Education – Great Britain – History – 19th century.
3. Feminism – Great Britain – History – 19th
century. 4. Great Britain – Social life and
customs – 19th century. I. Title. II. Series:
Studies in social history (Routledge & K. Paul)
HQ798.D85   305.2'3'0941   81-8578

ISBN 0-7100-0821-X   AACR2

To Alexandra

Contents

Acknowledgments

I should like to record my thanks to Professor Harold Perkin and Dr Eric Evans, the editors of this series, whom I first encountered as a graduate student on the MA course in Modern Social History at the University of Lancaster in 1970-1. Their interest in my work, and the encouragement they have consistently offered over a long period now, have been a great source of support. In addition to thanking my teachers, I must also thank my own students, particularly those who have participated in my seminars on the social history of women here at Sussex University, with whom I have had valuable opportunities to discuss many of the ideas which appear in this book.

I am grateful to the staff of Cambridge and Sussex University Libraries. In particular Marion Framroze and Joan Benning in the Inter-Library Loans Office at Sussex, and David Kennelly, Bet Inglis and Sheila Schaffer, working in the Documents Collection, have all proved endlessly patient in tracking down references and providing me with source material. I should like to thank Betty ffrench Beytagh and Margaret Ralph for typing successive drafts of my manuscript; and John Lowerson, who, partly through the accident of having his office situated just down the corridor from my own, provided an endless source of friendly advice and good cheer while this book was being written.

The Editors of the *Oxford Review of Education* kindly gave permission for me to re-use material which first appeared in an article entitled 'Good Wives and Little Mothers: Social Anxieties and the Schoolgirl's Curriculum, 1890-1920', published in 1977 (vol. 3, no. 1) of their journal. Faber & Faber also granted permission for me to use extracts from Winifred Peck's *A Little Learning, or a Victorian Childhood,* published in 1952.

I would not have been able even to contemplate writing this book without an enormous amount of non-academic support. In particular, I should like to express my gratitude to Maureen Ashby and Mary Kinsella; the staff of Sussex University creche and, more recently, Erna Metcalfe and Steve Greaves-Lord in the University nursery, for helping to look after my small daughter, Alexandra, during work hours. Camilla and John Dinkel provided accommodation during the miserable period when our house was being reconstructed. My parents were endlessly generous and helpful. Finally, and most importantly of all, I must thank my husband, Nicholas von Tunzelmann, for his incalculable patience and support, and for never even supposing that domestic organisation and childcare were anything other than our shared responsibility.

Introduction

This book is about the socialisation of girls — and the social construction of 'femininity' in late-Victorian and early-Edwardian England. I use the word 'socialisation' rather than 'education' advisedly because the latter is often understood to mean formal schooling. One of my major purposes here has been to show that the majority of girls living in the period 1860-1920 received at least a crucial part — if not the major part — of their education in the family, and not through schooling of any kind.

This work differs from most histories of women's education, then, in looking closely at girls' experiences in the family and in attempting to assess the influence of schooling in a broader social context. At the same time there are a number of other ways in which my aims have been different from the majority of those who have written on the subject to date. In the first place, I have been interested in the history of working-class, as much as middle-class, girls. Secondly, I have attempted to consider *experiences* of growing up and of school and family life, being anxious to avoid the kind of approach which is almost exclusively occupied with chronicling the history of educational *provision*. Where I have been concerned with the latter — with the structure and evolution of the school curriculum, for instance — I have been especially concerned with the wider ideological and institutional pressures which were brought to bear upon specific debates; such as the pressures which members of the Medical profession (insisting that the ignorance of mothers accounted for high infant mortality rates in the 1900s) exerted upon the Board of Education to include lessons in infant management and childcare to girls in elementary schools early this century.

1

A fundamental preoccupation with what I believe to be the social construction of 'femininity' has led me to scrutinise Victorian concepts of 'femininity' in both popular and 'scientific' thought. Centrally, the Victorian ideal of femininity represented economic and intellectual dependency; its prescribed service and self-sacrifice as quintessential forms of 'womanly' behaviour. From early childhood girls were encouraged to suppress (or conceal) ambition, intellectual courage or initiative — any desire for power or independence. The feelings of guilt and/or ambivalence which many strong intelligent women wrestled with in the attempt to reconcile their drives with what they had been taught to perceive as their 'feminine' social identity are a recurrent theme in the pages which follow.

The first chapter of the book examines girls' early experiences of the sexual division of labour in the family; the clear demarcation between the male/public and female/private realms so characteristic of nineteenth century middle-class life; the early initiation into sex-specific tasks further down the social scale. Relations between girls and their fathers, brothers and (particularly) their mothers structured learning about femininity through childhood and adolescent years. The second chapter is concerned with schooling and college education for middle-class girls: it argues that even the newer girls' high schools and colleges of the late-nineteenth century were in many ways highly conservative institutions, fostering conventional ideals of 'feminine' behaviour and reinforcing, essentially, the lessons of family life. In the third chapter I have set out to trace and analyse attitudes towards the socialisation of working-class girls, reflected in both the evolution of the curriculum in elementary schools and also in the organisations catering for adolescent girls which mushroomed during the period: the Girls' Friendly Society, for instance; 'Snowdrop Bands' and Guiding. The fourth chapter is concerned with theories about, and the early social-psychology of female adolescence, and particularly the work and influence of G. Stanley Hall. Finally, Chapter 5 examines feminist theory in relation to girls' education, focusing on the extent to which feminists were able to challenge the sexual division of labour and concepts of 'femininity' during the period 1860-1920. It is argued that even if the history of girls' education is narrowly conceived of as the history of the widening provision of 'educational opportunities' for middle-class girls, there is no simple tale of steady progress towards sexual equality.

2

1

First lessons in femininity:
the experience of family life

◇◇

Any understanding of the education of girls in the nineteenth century must commence with some study of family life. The family is the primary and most powerful agency of socialisation. Its role in the socialisation of girls, in particular, was even more important in late-Victorian and early-Edwardian society than it is today. It was then much more able to determine and control the influence of other social groups and institutions – especially the impact of schooling – on the growing girl. Up until the first world war, a significant proportion of upper middle-class girls never went to school at all, being educated at home under the aegis of governesses. Most of the middle-class girls who did go to school attended private schools over which the state had no control and the choice of which was entirely in the hands of their parents. In working-class families, in spite of moves towards compulsory elementary education in the 1880s and later attempts to lengthen the period of school life, girls' schooling remained a fairly short-term experience; judged by the majority, perhaps, as rather 'unreal', and commonly bitten into and ultimately curtailed by the much more real and pressing needs of the family.

Inside the family, relationships between parents and the organisation of domestic life constituted first lessons in the sexual division of labour, and if these relationships conformed to the patterns the child perceived in a widening world around her they were likely to be accepted as 'normal', part of the given order of things. Mothers provided small girls with their first models of feminine behaviour; fathers their first examples of paternalism – distance, indifference or benevolence, perhaps. They commonly appeared invested with authority or power. Where there were children of both sexes girls would be quick to perceive differences in treatment: even if they resented it they would have no choice but to realise that their parents entertained different expectations of and ambitions for their children according to sex. Then, if the household included servants, the growing understanding of social relationship and authority would be amplified by a class, as well as a sexual dimension. In this chapter I want to explore the ways in which girls learned about the sexual division of labour characteristic of their society; to see how patterns of authority were presented to them, and how they were encouraged to conceive of 'femininity' and to define themselves as 'feminine', from their childhood onwards in the family. I shall then move on to consider some of the conflicts of emotion and personality this learning implied.

Late-Victorian middle-class society had developed a very marked sexual division of labour. Men went outside the home to earn money to maintain the household. Their wives, on the whole, stayed in the home and were economically dependent on the male breadwinner. From mid-century onwards, particularly following the establishment of a railway system, urban growth had taken a distinct form which emphasised the sexual division of labour by widening the physical gap between home and workplace. Well-to-do, middle-class businessmen migrated in large numbers to leafy residential suburbs remote from the pollution and griminess of central commercial and industrial districts. Daily they travelled into work on commuter trains, leaving their women-folk and children stranded in suburbia. Katharine Chorley, growing up in Alderley Edge, a prosperous suburb of Manchester, late last century recalled that:

> After the 9.18 train had pulled out of the station the Edge became exclusively female. You never saw a man on the hill roads unless it were the doctor or the plumber, and you never saw a man in any-one's home except the gardener or the coachman.[1]

The pattern was repeated in suburbs characterised by greater or lesser degrees of affluence, all over urban England. Children of suburban households grew up in a world where they expected their fathers to be absent all day; seeing them briefly, perhaps, in the evenings, otherwise only at weekends. The distinction between mother's world — the private, comparatively leisurely routine of the home and neighbourhood activities; and father's world — distant, invisible — a public world

4

of regular time-keeping and rather vague but decidedly important activities, was abundantly clear.

In working-class families the sexual division of labour might be less clear cut. For those who remained in the central areas of large towns there was less separation of home and workplace. In the metal-working districts of Birmingham and Sheffield, for instance, families might still live alongside small workshops. Children would have seen their fathers working and fathers did not necessarily automatically absent them-selves from the daily life of the family. In areas where work was organised in larger factories, fathers might disappear regularly, but the kind of work they did might still have been more visible and familiar to their children. In some parts of England such as the textile districts of Lancashire or the Potteries a sizeable proportion of married women — even those with small children — remained in fairly regular, full-time employment. Further, working-class mothers almost everywhere were very likely to supplement the family income with some form of home or neighbourhood-based casual employment. In rural areas this might have taken the form of casual, seasonal work on the land: gleaning at harvest time, stone picking, or gathering fruit. In the towns women ran corner shops, or even set up shop in their front rooms. They often went charring or took in washing for other families. Sometimes there were lodgers to be seen to, or babies to mind for other working mothers.

All these factors served to blur the distinction between a father's world of paid work and a mother's world — dependent, and in the home — that most middle-class children took for granted. But it is important not to exaggerate the picture: working-class children were also presented with a society in which there were important differences between 'men's work' and 'women's work'. To begin with, the cate-gories themselves were distinct: that is, there were certain trades in which men worked, others dominated numerically by women. In trades which employed both sexes, there tended to be certain pro-cesses defined as women's work and different processes employing men. And women's work tended to be less secure and, of course, markedly less remunerative, than men's. Most important of all we should remember that if we take the figures for the country as a whole, the proportion of married women who remained in full-time employ-ment outside the home was relatively small. One cannot know the precise figure. The 1901 census for England and Wales recorded that 917,509 out of a total of 6,963,944 married or widowed women were returned as having a full-time occupation.[2] However, several historians

5

have pointed out that this is probably an under-estimate: many women, aware of social opposition to married women's work outside the home, may have preferred not to declare themselves as 'occupied'. The figure cannot indicate the extent of *casual* labour amongst women in working class areas.[3] At the same time, we are left with the impression that most married women did give up full-time paid work outside their homes. This was particularly likely when there were very young children at home: it should be pointed out that the figure of 13 per cent mentioned above would have included married or widowed women who were childless, as well as those whose children were no longer fully dependent on them.

The 1901 General Report of the Registrar-General suggested that the proportion of occupied married women had decreased over the country as a whole since 1881.[4] There were economic and social reasons for this. As real wage rates rose in some occupational groups after 1870, social aspirations changed. Middle-class ideals of domestic organisation filtered down the social scale.[5] Katharine Chorley, recording her closeted, middle-class upbringing could not

> remember any woman in our circle who had a career or a paid job
> of her own, either a married woman or a spinster. A paid job for one
> of his womenfolk would have cast an unbearable reflection of in-
> competence upon the money-getting male.[6]

Concepts of dependency may not have spread quite so far lower down the social scale, in that a workman would not necessarily have felt that it was his duty as a man to maintain his sisters. But in the last quarter of the century a 'respectable' working man aimed to support his wife and children in some degree of comfort. Married women's work – for a wage, outside the home – was decidedly *not* respectable. A working wife endangered a husband's status and self-respect, bringing into question both his class position and somehow, his manhood, because definitions of masculinity were so intimately bound up with a particular form of domestic life. So, too, were patterns of authority, still revealed in common speech. Men might object to their wives working lest they should want 'to wear the trousers' – a crime against what they would argue to be the natural order of things.

Social opposition to married women's work can be argued to have increased in early twentieth-century Britain. The contribution of women to industry and commerce during both world wars did little to break down barriers against the employment of wives and mothers in peacetime, indeed these prohibitions were made, if anything, more explicit. The Report of the Women's Employment Committee of the Ministry of Reconstruction, published in 1919, recommended categorically that: 'The employment of married women outside their homes is not to be encouraged', and added that 'Factory crèches in normal times are not approved of.'[7] During the 1920s, some local educational authorities instituted new regulations requiring teachers in their employ to resign on marriage.[8] In industry, women reluctant to relinquish jobs were castigated by the national press, accused of greed and avarice, ingratitude to war-heroes, of stealing the bread out of other (dependent, womanly) women's mouths. The 1921 census indicated that the proportion of women as a whole gainfully employed had actually shrunk since 1911.[9] The proportion of married or widowed women occupied between 1901 and 1931 stayed at about 13 per cent.[10] In the meantime the ranks of the widows must have multiplied because of war losses. But married women were still not encouraged to earn a living.

Fathers, then, were breadwinners, and children from both middle- and working-class backgrounds were likely to grow up in households organised round the man's needs as a wage-earner. The prosperous businessmen dressed for the City who lined the platforms of suburban railway stations each morning were setting off into a world remote from their children's experience. It was emphatically a male world of public events and finance. Ladies were excluded from this world as effectively as they were from a gentleman's club or from the port-drinking sessions that followed dessert. Katharine Chorley tells us that

> When I tried to sketch the neighbours on the station platform, I
> was thinking exclusively of the heads of families and their sons.
> That was partly because there would be no females on the platform
> except the occasional embarrassed one who had to catch an early
> train, and partly because the womenfolk moved across my daily
> scene and I cannot detach them so easily from it.[11]

Women wanting to go shopping in town were careful to avoid travelling on the men's commuter train: it was not seemly, even if one could guarantee the seclusion of an empty compartment. A small girl growing up in suburbia accepted as Katharine Chorley did, even without putting it into words, that this male, public world was inaccessible to her: for her brother, on the other hand, it was merely a time of waiting. One day, he would be automatically initiated into its mysteries.

7

Chorley adds further that she could not sketch women alongside men on the railway platform because

> it should not come natural to put them on an equality. For the men were the money-lords, and since for almost every family the community values were fundamentally economic, it followed that their women were dependents. They existed for their husband's and father's sakes and their lives were shaped to please masculine vanity.[12]

She had learned from the beginning that she lived in 'a man-made, and a man-lorded society'.[13]

There were many other aspects of organisation in a middle-class household which would have reinforced children's impression of the dignity and separateness of the male world. The existence of a study, for instance, into which fathers might retire in the evenings, a place into which the children did not normally venture, at least without knocking to announce their presence. Father's study, in many annals of middle-class childhood, had something of the atmosphere of the Gentleman's Club about it − leather armchairs, newspapers and account books, the odour of tobacco which would have been out of place in the drawing room. There was often a clear assumption that father's activities − from reading the newspaper during or after breakfast to struggling with the intricacies of family finance − were sacrosanct. His time was precious. A mother's time, however, mattered much less − her attention was often freely available to her husband, her children, the servants' needs and demands. Women generally were not expected to have any occupation which might stand in the way of their time being freely disposable for other people's needs, a fact bemoaned by many through the period − by Florence Nightingale,[14] for instance, and by Beatrice Webb.[15]

Lower down the social scale the status of the man in the family was often made just as clear to his children, albeit in different ways. Again the household was most likely to have been organised around *his* pattern of work. Mothers would often rush round to finish their own tasks, and to get the children fed and 'out of the way' so that they might have their husband's meal waiting for him when he came home from work. Fathers were likely to get the best food − if the supply of meat was limited, it was common for the rest of the family to make do with gravy and potatoes. Flora Thompson, growing up in a hamlet on the Oxfordshire-Northamptonshire border in the 1880s remembered that:

8

When the men came home from work they would find the table spread with a clean whitey-brown cloth, upon which would be knives and two-pronged steel forks with buckhorn handles. The vegetables would then be turned out into big round yellow crockery dishes and the bacon cut into dices with much the largest cube upon Feyther's plate.[16]

After the evening meal, the best chair by the fire might be as sacrosanct for father's use as the study was in middle-class households. Countless children must have grown up accepting it as quite normal for their father to expect time to relax and smoke his pipe, or to go drinking with his mates in the evenings, whilst their mothers toiled incessantly with household tasks.

Small boys in working-class households might be given to understand very early on that they would soon be able to make a more substantial contribution to their family's resources than would their sisters. This was especially the case in localities where opportunities for women's paid employment were scarce, or in rural areas where the large majority of girls just approaching adolescence were expected to go into service. Flora Thompson described how girls of twelve or thirteen were made to feel they constituted a drain on the family budget if they went on living at home, they were expected to go out at that age or even earlier to more affluent households as living-in domestic servants. From the time she left school the girl

> was made to feel herself one too many in the overcrowded home; while her brothers, when they left school and began to bring home a few shillings weekly, were treated with a new consideration and made much of. The parents did not want the boys to leave home. Later on, if they wished to strike out for themselves, they might even meet with opposition, for their money, though barely sufficient to keep them in food, made a little more in the family purse, and every shilling was precious. The girls, while at home, could earn nothing.[17]

First lessons in the sexual division of labour were not limited to observing patterns of activity in which adults involved themselves. As soon as they were capable, children were recruited into these activities in a way which was often highly sex-specific. M.K. Ashby, whose childhood was spent in rural Warwickshire at the turn of the century, vividly recalled the sexual division of labour in her home.

The girls helped their mother with housework, dairy and cooking, the boys went out on the farm with their father.[18] Saturday was a day of extremely hard domestic work, making bread, scrubbing tables and floors, cleaning everyone's boots ready for the leisure of the sabbath. Boys worked in the garden, girls in the house; the girls often feeling they had the worst of it:

> Sometimes the girls would feel that fate did not deal evenhandedly between the sexes. Father and brothers when dark fell or the weather was stormy could sit reading newspapers and books, but if Mother sat, it was to darn or patch and they themselves in the worst times spent evenings making next day's pudding, chopping suet in the cold kitchen or stoning raisins on the hearth.[19]

Hannah Mitchell, who grew up on a farm in the Peak District of Derbyshire in the 1870s and 1880s, recalled similar memories of how the girls had been expected to do heavy household tasks. Their mother

> made us sweep and scrub, turn the heavy mangle on washing days and the still heavier churn on butter-making days. Stone floors had to be whitened, brasses and steel fire-irons polished every week. On winter evenings there was sewing by hand, making and mending shirts and underwear. At eight-years-old my weekly task was to darn all the stockings for the household, and I think my first reactions to feminism began at this time when I was forced to darn my brothers' stockings while they read or played cards or dominoes.[20]

The boys, then, had time to themselves — the girls were rarely allowed this luxury:

> Sometimes the boys helped with rug-making or in cutting up wool or picking feathers for beds and pillows, but for them this was voluntary work; for the girls it was compulsory, and the fact that the boys could read if they wished filled my cup of bitterness to the brim.[21]

Similarly, Gladys Otterspoor, talking to Mary Chamberlain about her childhood in the fens in the 1900s, remembered:

> we had to knit father's socks. And make his flannel shirts they used to wear then. Them were too dear to buy. You had to buy a bit of stuff and make them into a shirt. We couldn't stop out to play much, especially as we got older. We all had to sit and sew. We didn't

go out and play. The boys, they had a better time than us.[22]

Examples could be multiplied. And in urban areas, too, girls were frequently expected to make much more of a contribution to domestic work than their brothers. Mrs Layton, whose childhood was spent in Bethnal Green in the 1860s, recalled that she and one of her sisters used to stay away from school to help their mothers on washing days, and that it was a common practice in her neighbourhood to keep the elder girls at home in this way.[23] And if the girl's own family did not absorb all her available time in household work, urban society generally furnished plenty of opportunities for carrying out domestic work such as step-cleaning or child-minding – often for a pittance – for other families in the locality.[24]

In middle-class households children were less likely to be required to make any contribution to domestic work. In highly prosperous households there would be an army of servants with carefully designated tasks and responsibilities according to their particular skill, age, experience, and even more important, their sex. The division of labour and structure of authority amongst servants in an upper-middleclass household often mirrored that of the family 'above stairs'. This pattern was likely to have been almost unconsciously accepted by the children of the employing family as a normal one. Male employees saw to garden, stables, estates. In the house itself, the senior male was the butler, his status and authority over the other servants unquestioned. His male precincts were the cellars, the butler's pantry. The cook was the senior female. Her attitude to her underlings might be protectively 'maternal' or tyrannous (as repressive, indeed, as the real mother-daughter tie could sometimes prove to be). The worst drudgery fell to the lot of the most junior female members of the servants' hall – scullery, kitchen or 'tweenie' maids.[25]

In more modest middle-class households with one or two servant girls only, boys' time, when they were not at school, might have been considered their own but their sisters would more likely have been expected to contribute to domestic work. According to her biographer, Dorothea Beale's comfortable middle-class upbringing failed to exempt her from 'the inevitable sock-darning which falls to a girl's portion in a family of so many boys'.[26] Minding babies or younger siblings was seen to be also the most natural duty of the elder daughters in the family if a nursemaid was not to be employed, or enjoying an afternoon's holiday.[27]

11

Girls were taught that deference towards brothers was part of the natural order of things. It is interesting to note Lilian Faithfull, who followed Miss Beale as the Principal of Cheltenham Ladies' College, discussing what seemed to her the advantages and disadvantages of co-education in the 1920s.[28] She noted that advocates of co-education commonly maintained that boys became more courteous and chivalrous towards women when educated alongside girls: she herself felt that this was a rather unnatural restraint on their exuberant energies and spirits:

> In family life sisters are not as a rule treated with this consideration until long after school-days. If there is a fishing expedition their lot it to put on the worms for the elder brothers or to stay at home, and they meekly choose to serve. Strength — yes, even brutal strength — is secretly admired by girls, and the age of the 'perfect gentle knight' is not the school age.[29]

Moralists and writers of manuals on 'womanly behaviour' in the second half of the nineteenth century constantly exhorted their young female readers to curb their spirits: 'natural exuberance' in a boy approaching puberty was 'hoydenish behaviour' in a girl. In the opening pages of *The Daisy Chain* (1856) Charlotte M. Yonge makes it clear that impulsive behaviour or argument with governesses may be tolerated in a young male, but constitutes an impertinence not to be countenanced for a moment in his sister. Girls should seek opportunities to wait on their brothers' comfort.[30] In their recent survey of fiction written for girls Mary Cadogan and Patricia Craig describe a story published by *The Girls' Realm* (which they describe as a relatively 'progressive' publication of its kind) in 1899.[31] The story was entitled 'The Strike of the Sisters' and featured two sisters who rebelled against having to wait on their inconsiderate brothers' needs. The boys refused to submit to their sisters' demands that they should become tidier round the house and deadlock ensued. Eventually, the grandmother persuaded the girls that they were misguided, that it was women's duty to make the house comfortable for menfolk, and both men and women stood to lose out if they did not work together, each with their allotted tasks, to keep up the family position in society.

Girls' magazines and journals told their readers that they might exercise an uplifting moral influence over their brothers by keeping before these latter a model of true feminine behaviour and refinement which the boys would learn to respect and cherish. But one doubts whether this respect for budding feminine refinement significant modified the balance of power between sisters and brothers when it was so generally weighted in favour of the latter. Molly Hughes, the youngest child and only girl in a middle-class family living in London in the 1870s, found herself alternatively petted and patronised by her four older brothers, whom she looked up to adoringly.[32] Molly argued that it was her mother's fear that as the baby of the family she would be spoilt which made her proclaim the rule 'Boys first':

> I came last in all distribution of food at table, treats of sweets, and so on. I was expected to wait on the boys, run messages, fetch things left upstairs, and never grumble, let alone refuse.[33]

This was said without any trace of resentment, Mrs Hughes adding that she had never ceased 'to thank her mother for this bit of early training'. Mrs Thomas, Molly's mother, retained deeply conservative views about a woman's role to the end of her life; views which she managed to pass on very successfully to both her daughter and her sons. Molly's descriptions of her eldest brother, Tom, in the first volume of her autobiography, are tolerant and reflect the fact that she idolised him but the reader is still left with the impression of a self-important young chauvinist. Tom was responsible for organising a kind of family club, called 'The Library', governed by a set of rules which he himself drew up. ('Now whatever else Tom had failed to learn at Shrewsbury,' Molly observed, 'he had acquired the knack of ruling others, and by common consent he became a kind of Dictator.')[34] The rules invaded every aspect of family life, from the use of the study to the brushing of one's teeth. Transgressions were punished with fines levied by Tom:

> For small misdemeanours, such as doing sums aloud, shaking the table, or spilling the ink, Tom executed summary justice by means of a big, round, black ruler, that always lay on the table like the mace in Parliament. 'Hold out your hand', he would say very quietly and down would come the blow, fairly softly if you were quick in holding out your hand.[35]

Molly herself, evidently, was exempt from these finger-rappings – a reflection, no doubt, of Tom's respect for her feminine frailty. However, one day, she recalled,

> I was foolish enough to defy Tom. He was busy, and told me to pick

up a piece of paper that had floated on the floor. 'No, I won't', said I, and dreading what he might do to me, I fled in real terror to my bedroom, and crouched down on the farther side of the bed and hid under the valance. Tom followed at a leisurely pace, came over, picked me up in his arms without a word, and carried me up to the study. There he made my hand grasp the bit of paper and place it on the table. I felt very foolish, and strange as it may seem, that is the only difference I have ever had with Tom throughout our lives.[36]

Tom (the reader will not be surprised to learn) soon embarked upon a career as a schoolmaster teaching classics in a boys' public school. From Molly's description he appears to have remained a rather conventional teacher, highly concerned with questions of authority, discipline and obedience all his life.

Molly's respect for her brothers was increased by the fact that they all went to school; first to a local private school, then Tom when on to Shrewsbury, the others on to Merchant Taylors'. Until she was twelve years old their sister stayed at home and was taught by their mother. Molly seems to have lived vicariously through her brothers' schooling. 'So much did I hear about the school and the masters', she wrote later, 'that I feel almost an old Taylorian myself (especially since I have had two sons there)'.[37] Quite substantial sections of the autobiography which she wrote in the 1930s are devoted to anecdotes from her brothers' school-days, and pen-portraits of the characters and idiosyncrasies of the masters who taught them.

The experience of being kept at home and being taught by mothers or governesses whilst brothers were sent away to school was one shared by large numbers of middle-class girls in the second half of the nineteenth century, and right up to the time of the first world war. Many of these girls envied their brothers, fully aware of the fact that a boy's education was considered a much more important affair by their parents, and worthy of more expenditure. Sisters waited eagerly for their brothers to return during vacations; when they did come back they sometimes felt rather overawed by their learning. The brothers, one senses from countless autobiographies, were likely to return home imbued with a new self-consciousness and sense of their own importance. They might patronise their sisters, lending them books sometimes or helping with homework if they felt magnanimous; sometimes too aloof to have very much to do with them at all. And the few occasions

14

on which the middle-class girl might come into contact with the public school world would be when she was given the opportunity to visit her brothers' *alma mater* on prizegivings, or school speech days, occasions which saw her invariably attired in frilly white muslin, probably nurturing half-formed romantic fantasies about her brothers' handsome friends. Vera Brittain's recollections of her visit to Uppingham, where her brother Edward had received his schooling, spring immediately to mind.[38] Few young men could have so distinguished themselves with academic honours as did her first love, Roland. But many adolescent girls would have shared memories of July lawns and dignified assemblies in school chapels, occasions when the majesty of the male world and the achievement of its gilded youth was amply confirmed.

The more intelligent middle-class girls who were educated at home sometimes profited indirectly from their brothers' education in school and college. Some apparently set out to conquer certain branches of learning ostensibly in order to help their brothers' studies. Nora Balfour (later Mrs Henry Sidgwick), living at home in Whittingehame in the late-1860s, decided to brush up her mathematics in order to be able to help her brother with trigonometry for his entrance examination to Cambridge.[39] Dorothea Beale, after leaving school herself, determined to follow Latin grammar lessons with her brothers (who were at the Merchant Taylors' school) partly in order to be able to help them, but also to develop her own understanding of the language.[40] But both of these women were exceptional. More usually the boys, initiated into the mysteries of mathematics and classics at their public schools, helped their sisters. Even when the girls were sent away to school the quality of the education they received was generally markedly inferior, in academic terms, to that of their brothers. Even Molly Hughes, privileged to receive the last phase of her schooling at the North London Collegiate School under Miss Buss in the 1880s, continued to need help from her brothers in classics and mathematics.[41] Their feeling of superiority survived unchallenged. Indeed, Tom's was amply confirmed on one memorable occasion when Molly 'imported' him to help the senior girls with their choice of a Greek play. Tom wrote the entire play for them – based on Pope's *Iliad*, and his masculine vanity must have been well flattered by Miss Buss's gratitude.[42]

Many women have written accounts of their upbringing which call to mind George Eliot's descriptions of Maggie Tulliver in *The Mill on the Floss*, eager to learn from her brother's books, disappointed and frustrated by a growing awareness that adults took her intelligence

15

lightly and expected little of her: she was only a girl. Hannah Mitchell recalled that when her brothers were sent away to school during the week (there was no school near enough their home for them to be able to attend as day scholars), she bribed them to lend her books and to share with her their new and precious learning:

> Finding that the schoolmaster was willing to lend the boys any books they wished to bring home at weekends, I made a bargain with them. I offered to do several small tasks, such as cleaning boots, or gathering firewood, which they were expected to perform at weekends, on the understanding that they brought me home a book each Friday; if no book were forthcoming, the work would be found undone the following week, I told them. But on the whole they played fair, and even asked the schoolmaster for books suitable for me. They also taught me the multiplication table and a few simple sums in addition.[43]

Hannah Mitchell's sister, Lizzie, followed their brothers to school, their mother promising Hannah that she should have her turn when Lizzie finished. But she failed to keep this promise. When Lizzie left school her mother decided that Hannah 'knew far too much "book learning" ', and should settle down to work more suited to her age and sex. Hannah's sense of betrayal, and her resentment of her mother lasted for the rest of her days.[44]

This raises a theme of crucial importance when we are considering the way girls were brought up and the way they learned about femininity: the question of a girl's relationship with her mother. Hannah Mitchell's relationship with her mother seems to have been bitterly hostile on both sides from a very early stage. The mother had not wanted a child when Hannah was born, and does not appear to have been a very happy woman, generally disliking the remote farmstead where she was destined to spend her married life: 'She had no love for animals', wrote her daughter, 'and detested the constant round of milking, feeding calves, poultry and pigs, while the dirt brought into the house during the process nearly drove her frantic.'[45] Mrs Webster apparently drove herself and her family into frenzied, relentless efforts to keep the household clean, her daughter accusing her of even using the left-over soap-suds on washing days to scrub and wash the pigs.[46] She had no sympathy at all with the ambitions of her dreamy and book-loving daughter, Hannah, and poured scorn on her efforts at intellectual self-improvement. The relationship deterioriated to such

16

an extent that Hannah eventually ran away from home. An antipathy had sprung up between them, Hannah wrote over fifty years later,

> Which lasted all our lives. I never quite forgave her my lack of education, and she never forgave me for my lack of interest in the things she considered important. Although she lived to the age of ninety, and in her later years owed much of her comfort to me, she never showed any gratitude, never regarded me as anything but the one failure among her children, and always spoke contemptuously of my desire for culture.[47]

Partly because of Mrs Webster's own profound unhappiness, partly because both she and her daughter were extremely determined women with violent tempers, this relationship was an exceptionally bad one. But it is by no means unusual to find those women who have left us autobiographical accounts of their childhood in working-class families, both urban and rural, complaining that their mothers treated them rather harshly, or at least that their mothers were consistently less tolerant of their daughters than their sons. It could be that the accounts are self-selective, that the women who eventually came to document their experience were themselves rather unusual personalities who would have been more likely to have clashed, when young, with the conventions of their families and their mother's ideas about proper womanly behaviour. Even so, many girls do appear to have felt that somehow their brothers received preferential treatment. Flora Thompson observed that even when daughters went dutifully away into service, skimping and saving on their own expenditure in order to send what meagre wages they could home to help their mothers, mothers seemed to favour sons:

> Strange to say, although they were grateful to and fond of their daughters, their boys, who were always at home and whose money barely paid for their keep, seemed always to come first with them. If there was any inconvenience, it must not fall on the boys; if there was a limited quantity of anything, the boys must still have their full share; the boys' best clothes must be brushed and put away for them; their shirts must be specially well-ironed, and tit-bits must always be saved for their luncheon afield. No wonder the fathers were jealous at times and exclaimed, 'Our Mum, she do make a reg'lar fool o' that boo-oy!'[48]

Since Freud we must suspect something Oedipal in this. But more

17

viously, mothers sensed they had rather less control over their sons n their daughters. Young boys were more often out of the home — working near their fathers and uncles on the fields in the countryside, perhaps, or in a variety of casual work, running errands, or delivering newspapers in the city. We have seen how daughters would be more likely to have been seen as a captive labour force by their mothers, overwhelmed by the constant demands of small children and by domestic chores in the home. At times their impatience with, and some-time bullying behaviour towards their daughters must have stemmed from sheer exhaustion. Several accounts recognise this. Maggie Fuller, who was born in Leith, the dockland area of Edinburgh, vividly re-called the hardship endured by her family after the first world war, when her father had been disabled and hence lost his job. Her mother had taken on a cleaning job and Maggie herself had left school early (at thirteen-and-a-half) to earn money. As well as working in a bakery, she also came home at lunch-time to feed the children and do house-work. One night, she remembers:

I had a rough time with the kids and I couldn't cope with them by the time I came home. You're young, you're fourteen, what can you do? There had been a right fight and I was a bit late with the tea and we always had somebody looking out the window for mum coming home because she was so tired. My mother was scrubbing for the school, we used to look for her and somebody would say, 'Here she's coming', and you ran to make the tea. Well this night there was only a wee drop of tea in the pot — I forgot that — and it stood up on this big high mantelpiece, and one of the kids came up against me and I just dropped this tea and it went all over the floor. And then she was up and into the house and she nearly killed me for that, somebody pulled her off, she was choking the life out of me. Mind I don't hold it against her, as I say — you've no idea what it was like with all these ruddy kids.[49]

Winifred Foley, growing up in the Forest of Dean in the 1920s, recalled a similar occasion when her mother had had to rely on her to cook the potatoes for supper while she had had to go out with the youngest children to find food. Winifred, engrossed in a book, had forgotten to do this. Her mother had returned, nerves frayed and utterly worn-out, but had miraculously managed to restrain the out-burst of violent temper which her daughter clearly expected in the circumstances.[50] This kind of episode must have been all too frequent

18

in large families with limited resources.

There is no shortage of evidence to illustrate the incredible hardships endured by working-class mothers of large families right through the period under review: in the early decades of this century the publication of studies like *Maternity: Letters from Working Women* (1915) by the Women's Co-operative Guild, and Margery Spring-Rice's *Working-Class Wives, their Health and Conditions* (in 1939) brought some awareness of this suffering before the middle-class public.[51] Large numbers of working-class women were prematurely aged and worn out by yearly childbearing and the toll this took on their bodies and spirits, particularly when the family's well-being was constantly threatened by a shortage of nourishing food. This sometimes engendered bitterness; more often, perhaps a grim fatalism — an acceptance of the amply demonstrated fact that the world was a joyless place for women, which must have coloured the relationship between mothers and daughters. Mothers could see no escape for their daughters — the best that they could hope for was that they would marry responsible men who kept out of the pub, and that they would be strong enough to cope with the round of unceasing drudgery that would inevitably be their portion.

There was no sense, then, in coddling a girl. Better to accustom her from the start to the kind of work she would eventually have to do. At the same time, accounts sometimes suggest that even the most authoritarian and unsentimentally inclined mothers might be fiercely protective of their daughters, especially when they were being overworked or bullied by others outside the family. Mothers commonly intervened on a daughter's behalf, for instance, when the latter went into service and the mother considered the daughter was not being treated well by her employer. Maggie Fuller, who has just been mentioned, eventually left home because she felt she was being bullied by her mother. When she went into service she was expected to rise at six to scrub steps, but Maggie's mother thought otherwise:

> My mother said no, that day and age was done. She said, 'You can go down and give them a brush, but she's not doing that.' So my mother came another time and I was out. She was waiting when I came back and she said, 'Am I not going to get a cup of tea?' I said 'I'll see what there is', and there was a slice of bread with a wee drop of jam and butter on it and one dry biscuit and that was my tea. And my mother said, 'Is that your tea?' And I said 'Yes'. 'Take me

to her', she said. 'No lassie of mine — you canna work for that'.[52]

In the nineteenth century it was not only the working-class mother who might suffer ill-health through constant child-bearing. The middle-class mother was well-fed and may have had servants to look after her, but she might still suffer. A remarkable proportion of the women who have left us accounts of their upbringing seem to have shared the experience of having sofa-ridden mothers at some stage in their youths, and even if some of these were suffering from *maladies imaginaires*, their neuroses, as much as the physical symptoms of weakness and ill-health, must have made a marked impression on their children. Daughters on such occasions might feel they had to 'stand in' for their mothers as well as nurse them through their ailments. A.J. Clough and Eleanor Sidgwick, née Balfour (the first two principals of Newnham College, Cambridge) and Constance Maynard (mistress of Westfield College, London) all spent long periods in their youth nursing their mothers.[53] The young men in such families might well have grown up accepting it as 'natural' that women's health would be damaged by maternity and that the female sex was weaker than the male. And daughters would surely have entertained mixed feelings about their own futures. In 1935 Winifred Holtby remarked,

> It often happens that, just as the girl is first facing the complexities and problems of the adult world, her mother is going through the physical and nervous disturbance of the climacteric. With some women this creates little trouble; but it would be stupid to deny that under present conditions the majority of women do, from the ages of about forty-five to fifty, suffer from headaches, indigestion, low blood-pressure or some other form of disabling if not crippling disability. The fact that later most of them regain their second youth, and live to a longer, healthier and more active old age than their husbands, is a truth which their daughters, aware chiefly of the domestic scene below their noses, are tempted to ignore. To most young people in their twenties, middle-aged women all-too-often appear as physical crocks. And that discourages them.[54]

At least, she might have added — the girls.

One important aspect of the relationship between mothers and daughters in all social groups concerned the sexual education of the daughter. We don't have enough evidence to be able to generalise about dominant patterns. But few oral historians or others who have talked to women born early this century have failed to uncover stories of girls kept in astounding ignorance about their sexuality. Letters written to Marie Stopes in the 1920s show that extreme ignorance about sexuality and reproduction pervaded all social levels.[55] Mothers too prudish to discuss even the existence of the menstrual cycle with their daughters often condemned them to a frightening experience at puberty. The only information Maggie Fuller's mother passed on to her when she began to menstruate was the cryptic injunction that at such times she should 'keep away from men'.[56] Other women talking to Jean McCrindle and Sheila Rowbotham had had similarly traumatic experiences. Fiona MacFarlane, who grew up in Glasgow in the 1930s and 1940s, remembered running, screaming with fear, to her mother when her periods started. Her mother merely told her to stop her nonsense; that she was a woman now, but failed to warn her that the bleeding would return each month.[57] Fiona was too embarrassed to mention the subject again, and nursed her shame in secret, eventually working out from advertisements for sanitary towels in women's magazines that her experience was normal.

A mother's own embarrassment over the subject of menstruation inevitably communicated itself to her daughter who was likely to feel somehow shamed, unclean. Naomi Mitchison (née Haldane), brought up in a prosperous, intellectual upper middle-class family in Oxford in the 1900s, vividly described her experience of puberty:

I was twelve, still at the Dragon School unsuspecting. I had little or no pubic hair, my breasts were ungrown and did not in fact develop until my mid-teens. And then there was blood on my blue serge knickers. I was quickly pulled out of school and I never went back. I couldn't quite understand why, only it seemed that it was something about me which was shameful and must above all never be mentioned to a school friend. It had been a complete surprise, because I had not taken in my mother's carefully veiled and no doubt physiologically inaccurate information. The process was not at all well-known at that time, and there were many superstitions about it and little medical help. Even for unbelievers a reading of the Old Testament (those bits of *Leviticus* probably gobbled while one was supposed to be merely taking in the bloodthirsty tribal adventures of *Kings*) with its perpetual reference to uncleanness added to one's unpleasant feelings. For many years I had monthly pain, distress and acute embarrassment; I was taken to various

21

doctors, but, as nobody understood the physiological process, this did not help. The curse, as it was always called, was a main trouble all my life.[58]

Femininity, in this kind of context, would be understood as something of a secret pollution: mother and daughter feeling themselves involuntarily bound together in the possession of this guilty, shameful secret. This was unlikely to increase their respect for each other as women because they were both cursed with the misery of their sex. (The widespread use of the term 'the curse' to mean menstruation is of course significant.) One might judge this one of the most important roots of repression.

Prudery in some middle-class homes could be so extreme that it was impossible even to mention the lavatory by name. Ursula Bloom, the daughter of a clergyman, remembered that in the 1900s her family and friends suffered agonies of shame when they were unable to visit the lavatory in total secrecy.[59] Both she and Naomi Mitchison recall that servants, men and women of the family used separate lavatories. It would have been degrading for the women to use the gentlemen's and impossibly contaminating even to *consider* using the servants' toilet.[60] Ursula Bloom remarked that girls even refused invitations to go out or to visit other houses, sometimes out of a secret terror lest they should need to visit the lavatory. At children's parties, she recalled,

One's Nanny had the jitters, for this was the thorn in her flesh, and she always got agonized. No-one would tell her where 'it' was. What did she do? Enquire from the butler, and he a MAN? Most certainly not! From the hostess, who being a lady could not possibly know of the existence of such places? What indeed? She would not speak to a lower servant, who took the coats and scarves, for upper servants did not consort with those beneath them in position, so this was another dead end. Frustration would give Nanny the hot flushes and she would say 'Whatever you do, dear, don't drink too much'.[61]

Women undoubtedly suffered much more than men from this kind of prudery, because of the rigid conventions which had grown up around ideals of feminine purity and modesty. Mothers, of course, played a central role in educating their daughters in these conventions of feminine modesty. Inwardly, to be a woman might imply a guilty feeling that one was somehow impure — but this had to be repressed:

22

the essence of femininity was defined as purity, and little girls should appear innocent, virginal, and unsullied in every way. Dressed in white muslin frills, they were adjured to keep clean, to keep quiet, and to keep still. Improprieties might be ruthlessly censored when a mother had a very particular sense of what constituted 'ladylike' behaviour. Lady Henry Somerset remembered that as a young debutante she had been staying with her mother, Lady Somers at Strawberry Hill. After dinner the house-guests had played a game called 'Wishes' in which they took it in turns to confess their most cherished desires to the company at large. Young Isabel declared that it was her dream 'to live in the country and have fifteen children'. This brought her a violent retaliation from her mother when they left the drawing-room: 'Of all the horrible indecent things for a young girl to say', remonstrated Lady Somers, 'What do you suppose they will think of the mother who has brought up such an indelicate daughter?'[62] Isabel recalled that she had sobbed herself to sleep that night.

At the top of the social scale nursemaids and nannies were likely to be employed to take charge of the children when young. Women brought up in aristocratic and upper-class households sometimes recalled their parents as rather remote figures whom they saw at specified times, such as after dinner in the evenings when they were brought down, freshly scrubbed and neatly dressed from the nursery. Sonia Keppel, daughter of a High Society family in Edwardian England, recorded that her childhood was largely spent living on a different floor of the house from that inhabited by her parents. Her visits to them followed a daily pattern. In the morning she visited her mother's room and was allowed to play with the jewels, feathers and beads she had worn at dinner the night before. Then she visited her father in *his* dressing room. In the evening at six o'clock, she met her parents again, this time in the drawing room. Sonia's early images of her mother are mostly of a magnificent, perfumed and exceedingly well-dressed being whom she saw as a kind of goddess (a word she often uses in her descriptions of her), inhabiting a separate plane from her own.[63]

If mothers remained rather distant figures through the early years of childhood in upper-class society, their relationship with their daughters was destined to become closer when these latter came down from the schoolroom and were groomed in fashion, deportment and etiquette ready for the 'coming out' party which would celebrate their entry into society, and more importantly, the marriage market. Hair was put up, hems would come down, and in 'the best circles', as Leonore

Davidoff has described in a book of that title, large sums of money would be invested in elaborately coutured gowns ready for 'the season'.[64] If the girl was to be presented at Court, the rules of procedure she had to familiarise herself with were particularly elaborate. And even in less exalted circles there was a formidable body of etiquette to be learned — how to fill in dance-cards, how to respond when asked for more than one dance by the same partner, how to address those of higher or lower rank, how to enter the dining room and conduct oneself at the dinner table. Mothers were responsible for initiating their daughters into these mysteries.[65]

Most middle-class women with leisure on their hands played their part in the elaborate social ritual — interpreted by them as a duty — of 'paying calls'. The rules of this game were extremely complex, governing the question of who might or ought to call on whom (depending on social rank, the length of time the family had been established in the neighbourhood, and whether or not there had been previous social engagements). There were 'dinner calls' (*de rigueur* one or two weeks after a dinner party had taken place) and afternoon 'At Homes' when there were strict conventions about procedure — which room maids should show visitors into, who should stand up for whom when anyone entered the room, who should rise first to leave and so forth. A concomitant of the whole business was the leaving of personal visiting cards on the hall table in correct numbers. Matrons and their husbands had their own cards. Daughters, when they 'came out', had their names printed beneath their mother's (or widowed father's) cards for a year or two. Ursula Bloom recalled:

> Cards were printed. They must be the right size, they must give the lady's name in the centre and her address in the left-hand bottom corner. Most people left them personally, with the right-hand top corner turned down to show it was a personal call, but if you were very grand and did not want to encourage the friendship you sent a footman round to do it for you, and then the top corner was *not* turned down. It was something of a snub and always left a bad taste in the mouth. Only cads did it.
>
> A lady left a card on the lady of the house, and her husband left two smaller cards, one for the lady and one for the gentleman. These were kept on a tray in the hall, and one liked to have an overflowing tray, for it showed that people wanted to know one, which was the right thing.[66]

24

Although the increasing number of journals addressed to the adolescent girl, and encyclopedias of advice on etiquette, featured guidelines to such complexities of social behaviour, mothers remained the main advisers and tried to instil what they deemed to be the correct forms of behaviour into their daughters. Daughters learned by accompanying their mothers on calls – not always wholeheartedly, social duties might have appeared tiresome, but they had to be carried out. Katharine Chorley remarked:

> The day was indeed a black one on which we found that our mothers had had their cards reprinted and that our names figured below theirs on the disgusting little white slips. But we, too, were drilled and disciplined.[67]

It is important to emphasise that these patterns and routines of social life into which middle-class mothers initiated their daughters were seen as *duties*.[68] It was considered right and proper that girls should rank the claims of social life, the whole business of maintaining the family's reputation in society, high among their obligations. Schooling and intellectual work were not nearly so important. A tract published by Henry Robinson in 1881 addressing itself to middle-class girls is representative of a whole body of literature on similar themes and can be used by way of illustration here. The full title of the publication was *A Conversation with some Home Daughters on the question 'Wherein does a girl's Usefulness Really Lie?'*[69] The author proceeded to describe a middle-class drawing room where two sisters were arguing about whether it was acceptable for women to develop 'some definite interest or plan' in life. They consult their favourite aunt on the theme, Aunt Ursula (presented by the author as a perfect specimen of late-Victorian womanhood who might have walked out of the pages of Ruskin's *Of Queens' Gardens*). There follows a long, sentimental narrative describing the conversation which ensued. One of the sisters, Winifred, impulsively confesses her secret dream: 'to work for the Higher Local Examinations at Cambridge next June'. Aunt Ursula gently expresses her reservations: it *might* be a good idea, but only if the girl could be *absolutely sure* that her studies could be reconciled with 'those home duties in which success is her pride and pleasure', 'Such a large and an important item in a girl's life'.[70] Thirty years later, Amy Barnard, in *A Girl's Book About Herself* (1912) offered similar pearls of wisdom.[71] Many elder sisters, she observed, found that their educational opportunities were cut short by the need

25

to be companions to their mothers and to help with younger children. She realised that 'if the girl was intellectual and keenly interested in study' this might prove a heavy cross to bear. But she brightly exhorted those of her readers who should feel themselves overburdened in this way not to despair:

> It is possible to do something by snatching spare moments. . . .
> Poems have been composed at the wash-tub, mathematical problems
> solved in bed, French remembered by reading a French Bible in
> church, lessons prepared in a train, and all manner of subjects kept
> fresh by helping the children with their home studies.[72]

One doubts whether this kind of advice offered much comfort to those with real yearning for study. At the same time, it is worth re-calling some of the many Victorian and Edwardian women who *did* manage to cram every hour they could wrest away from domestic and social duties with solid reading and intellectual work. Beatrice Webb, for instance, rose every morning in the very early hours in order to labour away at her studies before breakfast.[73]

If one searches for some dominant theme in the understanding about femininity mothers of all social levels passed on to their daughters, it can probably best be found in the ideas of service and self-sacrifice. Women were expected to occupy themselves in providing an environment — a context in which *men* could live and work. As the nineteenth century progressed, middle-class women particularly were likely to have much of the burdensome domestic work involved in running a house-hold taken off their shoulders by domestic servants. Lower down the social scale wives did their own household chores but this was no longer defined as *work*. Their husbands *worked* — the women 'stayed at home'. Closely related to this emphasis on the idea of women creating a context for men to live and work in was the ideal of femininity as representing self-sacrifice. Women of all social groups were encouraged from childhood to consider it selfish to become wrapped up in their own interests, for the ideal was to serve others, and always to consider the interests of their menfolk first.

Middle-class conceptions of dutiful daughterhood are succinctly expressed in an engraving entitled 'Evenings at Home' by T. Allom which formed the frontispiece to Fisher's 1842 edition of Sarah Ellis's *Daughters of England*.[74] The scene, as the title suggests, is a middle-class drawing room after dinner. Father sits by the fire. One diminutive daughter — aged about five years old — is taking her father's shoes off and gently rubbing his feet. Her slightly older sister is stroking his hair. The mother of the family sits away from the fire with two older daughters, one at each arm, both obviously mainly solicitous for *her* comfort. A fifth daughter pours tea for her parents, at the same time keeping an eye on another tiny female child engrossed with her doll on the floor. The seventh and last daughter is seated at the piano, gazing affectionately into the eyes of a young man for whom she is evidently primarily playing – a brother, or sweetheart, no doubt. The whole picture amply illustrates Mrs Ellis's conviction that women were born to serve and that girls should be taught this, in the family, from as early an age as possible.

In working-class households, as we have seen, girls learned to perform household tasks, to sew and mend for their fathers and brothers from childhood. Where women bore large families in poverty and poor conditions, self-sacrifice was built into the physical facts of their existence. Women stinted on food that their husbands and children might be fed. In a middle-class home there were servants to cope with domestic work but wives still waited upon their husbands – they might toy prettily with the tea-cups or, more importantly, it would have been their responsibility to supervise the servants, to secure the service necessary for the comfort of the family. Ursula Bloom recorded that as a child she saw her mother

> rush out of her room when a bell rang violently from my father's study, and heard her agitated demands of the maid who had dallied: 'It's Mr Bloom's bell! You simply must answer Mr Bloom's bell, he has rung twice already.'[75]

She added that 'nobody would have been chivvied had it been Mrs Bloom's bell because nobody would have cared, and this was as it should be and existed in all households.'[76]

Although, according to common law, the fathers of legitimate children were vested with the right to custody, and hence in some sense defined as the 'owners' of their children,[77] wives were, of course, those who looked after them (or those who supervised the nannies and nursemaids employed to look after them). This was one of the most important services rendered to a husband by his wife. Another crucial area of service was the care of the sick and the elderly. The nursing of sick relatives was seen as a particularly feminine role in a period when what few hospitals there were were often dangerous, insanitary places designed for the poorer classes. Many Victorian and Edwardian women spent long periods of their youth giving comfort to ailing relatives. Anne Jemima Clough nursed her mother, Beatrice Webb her father, Rachel McMillan her step-grandmother.[78] There are plenty of examples to be found amongst those who later merited biographies or who wrote autobiographies: the number of ordinary working women who must have nursed elderly relatives through their last years defies estimation.

In those middle- or upper-class families where women had sufficient leisure, the ideal of service might be extended to include philanthropy. The Evangelical Movement had played an important role in helping to define the feminine mission as one of service.[79] In *Strictures on the Modern System of Female Education*, Hannah More had argued that 'ladies should consider the superintendence of the poor as their immediate office.'[80] She had suggested that

> Young ladies should be accustomed to set apart a fixed portion of their time, as sacred to the poor, whether in relieving, instructing, or working for them, and the performance of this duty must not be left to the event of contingent circumstances, or the operation of accidental impressions; but it must be established into a principle, and wrought into a habit. A specific portion of the day must be allotted to it, on which no common engagement must be allowed to intrench.[81]

The influence of Evangelical ideology and particularly this ideal of womanhood can be traced at all social levels. Lady Blanche Balfour aimed to educate her daughters in social service by encouraging them to set apart a fixed proportion of their incomes for philanthropic purposes.[82] Hannah More had expressed mixed feelings about this kind of practice because she felt the money was properly the parents', and that to give it away was to impose too small a sacrifice on the children:

> The sacrifice of an orange to a little girl, or a feather to a great one, given at the expense of their own gratification, would be a better lesson of charity on its right ground than a considerable sum of money to be presently replaced by the parent.[83]

It might be contended that boys, as well as girls, were encouraged to make this kind of gesture, but there were other kinds of training in social service more specifically directed at girls. Lady Somers, for instance, gave her daughters Isabel and Adeline special baskets which they were to keep for carrying puddings, jellies and grapes to elderly or sick tenants on the family's estate at Eastmor.[84]

In families where the mother's religious beliefs had a strongly evangelical flavour, daughters might be schooled in forms of self-denial even more stringent than the prescriptions of Hannah More. Constance Louisa Maynard's mother, whose profound belief in the necessity for self-sacrifice as a form of personal atonement for sin seems to have reached the level of fanaticism at times, was such a parent. Her children were endlessly exhorted to abjure worldliness, enjoyments and pleasures in almost every form in order to prove themselves worthy of God.[85] Her daughters inherited both her conviction of sin and her terror of worldliness. They were taught that regular acts of voluntary renunciation were necessary if one sought to approach a state of grace. Constance recorded that as a girl, she and her sister Gabrielle (Gazy) had been holidaying with their father on the Isle of Man:

We stayed in a very splendid hotel called Castle Mona at Douglas.
It was the height of the season, and on the Saturday night there
was dancing on the floor of the great *salon*. I had never before seen
grown-up people dancing, and quick wishes came into our minds
that we might join them. Only just for an hour of play, only to be as
glad, as gleeful as some of these girls looked as they gave their hands
right and left in the chain of the Lancers. As I sat quietly by, I tried
to fix in my mind how dear Cowper had looked on at just such a
sight. 'As the gambols of lunatics that one regards with uneasiness
rather than with any desire to join them.' I tried, but no, I could
not. There was something about the scene so natural, so pleasant,
so suitable to rosy cheeks and springing footsteps that I felt stag-
gered and I could only say in my heart, 'I will refrain, not because it
is wrong, but because it is something a little extra to give up for
Jesus' sake. The footsteps of the flock do not point that way. I will
be content'.[86]

Later that night Constance remembered she had discussed her feelings with Gazy:

She was always a sympathetic friend on such matters, and then and
there we agreed solemnly and heartily that it was the better part,
although the more difficult, not even to taste and try the world, but
'to take God's opinion of its worthlessness, and reject it while we
were still young and it still looked fair and pleasant'.[87]

From their childhood Constance and Gazy had learned from their mother that self-abnegation and service should go hand in hand. Personal ambition was to be stifled at birth by a desire to serve others. When Constance spent a short period away from home, at school, and was soon promoted on account of her zeal and capacity for study, Gazy wrote to her begging her to conquer any thought of her own success. She suggested that Constance occupy herself by looking after the new intake of children arriving for the first time at school:

> Think *every minute* what you can be doing for them, remembering that it is a great and *passing* opportunity for being really useful that you now have, so I would not advise you to think of drawing at odd times or such things for yourself, but use the minutes for others, and you will soon feel all the pleasant *busy* feelings of a real First Class child. You must give up anything, and torment yourself no end with being tidy, etc. . . . to be all that is expected.[88]

Through her mother and from her sisters, then, Constance absorbed a complex mixture of guilt, an obsession with self-denial (not unmixed with an arrogance stemming from the conviction that she was one of the few who followed the true spiritual path), and the profound desire to serve others, and through them, God, which characterised her whole life.

In sum: family life taught girls growing up in late-Victorian and Edwardian England about a sexual division of labour in which men were regarded as the major breadwinners, and women were generally occupied at home. Men worked, women did not. Boys and girls were treated differently and girls were likely to perceive the male world as distant, authoritative and closed to them. Relationships between mothers and daughters were extremely important. Mothers provided daughters with some image of how their own lives might take shape. Their daughters also learned that women's interests were of secondary importance in a society dominated by males. Women were expected to serve; this was seen as 'natural', and 'femininity' was socially defined in terms of dependency, self-sacrifice and service.

Families play a major part in moulding personalities and it is not surprising that so many women accepted what they were taught. Florence Nightingale had pointed out in the 1850s that any good affectionate girl would inevitably find that her family would 'have more influence with her than the world'.[89] She went on to catalogue all the obstacles in the way of middle-class girls achieving any important work in life, speculating on the hundreds of lives (or rather deaths) of persons who cannot fight with society, or who, unsuppported by the sympathies about them, give up their own destiny as not worth the fierce and continued struggle necessary to accomplish it.[90]

It is often easier for the historian to find out about the attitudes and experiences of those women who rejected conventional expectations about their role than about those who accepted these expectations and shaped their lives accordingly. The latter group were less likely to leave autobiographies or other written records, or to inspire biographers. This is true for the middle class, but even more the case when one is mainly concerned with exploring the experience of those vast numbers of working-class women who lived ordinary, married lives and who have remained so notoriously 'hidden from history'. But even if the written accounts we do possess are few in number, it does not follow that the experiences they document were wholly exceptional. We must certainly be careful not to fall into the trap of assuming that because women were silent about their lives (in the sense of leaving no written record) – they *accepted* the conventions, let alone rested happy or content with the existing order of things. Twentieth-century accounts of working-class women's lives often reveal a good deal of rational resentment, pain and bitterness – even if numbed by the fatalism which long years of suffering might produce.

I have suggested that the anger and resentment which women such as Hannah Mitchell or Maggie Fuller felt towards their mothers as young girls was not uncommon. However, both women retained this resentment through their adult lives to what may have been an unusual extent. When Young and Willmott investigated the structure of working-class communities after the second world war, one of the aspects which interested them most was the strength of the relationship between mothers and daughters.[91] It seems probable that the majority of adolescent girls who experienced conflict with their mothers would have become less hostile to them as they themselves grew older, married, and in their turn bore children. Grandmothers commonly provided an important service, helping and advising their daughters with their young children. This might certainly have raised new forms of conflict – daughters resenting their mother's interference – but the conflicts were perhaps likely to be less bitter than when both were younger, because mother and daughter would now be united by more common experience. Many daughters would have grown up to

31

replicate, in all essentials, the details of their mother's own past.

We cannot know the proportion of girls in any particular social class who would have found themselves in constant conflict with their mothers, or otherwise resentful about the role they were expected to play in family life. Advice columns in girls' magazines, chapters in manuals and encyclopedias of useful knowledge written for adolescent girls at the turn of the century frequently discussed the difficulties of mother-and-daughter relationships, and convey the impression that, at least in middle-class families, tensions were very common. Oral history might go some way towards illuminating girls' experiences in working-class families. But generalisations will remain somewhat hazardous. Even if one tried to construct some kind of representative sample (notoriously difficult to do when one is interviewing old people, since those who survive are already a selected group, and so forth), then we are still left with the problem of *measuring* resentment. Anger and resentment may take a variety of forms. It may be argued, for instance, that anger or resentment which could not find outlet in speech or action sometimes manifested itself through symptoms of hysteria, asthma, or other physical malaise. Florence Nightingale certainly used illness as a weapon against and a refuge from the suffocating claims of her mother and sister in the 1860s.[92] Victoria Glendinning entitled her biography of Winifred Seebohm *A Suppressed Cry*, because she believed that Winifred's loving but repressive Quaker family background was responsible for the nervous asthma which haunted Winifred's youth, bringing to an end her intellectual career at Newnham and ultimately causing her death.[93]

Vera Brittain's autobiographical *Testament of Youth* records the agonised resentments she suffered being brought up as a young lady by middle-class parents living in Buxton in the 1900s. A staunch feminist all her life, she suggested that

> Probably no ambitious girl who has lived in a family which regards the subservience of women as part of the natural order of creation ever completely recovers from the bitterness of her early emotions.[94]

It is tempting to assume that she was right, but that would mean ignoring the testimonies of other women, undoubtedly intelligent and not without ambition, who appear to have been able to tailor their ambitions to fit the conventions apparently without resentment: M.V. Hughes, for instance. We have seen how as a girl Molly's mother trained her in habits of deference to her four older brothers. Mrs Thomas'

32

husband died while their daughter was twelve years old. The boys in the family immediately offered to provide for their mother and sister and promised to maintain them in ladylike comfort. However, Molly decided that she would prefer to earn her own living and it was decided that she should become a pupil of Miss Buss at the North London Collegiate School, in order to secure the kind of education which would enable her to become self-supporting.[95] After a successful career at the North London School, Molly went on to train as a teacher in Cambridge. She then took a teaching post in the north of England. Her mother went with her, taking lodgings near the school. Later Molly took a post in London, again taking her mother with her. Their relationship seems to have been extremely intimate. When Molly became engaged to be married, her mother's approval of the man in question, Arthur Hughes, was crucial. Molly shared all her love letters with her mother. In the second volume of her autobiography she describes the formula her mother offered for a happy married life. Mrs Thomas thought it absolutely essential for a woman to follow her husband everywhere, have no money of her own, and to submit willingly to becoming totally dependent on him. 'Obviously in her scheme of things', Molly pointed out, 'men were the important people', adding, wholly without irony, 'Well, they are. And I shall never cease to be grateful to her for training me from childhood to appreciate this point.'[96]

By the time Molly eventually became Mrs Arthur Hughes (a long time later), she had developed a flourishing career of her own, having pioneered the development of a new department for training teachers at Bedford College, London.[97] Her marriage proved the occasion for her to resign this career — apparently without regret. She proudly records that she promised to 'obey' her husband in her wedding vows — contemptuously dismissing the ideas of feminists who felt this better left out — invested in cookery books and set out to prove herself a perfect angel-in-the-house.[98] The reader is then coyly treated to her own recipe for a happy marriage — 'Two guiding stars were the outcome of my own experience: (1) never to keep Arthur waiting for his meal, (2) never to give him cold mutton.'[99]

This was in the 1890s. Perhaps Vera Brittain's voice was more representative of the younger generation. But Molly Hughes' account is instructive in demonstrating the persistence of conventional attitudes, learned in the family, even in highly able and articulate women. Of course one way in which women of ability and some ambition sought to reconcile these qualities with that image of themselves as feminine, submissive beings they may have inherited from their childhood, was through marrying men whose achievements seemed greater than their own. In this way they might serve, and sacrifice themselves, whilst indirectly fulfilling something of their own ambitions. Emilia Francis Strong — young, intelligent and beautiful — married the somewhat grey and elderly but very scholarly Rector of Lincoln, Mark Pattison. Their union is said to have been one of the sources of inspiration for George Eliot's depiction of the marriage between Dorothea Brooke and Casaubon in *Middlemarch*, although most contemporaries who remarked upon this hastened to add that Mark Pattison was much more distinguished than Dorothea's desiccated patriarchal lover.[100] Agnata Frances Ramsay, after winning high honours in Cambridge's classical tripos in the 1880s, married the Master of Trinity. Mary Paley, one of the first students at Newnham College and a distinguished scholar in her own right, married the well-known economist (and inveterate anti-feminist) Alfred Marshall. Eleanor Balfour married Henry Sidgwick, after a period of wholeheartedly devoting herself to the work of her brother-in-law, Lord Rayleigh, on the measurement of electricity.[101] (She had kept notebooks for him, and checked his arithmetic.) She then proceeded to switch her attention and service to her husband's work. 'At the time of her marriage', wrote her niece and biographer, Ethel Sidgwick,

> she was reading for the Higher Locals, and her coach in mathematics, Professor Ferrers, was known to be of the opinion that she would have been a High Wrangler if she had read for the Tripos: but, though undoubtedly tempted by the course, she did not long toy with the idea. She decided that marriage, with its tail of obligations and the care of her husband, and her husband's books, sufficed to absorb her time; and she renounced, silently.[102]

In her youth Eleanor Balfour had explored Florence with her brother, with George Eliot's *Romola* as a guide.[103] It must surely have been a novel which exerted a strong appeal to one of her temperament. Possibly the feats of self-sacrifice and martyrdoms of Eliot's heroine reinforced the teaching of her mother and helped to inspire that life-long capacity to put others' interests before her own for which Mrs Sidgwick was long remembered.

A *total* rejection of the understanding about femininity and the patterns of relationship between men and women learned in the family was probably comparatively rare. It is much more common to find mature women who were still in some way troubled about their self-image, their femininity: consciously or unconsciously ambivalent about their feminine role. Women who stepped aside from convention and carved out careers for themselves outside the home — particularly those who became feminists — illustrate these conflicts in their attitudes and personalities, sometimes in an acute form. Many of those involved in the movement to expand educational opportunities for women, and in other forms of intellectual pursuit, for instance, retained an intellectual timidity, a deference to male academic values and intellectual authority which was surely closely bound up with the ideas about feminine modesty and male precedence they had been taught from childhood. The example of Anne Jemima Clough immediately springs to mind. In her youth she had learned to 'look up' to her brother Arthur, to seek his advice on most intellectual issues and to trust his judgment more than her own. Her journal, written through adolescence, shows her constantly battling with her own ambitions, aware that society regarded these as unseemly in women, and trying to school her own spirit and intellect into submission, to repress her own interests and substitute the interests of others.[104]

Anne Jemima Clough and Constance Louisa Maynard are just two of the many examples of women who eventually carved out careers for themselves in a quintessentially 'feminine' way. Both became heads of colleges of women students whom they governed in a self-consciously 'maternal' fashion. Miss Clough managed to appease 'respectable' Cambridge society by her conventional retiring and 'feminine' manner.[105] Constance Maynard's world of Westfield College was more insulated from the male academic world. Neither woman ever married and Constance, through most of her life, seems to have sought emotional stability (not always successfully) through intense relationships with other women.[106] Her ideal of herself as a teacher was wholeheartedly one of self-sacrifice and service. This was an extremely common pattern amongst nineteenth- and early twentieth-century women teaching heads of schools and colleges. They 'mothered' their schools in a devoted, self-sacrificing way, speaking of their pupils as 'daughters' or 'children', and not infrequently regarding their careers as a religious vocation or duty.

Another common pattern of acceptance and rejection, of ambivalence about femininity can be seen manifested in women who intellectually rejected the ideal of themselves as self-sacrificing beings, serving the interests of others but never pursuing their own; yet at the same time remained emotionally divided — unable to break free from the pattern of giving and attending to those close to them which they had learned from their mothers as 'feminine'. Such women could rarely be free of guilt when they followed their own goals — a guilt inspired by the feeling, at some level, that the work they were engaged in was selfish; that the needs of their parents, their elderly relatives, their husbands, their children — the needs of anyone but they themselves, should come first.

Again, there are many examples one could give. Two women writers this century, Virginia Woolf and her less well-known admirer and contemporary, Winifred Holtby, were both aware of these conflicts in their own lives: neither was able to resolve them. In an essay on *Professions for Women*, Virginia Woolf argued convincingly that in order to achieve, to write, or even just to be themselves, women had to murder the phantom of 'the angel of the house' — meaning the Victorian concept of femininity, 'always charming, always sympathetic, conciliatory, sacrificing herself daily to others'.[107] Winifred Holtby echoed these sentiments:

> This tendency to consider everybody else's interests more important than their own is one of the major expressions of women's inferiority complex. If they dared to believe in their own capacity, if they had learned that the price to be paid for in achievement is not merely the sacrifice of oneself, but often the sacrifice of others, their achievements would appear less mediocre. When a woman believes enough in her own mission to be ruthless — a Mrs Siddons, a Florence Nightingale, a Mrs Pankhurst — then, indeed, something happens. But most women dread before anything to 'cause an upset', or inconvenience a family; and their work suffers.
>
> I believe that this is one of the most formidable handicaps confronting women.[108]

Winifred Holtby saw clearly that those services to husband and family which society defined as exclusively 'feminine duties' constantly interrupted the work of even the most highly talented, capable professional women she knew — especially once they were married:

> The woman doctor, architect or engineer may do her work effectively, but the illness of a relative or a catastrophe in the household arrangements throws a double burden upon her. Husband and wife in a home may both be professional workers; but it is the wife who

36

is expected to order the meals, superintend the nurseries, arrange the entertainments and engage the domestic staff, just as in the case of industrial employees, though both may go to the factory and the wife's may be the hardest work, it is she who is expected to prepare the food, clean the house, and mend the children's clothes in her so-called leisure.[109]

This passage is interesting and shows clearly that she perceived the sexual division of labour in both middle- and working-class families to be at the root of the problem: her analysis of women's plight throughout *Women and a Changing Civilisation*, from which these passages are taken, is both profound and lucid. Yet if both Virginia Woolf and Winifred Holtby recognised in their rational minds the trap that concepts of femininity and feminine responsibilities constituted for women, they had both internalised these concepts from childhood and were emotionally unable to free themselves in the way they sometimes urged others to do. This is apparent both in their novels, and in their lives. Winifred Holtby's career, particularly, seems to have been constantly interrupted by her sensitivity to other people's needs. Her friend, Vera Brittain, recorded that she was ever ready to help others with their work, their ambitions and the burdens of their domestic life — at the expense of her own writing. Others endorsed this.

Her most successful novel, *South Riding*, published in 1936, shows Winifred Holtby beginning to explore some of the problems about 'femininity' and the self-image of successful professional women with which she was so concerned.[110] The central character is a strong-minded, intelligent and competent woman, Sarah Burton, with an established position as head of a girls' school in the north of England. The novel explores many aspects of provincial life and is structured around the theme of local government — Sarah's predicament is made to encompass a number of larger concerns about suffering, history and socio-political change. One strand of the novel narrates the story of Sarah's relationship with Robert Carne, a local squire and potentate of declining fortunes. (He is badly in debt, the estates are falling apart, and his wife is in a mental hospital.) Carne is a man of conservative political persuasion and Sarah — a social and political radical — is drawn into constant conflict with him. There is one scene in the novel which consciously echoes Charlotte Brontë. Carne is for a moment paralleled with the dour, masterful and remote figure of Rochester; Sarah with Jane Eyre.[111] Not surprisingly Sarah soon comes to the painful realisation that she loves Carne, in spite of their professed enmity and her own better judgment. The book comes to a climax when Sarah meets Carne by chance in a hotel where they were both staying independently, and cautiously (she does not want to injure her 'femininity' in his eyes by appearing too bold) takes the initiative in suggesting they go to bed together. The action is significant because Holtby is making it clear that Sarah knew that she was jeopardising her career for the passion of a moment and yet is wholly carried away by her sexual attraction for Carne (a strong, silent male chauvinist), and even, deep-down, the desire to bear his child. The author appears to be saying that underneath the brisk, capable, feminist, radical exterior Sarah was a woman with a 'feminine' desire to forget herself, to swoon in the arms of a hero — even at the expense of sacrificing her whole career. It is difficult to know exactly what Holtby want us to understand by this for the moment never comes. Carne appears at the door of Sarah's bedroom and is suddenly struck down by a heart attack.[112] Sarah is not made to face the consequences of her impulse — and neither, more significantly, is Winifred Holtby. The book reveals a great deal about the problems the author herself must have faced in reconciling the image of herself as a capable — even powerful — woman with her sexual identity and what she had learned to recognise as 'femininity'.

Virginia Woolf's novel, *To the Lighthouse* (1927) seems even more centrally to reveal a profound ambivalence about 'female values' and femininity.[113] On one level the author is critical of the kind of life led by Mrs Ramsay, a woman who is always giving sympathy, responsive to the demands of those around her, yet at the same time the novel sets up a clear distinction between 'masculine' and 'feminine' values and celebrates the latter. Male values are condemned as harsh, insensitive, instrumental: Mr Ramsay is a selfish figure who creates discord amongst those around him. By contrast, Mrs Ramsay — soothing, ordering, consoling — creates harmony. Lily Briscoe has her art. With no lover, no children, her art is not interfered with by services she must as a woman perform for others. But something is lacking, and she looks at and later remembers Mrs Ramsay with a feeling approaching longing. In many ways she represents Virginia Woolf herself. Lily Briscoe's wistfulness, perhaps, echoes the wistfulness with which the childless Virginia sometimes looked at her sister Vanessa, so happy with her small children; or the wistfulness with which she recalled memories of her own mother. It was with the rational, intellectual part of herself that Virginia Woolf had spoken when she had written of the necessity to kill 'the angel in the house'. At heart she remained more divided. For Mrs Ramsay, the apotheosis of that Angel, was in large part the memory of her mother.

2

Schooling, college and femininity: some experiences of middle-class girls

Schooling was generally regarded as one of the most important forma-tive influences on middle-class boyhood: the reformed public schools saw themselves as moulding 'character', and an education received in one of these schools became increasingly a passport to success in pro-fessional and public life. Hence middle-class parents in Victorian and Edwardian England selected schools for their sons with great care. The expense was usually considered a vital investment in a boy's future. With girls it was different. In the wealthiest sections of the middle class a small number of daughters would be sent to extremely expensive, fashionable boarding schools (the equivalents of the school attended by Frances Power Cobbe in Brighton in the early nineteenth century; or Heathfield — expensive, modish and select — in the Edwardian period).[1] These schools were few, and mainly situated in the south of England. But it was common in the upper region of the middle class not to send girls to school at all.

A wealthy family provided a more 'select' and sheltered environ-ment than even the most carefully chosen boarding school. Prosperous households would contain both nursery and schoolrooms; usually on the upper floors. Girls left the nursery and progressed to the school-room as soon as was considered appropriate. They would be taught by resident or visiting governesses; and if income ran to it, by 'visiting masters' who might be expected to polish up the accomplishments of their young charges in dancing, singing or painting. If the family cared enough for intellectual accomplishments, visiting masters might tutor young girls in some mathematics, classics or science, but parents who considered such subjects of any use to their daughters were rare. Girls might sometimes share their brothers' lessons, before the boys were deemed old enough to be sent away to school. In this way they might pick up the rudiments of mathematics, or classics. But once brothers left for school their sisters were more likely to be left in the charge of French or German governesses: in the upper middle classes, languages were seen as a necessary part of the curriculum for 'home daughters'.

This custom of educating girls at home was noted by the Schools' Inquiry Commission in 1867-8 as typical in the wealthy middle classes.[2] By the turn of the century it was being modified somewhat. New public schools for girls in St Andrews (St Leonard's), Roedean and elsewhere aimed to attract daughters of the upper class and soon succeeded in doing so. But many of these families still preferred to keep their daughters at home. It will be recollected that Naomi Mitchison's parents took her away from the Dragon School, Oxford, suddenly and without explanation when she reached puberty.[3] And her father was a man of liberal intellectual views. Probably her mother – much more conservative and conventional in outlook – was mainly responsible for the decision that a home education under a governess was more seemly for an adolescent girl. Loelia Ponsonby, whose parents lived in the centre of High Society circles on the eve of the first world war (her father had been Equerry to Queen Victoria and later became Head of the Royal Household) recalled that her parents had felt self-consciously 'modern' in sending her away to school.[4]

Further down the social scale, among the prosperous sections of provincial middle-class society throughout the period 1865-1914, it was still common for girls to receive a large part of their 'schooling' in the parental home. James Bryce, serving as Assistant Commissioner to the Schools' Inquiry Commission, described the pattern which he found amongst the merchant and professional class in Lancashire as fairly typical of the country as a whole.[5] Daughters of these families, he reported, were commonly taught at home by nursery or visiting governesses until they were about ten years old. They frequently shared lessons with their brothers at this stage. They were then often sent for two or three years to a local day school. At about twelve or thirteen until about seventeen years of age they might be sent to a select boarding school. Then they either came home for good, or were possibly sent for a year to a 'finishing' school. The aims of this kind of education, Bryce emphasised, were social, not academic. The more select or exclusive the school, the better. 'The finishing school', he

41

commented, 'is not so much an educational agent as a tribute which the parent pays to his own social position.'[6]

The pattern Bryce outlined in the 1860s seems to have persisted, in the social groups he was referring to, right up until the first world war. Katharine Chorley's experience was similar: her nursery governess was replaced by first an Italian, then a French governess. She was taught in the schoolroom at home until fourteen years of age, then sent to a boarding school in Folkestone of the kind which was determined to turn out 'high-minded and cultured home-makers'.[7] Vera Brittain recorded that she had shared a governess with her brother, Edward, until eleven years old. Then her parents moved from Macclesfield to Buxton so that the children might attend 'good' day schools. For two years she went to a day school advertising itself as a school for 'the daughters of gentlemen'. Then she was sent away to St Monica's, a boarding school in Surrey.[8]

In the lower regions of the middle class a different convention again prevailed, and again this seems to have remained fairly stable through the second half of the nineteenth century and up until the war. Here again the care of very young girls was likely to be shared between nurse-maid and mother, even if the nursemaid was herself only young and a kind of maid-of-all-work rather than a more specialised assistant. In this social group girls were likely to attend small local day-schools for about four or five years, beginning around the age of ten. Bryce had commented:

> Mothers belonging to what is called the lower middle class are able to make their daughters useful at home; they can help in the house-work and mind the baby, whereas boys of the same age are only, as they express it, 'a plague and a worrit'. Hence it often happens that girls are not sent to school till long after the age when systematic instruction ought to have begun, and that they are kept away upon slight grounds.[9]

Bryce found the norms of educational achievement amongst girls particularly low in this social group. Where the family aspired to middle-class standards of domestic life, but resources could not be stretched to purchase adequate domestic help, mothers' demands for assistance with household tasks might fall heavily on their daughters, and then school-ing would suffer accordingly.[10]

After leaving school (at any time between the ages of thirteen and seventeen) daughters of middle- or lower middle-class families were expected to stay at home and attend to the kind of social duties discussed in the previous chapter. Their 'intellectual' education, in so far as it had existed at all, was over. Bryce remarked that

> as a rule, an unmarried young lady, living at home, reads only the novels which the circulating library supplies, spends her morning in letter-writing, fancy work, and other approved means of killing time, her afternoons in shopping and visiting, her evenings in concerts, parties and tea-drinkings.[11]

What he regarded as this 'listless, purposeless life' was likely to continue until the girl married.

It is not easy to pass judgment on the quality of an education mainly received at home. It should be remembered, in the first place, that the goals of a home education were not primarily academic. The vast majority of middle class parents had no interest whatsoever in cultivating scholarly qualities in their daughters. They wanted them to grow up as decorative, modest, marriageable beings. The Report of the Schools' Inquiry Commission admitted that the Commissioners could see nothing wrong with this, for they believed these ideas to be rooted in human nature.[12] The Report noted:

> Parents who have daughters will always look to their being provided for in marriage, will always believe that the gentler graces and winning qualities of character will be their best passports to marriage, and will always expect their husbands to take on themselves the intellectual toil and the active exertions needed for the support of the family.[13]

This being the case, they confessed they felt a home education distinctly advantageous in many respects. Day schools, they decided, were preferable on the whole to boarding schools, because day schools allowed the home to continue to exert a strong influence on the growing girl:

> Assuming, as we may fairly do, that the homes of our middle class are commonly favourable to the growth and development of the female character we are ourselves inclined to the opinion, which also appears somewhat to preponderate in the evidence, that in the case of girls more than in that of boys, the combination of school teaching with home influence, such as Day Schools admit of, is the most promising arrangement.[14]

As Bryce pointed out, the Victorians educated boys for the world, girls for the drawing room.[15] 'Masculine' characteristics of independence, self-reliance and enterprise were seen to be developed in a public school environment, away from the intimacies and emotional dependences of the home. 'Femininity', conversely, might best be cultivated in the home.

Those sections of the Report of the Schools' Inquiry Commission which deal with the education of girls, then, are deeply ambivalent in tone. On the one hand the commissioners were extremely critical of the shoddy intellectual content, the academic incompetences of prevailing systems of girls' education. On the other hand, their basic acceptance of the sexual division of labour as natural and desirable blunted the edge of their analysis. Girls' schooling should be improved, and their minds sharpened — but not too much, lest their 'femininity' should suffer. Women, after all, should be pleasing, supportive individuals. They might ideally help their husbands and share their interests, but no more than this.

A home education cultivated 'feminine' virtues in a number of ways. The daughter was schooled in dependence and protected from undesirable social contacts. The adults with whom she would come into contact would demonstrate perfectly acceptable forms of social behaviour. The relationship between governess — with her own dependent status, teaching general knowledge and ladylike behaviour, and visiting masters — generally of higher status and teaching higher-ranking subjects such as the fine arts (painting or music), provided yet another model of the 'proper' sexual division of labour. Cut off from frequent informal contact with her adolescent peer group, the young girl might well become shy and retiring when she was faced with this kind of company. Too much social confidence might after all injure the appearance of feminine modesty beloved of the Victorians.

A home education aimed fundamentally to school a girl in femininity. Academic goals may have been considered of minor importance, but this is not, of course, to say that all educations received in the home were intellectually worthless. Middle-class homes, like their owners, varied infinitely, and the academic value of a girl's home education would vary with the extent to which her parents cherished intellectual, literary, or other cultural values, and in connection with this, with the parents' choice of a governess. Some parents taught their daughters themselves. M.V. Hughes was given lessons by her mother until she was twelve years old.[16] When she did go to school she was markedly more literate than those of her age group she found there. Her mother had also, rather surprisingly, started to teach her Latin. However, Mrs Thomas seems to have left a lot to be desired as a teacher of arithmetic, and Molly found herself disturbingly innumerate in relation to her peers.[17] It is interesting to find that Sophie Bryant, who succeeded Miss Buss to the Headship of the North London Collegiate School for Girls, a distinguished mathematician and the first woman in England to receive a doctorate for her academic work, never attended any school. She apparently received a large part of her education from her father.[18] Lists of women who had achieved successful careers at university, published in the *Journal of the Women's Education Union* in the 1870s and 1880s show that a significant proportion of these women had been educated at home, and had prepared themselves for University entrance through 'private study'.[19]

On the whole the historical literature on governesses has tended to concentrate on their ambivalent status in middle-class households, and the lack of facilities for their education and training in mid-Victorian England.[20] Undoubtedly many girls must have been educated by a succession of governesses without any real inspiration as teachers. Dorothea Beale recorded that her many governesses left 'little impression on my inner life'.[21] The novelist Dorothy Richardson, brought up in a middle-class household of somewhat unstable fortunes, remembered little of her governess except how boring she had been, and how she had bribed the children with chocolate mice.[22] Loelia Ponsonby suffered agonies as a child from the punishments of a sadistic governess.[23] But others were looked after by women who seemed to have cared for their charges and taught them reasonably efficiently. Katharine Chorley's early education, although cramped by her parents' concept of what was proper for a young lady, seems to have been reasonably sound from an intellectual point of view. Her French governess saved her from an uncritical acceptance of the patriotic English view of European history as well as teaching her the French language. Her father supplied lessons in mathematics and English poetry, and her mother taught her Scripture.[24] If it is impossible to generalise about the pedagogical skills, academic attainments and humanitarian qualities of Victorian and Edwardian governesses, it is still worth remembering that countless girls received a reasonably sound early education in their charge. At any rate, they generally learned to read and write. Numerical skills were much less likely to be developed, at least without the aid of a visiting master or brothers' tutors. Once she could read and write, if

45

she were not later sent away to school, any progress the girl might make would depend on the cultural tenor of her parents' home, the books she could gain access to, the circle of her parents' friends. Not infrequently, as Vera Brittain's provincial middle-class upbringing reminds us, these were cripplingly narrow.[25] A few middle-class girls were privileged to grow up in an extraordinarily stimulating intellectual milieu. Families such as Beatrice Potter's, Nora Balfour's, or Naomi Haldane's entertained successions of distinguished visitors and were closely in touch with the leading intellectual movements of their day.[26] All three of these women gained immeasurably, when young, from their families' contacts with great minds. But these minds, of course, were male minds – the world of learning, they learned, was dominated by men.

The majority of schools attended by middle-class girls in the 1860s and 1870s were small private establishments. Bryce found it extremely difficult to ascertain exactly how many of these institutions there were in Lancashire when he was investigating for the Schools' Inquiry Commission in 1866 – but guessed around 500.[27] Very few of these schools, he noted, took more than fifty pupils: indeed the majority took less than thirty girls. Many were catering for as few as six to eight children only. Such ventures were usually carried on in private households; one or two rooms being set aside for teaching purposes.[28] In Bryce's opinion this kind of school was often inefficient and uneconomic. The final Report of the Commissioners echoed this judgment when they looked at the running of these small private girls' schools over the country as a whole. But at the same time they argued that women teachers preferred small schools, and that parents saw them as providing a more homely environment for their daughters:

> Our Assistants report that ladies are generally found to shrink from the labour and responsibility of large schools, and that parents have the impression that smaller schools 'are conducted more like private families', are 'more like home', allow of more personal influence, and tend more to the production and confirmation of gentle and feminine characteristics. Right or wrong such feelings are probably too natural ever to pass entirely away.[29]

Small 'homely' schools, then, cultivated femininity. In many ways their organisation was modelled directly on the family. The Lady Proprietor or governess would adopt a maternal role towards the girls in her care. Lessons would take place in an intimate, sheltered and informal environment. Ties of affection, dependence, and close personal obligation might be relied upon to secure discipline — there would be less need for the codes of a formal rule-book. Bryce reported that discipline did not appear to be a problem in the majority of girls' schools he visited in Lancashire. Questioning one Lady Proprietress on how she dealt with any signs of insubordination amongst her pupils, she had replied that: 'I say that I don't love them, that is always enough'.[30] Such sheltered, intimate environments did not leave space for external disobedience on any scale, and allowed teachers ample scope for exercising personal influence and emotional pressure on their charges.

In a more direct sense these small private girls' schools were sometimes merely an extension of family life. Alice Ottley, the first Headmistress of Worcester High School for Girls, gained her early teaching experience in a school organised by her mother in Hampstead.[31] After her clergyman husband's death, Mrs Ottley was faced with the problem of meeting the expenses of educating a large family. She moved to Hampstead, and decided to take into her house a few girls aged between fifteen and twenty, whom she could educate along with her own younger daughters. Alice, then aged twenty-one, undertook to help her in this venture.[32] J.B.S. Pedersen, who has recently made a detailed study of girls' schools in the second half of the nineteenth century, has shown how common this kind of arrangement was, not least because the opening of a small school in one's own household for a few 'daughters of gentlemen' was one of the extremely few options facing a distressed gentlewoman who had to secure some means of self-support.[33] This goes some way towards explaining the inadequacies and inefficiencies of so many of these schools — their proprietresses were frequently without qualification, training, or even any real enthusiasm for their task.

The school which was in essence a kind of extended family unit, Pedersen reminds us, 'shaded almost imperceptibly into the familylike school'.[34] The original intake of Ashcliffe, the school run by the Sewell sisters on the Isle of Wight, had included nieces of the Proprietresses, who were addressed as 'Aunts Ellen, Elizabeth and Emma' by all their pupils as a result. The school became highly successful, with a long waiting-list of would-be entrants. But the Sewell sisters determined to keep numbers down — there were generally under seven pupils — in order to preserve the family atmosphere. The sisters continued to be addressed as 'Aunt' by succeeding generations of girls.[35] The career of Hannah Pipe as a schoolmistress also illustrates the way in which a tiny family concern could expand by taking more pupils but still retain an essentially 'domestic' form.[36] Hannah Pipe began her career by opening a small school in a house she inhabited with her widowed mother, in Manchester in the late 1840s. She herself taught the girls, her mother acted as housekeeper. The first pupils came daily but later some were taken as boarders. In the 1850s they moved to London and established a small boarding school again on the private household model. The venture prospered and fees went up, but Hannah kept the number of her pupils small. By 1860 the school, 'Laleham', was housed in an elegant private residence with its own attractive grounds. There were generally twenty to twenty-five pupils.

Hannah Pipe herself seems to have been a woman of some intellect but with decidedly conventional views about woman's place. In her educational views she was influenced by Thomas Arnold: hence the choice of the name 'Laleham' for the school. Willow trees were imported from Rugby and planted around the pond in the school's grounds. Character, to Hannah Pipe, was the aim of education; but the feminine character, she believed, differed essentially from the male. For her, woman's highest mission was in the home. In a letter to an old pupil she quoted Ruskin: ideally, woman was 'Queen of the home', her husband King.[37] She went to considerable lengths to ensure that Laleham retained the characteristics of a leisured, cultured, middle-class home; for her the only place to raise the daughters of gentlemen. Miss Pipe was generally known as the 'school mother' — she called her pupils her 'school daughters', and frequently spoke of being 'wedded to her school'. Her biographer, Anna M. Stoddart recalls that her gravest rebuke to the girls was to call them 'unladylike'. She remembered one occasion when Miss Pipe reduced a wayward girl to tears with the words: 'Your father is a gentleman. Your mother I know to be a Lady — but what *you* are, I don't know.'[38]

Laleham offered its pupils an excellent library, and lessons from distinguished teachers. Alice Gardner, who went on to teach history at Newnham, was educated there, and many of the girls went on to various kinds of higher education. But Hannah Pipe herself remained hostile to feminism.[39] She retained a deep conviction that examinations, competitiveness, achievements in the *public* arena were unseemly for women. If they insisted on going on to higher education, she thought Newnham less damaging than Girton. She saw herself as fostering intellectual 'accomplishments': not achievements to be measured against those of men.

48

The school in Hampstead run by Mrs Ottley and her daughters, Alice and Agnes, through the period 1861-80, remained much smaller than Laleham: as with the Sewell sisters' school, there were generally up to seven pupils. The aim of the school was to foster femininity in a deeply religious atmosphere.[40] Again, the distribution of duties was that of a conventional middle-class household. The bulk of the general, everyday teaching was carried out by Alice with Agnes as helper; together they presided over the schoolroom. Visiting masters handled more specialist branches of knowledge. Mrs Ottley held undisputed sway over the drawing room and over the rest of the household. The atmosphere was always 'homely'. An ex-pupil recalled that:

> In the Hampstead surroundings the girls were emphatically made to feel they were part of the home, and being few in number, were brought into closer personal touch with Alice than could be possible with larger numbers; she was their elder sister and never-failing friend, sharing their sorrows, joys, and difficulties with true and strengthening sympathy.[41]

Alice herself furnished a most exemplary model of conventional femininity — another early pupil recorded that:

> I don't think it ever occurred to us that she was especially clever or powerful; but we all loved her for her gentleness, and we thoroughly realised and admired her extreme unselfishness and devotion to her family, and the way in which she worked, and was ready to sacrifice everything, to enable her younger brothers to have all the educational advantages possible. She never seemed to want anything for herself, but everything for them.[42]

Agnes Hitchcock, a friend of the family in Hampstead during the 1870s, later wrote to Alice Ottley's biographer confirming this impression that Alice's early efforts in teaching were all motivated by the desire to help meet the expenses of her brothers' educations.[43] Mrs Ottley seems to have had rather more affection for her sons than her daughters, and certainly to have spent much more on their education. Agnes Hitchcock mentions this, but comments that 'it was a weakness shared by so many mothers in those mid-Victorian days, that it was very easily overlooked'.[44] However, friends marvelled at how, in the midst of devoting so large a proportion of her energies to others, Alice ever found space for her own studies:

When she found time for any work of her own was a mystery. She was always at hand — always ready to respond to other people's needs, never attempting to withdraw herself from the constant claims on her time and attention. The life she led was essentially a home life — as home life for women was understood in those days; it admitted of little privacy for quiet reading, or for occupations that could not be carried on in the midst of the family circle. To Alice this seemed to matter the less, that she had at all times the power of concentration, and had early learnt to make the most of the few quiet moments that came in her busy life.[45]

Modesty, service, forgetfulness of self; these were the characteristics which Alice Ottley constantly kept before her pupils throughout her long teaching career as the quintessentially feminine virtues, the hallmark of what she defined as a 'gentlewoman'.

An early historian of women's education, Alice Zimmern, estimated that even towards the close of the nineteenth century, probably around 70 per cent of the total number of girls who could be described as receiving some kind of secondary schooling were being educated in private boarding schools.[46] We cannot know how many of these schools there were. Around 1895, the total number of girls' private schools (both day and boarding) in England was variously estimated at between 10,000 and 15,000.[47] The Bryce Commissioners, investigating the structure of secondary education in England in 1894-5 learned that in some of the more rural counties especially, virtually no secondary schools for girls other than the proprietary schools existed.[48] Even at the end of the century, a large proportion of these proprietary schools remained small ventures, organised on the domestic model. Mrs Ella Armitage, who reported on girls' schools in Devon, found that in that county the school of around twelve pupils was ubiquitous and most popular with parents.[49] Such schools still tended to be lodged in private households. It was still evidently common to find that in the cheaper schools, the schoolmistress selected the best room in the house for her parlour — the schoolroom was too often relegated to the gloom of a basement, or girls might be taught in cramped conditions in the dining room, or back parlour.[50] Mrs Kitchener, describing the state of girls' education in the Salford and West Derby hundreds in Lancashire for the same Commission, thought that the cheaper private schools seemed in many cases to have remained totally unaffected by the reforms in girls' education which had taken place in the last quarter of the century.[51]

Lower middle-class girls were still frequently sent off to spend three or four years in the kind of shabby-genteel 'Ladies Seminary', so bitterly condemned by Bryce for the Schools' Inquiry Commission of 1867-8; establishments which offered an education he had found almost guaranteed to 'dwarf and distort' their minds.[52]

In Devonshire, Mrs Armitage reported that the upper layers of a society deeply divided by distinctions of social class and status still clung snobbishly to the idea of the 'select' Ladies' Academy:

> The dominant idea about girls' education is that it should be as far as possible claustral, that girls should be kept from any contamination with people who drop their H's or earn their salt. It is thought that careful seclusion is absolutely necessary for the development of that refinement which should characterise a lady.[53]

She was full of invective against the mistress of one establishment she had come into contact with, who had accepted the daughter of a tradesman as a pupil on condition that the girl never mentioned her home circumstances to her fellow-pupils.[54] This kind of intense snobbery and hypocrisy was apparently very common in the girls' schools of the time — as many accounts bear witness.[55]

It is probably worth quoting Ella Armitage's verdict on the quality of girls' private schools in Devon in a little more detail as an interesting attempt to generalise about conditions, albeit that Mrs Armitage herself insisted on the infinite variety and widely ranging degrees of competence and efficiency she found in these schools.[56] Mrs Armitage estimated that she had become acquainted with a total of about seventy schools, either through having made personal visits to them, or through having received trustworthy accounts from assistants. Out of this total there were only seven schools she was prepared to describe as 'excellent', thirty-five were 'fair', twenty-one were 'indifferent', and seven she would judge to be 'perfectly worthless'. 'It will be observed', she pointed out, 'that the indifferent and worthless schools form very nearly half the total amount.'[57] By far the majority of private schools were distinguished by their 'unblushing assertion of caste exclusiveness', she concluded:

> Perhaps it is difficult to overrate the evil which this kind of idle education . . . must have on the minds of the pupils. Large views of life are not seen from the windows of these schools; thoughts that live and quicken do not enter through these doors. The prim

51

conservatism, the fixed hostility to new ideas which characterise the average British matron of good position are fostered in these seminaries.[58]

Winifred Peck has left us a fairly vivid account of her personal experiences as a pupil in one of these snobbish, intellectually unexciting young ladies' academies of the late-nineteenth century.[59] After the loss of her mother, she and her sister were parcelled off to stay with a great aunt in Eastbourne, who arranged for them to attend a small school presided over by the proprietress, Mrs Quill. Winifred Peck's perceptions of the inadequacies of the establishment were sharpened by the fact that she had earlier been a day-girl at a fairly efficiently organised girls' school in the Midlands, Edgbaston Ladies' College. She was shocked, first by the unsuitable accommodation offered in Miss Quill's household (a villa on one of Eastbourne's less fashionable Southern-facing slopes):

The building itself was not well-suited for a school. There were two big sunny rooms divided by folding doors on the ground floor; the bigger was used as the school hall for prayers, and for the studies of the two top forms; the smaller had been kidnapped by the all-powerful French colleague of Miss Quill, who was her intimate friend and the only good instructress on the staff. In what house agents would call the semi-basement was a large, low, dark room, in which the three or four lower forms all had their lessons from their respective mistresses at separate tables. Such a noisy and distracting background for study was of course common form in the 1860s and 1870s, but was a real shock to my sister and myself after our orderly desks in our separate formrooms in the Edgbaston School. . . . The dining hall – a gloomy annex with windows in the roof – may well have been the old coach-house; off it opened three or four slips of bedrooms dedicated to the head girls. We all knew these rooms because, mere boxes as they were, they each contained a piano, sandwiched between bed and wardrobe, and here we, in turns, did our 'practising'. Their windows opened – if they ever were opened – onto a back yard on one side and into the dining-room on the other, so that they were haunted by the smell of damp cobbles from the yard and of boiled cabbage and steamed pudding, that immemorial scent of English educational establishments, from the hall. The dormitories upstairs had no cubicles, or curtains for privacy of any kind.[60]

Winifred Peck thought Miss Quill's typical of girls' private schools in 'middle class Mid- or indeed Early-Victorian England'. However, some features of the description just quoted place it more clearly in the later years of the century – the division into 'forms', the appointment of 'head girls' – these show the influence – however slight – of more modern educational models. The system of discipline which prevailed in the school was similarly a mixture of old and new. There was an extremely elaborate system of 'conduct marks' in operation: conduct marks could be deducted from each girl's total for 'orders', 'punctuality' or 'carriage'. The idea of the system itself was not unlike those operating in Girls' High Schools of the day (although the emphasis on 'carriage' reminds us that the use of instruments like backboards to correct posture was not yet obsolete). However, the conduct mark system itself scarcely sufficed to maintain discipline – girls became rather *blasé* about their totals – and Miss Quill regularly resorted to the forms of emotional and sentimental blackmail which Bryce had noticed in small private schools earlier in the century. Winifred Peck recalled that Miss Quill would burst into tears or sniff at *sal volatile* when rebuking pupils who had lost too many conduct marks.[61] On one fateful occasion (when Winifred and her sister had committed the awful crime of tearing away from the control of a mistress-in-charge in order to buy sweets) Miss Quill actually succeeded in striking terror into their hearts with the awful pronunciation that 'so shocking an affair must be reported direct to your father; I can only hope that the news will not break his heart'.[62] The upshot of all this was that the girls' father collapsed with uncontrollable merriment and then promptly removed them from the school, but too late, of course to save them from a longish period of dreadful anticipation about how he might react on their homecoming.[63]

Miss Quill's establishment was a bad example of its kind and one should balance this account with some descriptions of a rather better private school existing in the same period. Katharine Chorley spent four years at a school which her parents carefully selected for her in Folkestone; the headmistress of which, Miss Abbott, was a woman of considerably more intellect and cultivated taste than the unfortunate Miss Quill.[64] The girls were taught mathematics and some Latin, although no science at all, not even botany or physical geography, which as Chorley points out were two subjects 'generally considered sufficiently lady-like to receive some attention from the female young'.[65] History seems to have been comparatively well taught by Miss Abbott herself, with the aid of Oxford University Extension lecturers. Even so, the aims of the school were not primarily intellectual ones. Katharine Chorley felt that lessons 'provided us only with a top-dressing, a sprinkling of soil in which an appreciation of the arts and intellectual matters might flourish without raising any dynamic issues in our minds'.[66] The girls were certainly discouraged from developing any interest in controversies of the day of a political or social nature. 'We were discouraged from discussing politics at all and no newspapers were allowed to us.'[67] This last restriction was extremely common in girls' schools of the day. Vera Brittain later considered that the headmistresses of the private school she had attended in Surrey at the turn of the century had been particularly enlightened in allowing the girls to read newspapers. Even then, she pointed out, they were only allowed selected cuttings:

> We were never, of course, allowed to have the papers themselves —
> our innocent eyes might have strayed from foreign affairs to the
> evidence being taken by the Royal Commission on Marriage and
> Divorce or the Report of the International Paris Conference for the
> suppression of the White Slave Traffic — and the carefully selected
> cuttings invariably came from *The Times* or the *Observer* unmodi-
> fied by contrary political opinions, but the fact that we had them
> at all testified to a recognition of the importance of current events
> far from customary at a time when politics and economics were still
> thought by most headmistresses to be no part of the education of
> marriageable young females.[68]

This prohibition on newspapers in so many girls' private schools stemmed, of course, from the belief that the public world of newspapers and business was a male concern — women needed to be insulated from the world.

The pupils at Miss Abbott's school in Folkestone were kept under careful and constant supervision to keep them away from the contaminating influences of men or of other girls beneath them on the social scale. Katharine Chorley remembered that they were not allowed to write letters to anyone except their parents unless letters were left unsealed for inspection or enclosed in those they sent home. Even contact with brothers was regarded with some suspicion.[69] As for contacts with girls from dissimilar class backgrounds, Chorley records that even on the playing-field, these were strictly taboo — matches with other schools were rare since only three local schools were deemed to be socially acceptable:

The necessary accomplishment of refusing invitations politely on secret grounds of social ineligibility was thus taught us early. The Games Captain knew exactly what she had to reply when a challenge was received from this or that establishment whose pupils were 'not quite like ourselves'. She sat down at her desk with a sheet of best note-paper and indited an answer to the effect that all Saturdays were regrettably filled until the end of term.[70]

Social snobbery, then, formed part of the 'hidden curriculum' of the school. There is no doubt that the girls were made fully aware both of their own privileged class position and also of the fact that their social status throughout life would depend on that of their fathers, brothers and future husbands. Katharine Chorley recalled that in one term the girls had developed a craze for wearing their sailor-ties in the colours of schools and colleges and clubs which had been patronised by their fathers and brothers.[71] She herself had sported 'an Emm. College Cambridge blue and salmon'. The episode signified rather more than 'the comic expression of old school-tie snobbism' as she dismissed it: it showed the girls' awareness of the fact that their fortunes depended not on their own efforts, but on those of their male relatives.

For the main purpose of the schooling she received in Folkestone, as Katharine Chorley admitted, was to train the girls for suitable matrimony. To this end the curriculum included dancing, elocution and deportment. Miss Abbott made efforts to teach Katharine 'how to enter or retire from a room with a degree of elegance and assurance'.[72] One mistress, Miss Foggarty, busied herself trying to obliterate what she claimed to be Katharine's undesirable Lancashire accent.[73] Visiting masters (heavily chaperoned) supplied the refinements of music and art. These, with religious teaching (Miss Abbott was a devout Christian) constituted the 'core curriculum'. Proficiency in intellectual work was an added accomplishment.

New types of girls' schools came into existence during the second half of the nineteenth century, and universities to some extent opened their doors to women.[74] It should be emphasised at the outset that these reforms only affected a very small minority of middle-class girls.

At the risk of over-simplification, we might say that three main types of girls' school evolved. There were, first, the Ladies' Colleges. Queen's College, London, founded in 1848 originally with the aim of improving the education of governesses, developed into an institution offering what can best be described as a 'secondary' rather than university level education.[75] Bedford Ladies' College was founded one year later, in 1849.[76] Originally intended to be an institution of higher education, it still had for fifteen years a secondary school attached to it. Cheltenham Ladies' College was opened in 1854 and Dorothea Beale appointed as its second Principal in 1858.[77] This foundation rose to national fame in the 1860s and acted to some extent as an inspiration for Ladies' Colleges elsewhere – in Grantham, for instance, in Edgbaston, and in Eastbourne.

The second group of schools were those to a greater or lesser extent modelled on the highly successful North London Collegiate School, founded by Frances Mary Buss in 1850.[78] 'High' schools for girls all over the country, including the group belonging to the Girls' Public Day School Company (which was founded in 1872 and responsible for thirty-six schools by 1896) and those of the Church Schools Company (founded in 1883, and with twenty-four schools by 1896) came into this group.[79] So do the endowed high schools for girls such as Manchester High School, and the High School endowed under the King George VI Trust in Birmingham. We might further include the 're-formed' endowed grammar and 'middle' schools for girls in this group. Endowed 'middle' schools like the Skinners' School in Stamford Hill, Haberdashers Aske's at Hoxton, and Dame Alice Owen's School, Islington, charged lower fees than the average 'High' School and discharged their pupils rather earlier into the world.[80] Their organisation and curriculum was, however, similar, and they seem to have catered for much the same social group. Finally, many of the newer Municipal girls' secondary schools might be considered under this heading.

The third main category of new types of school consisted of the large public schools for girls which were intended by their founders as the counterparts of the leading boys' public schools of the time. In this group one can include St Leonard's (founded in 1877), Roedean (1885), Wycombe Abbey (1896), and twentieth century foundations such as Benenden (1923) and Westonbirt (1928).[81]

These divisions are in many ways arbitrary and unsatisfactory. A school such as Worcester High School for Girls (1883), for instance, in spite of its name, is difficult to place in this scheme. Under the headmistress ship of Alice Ottley (1883-1912) the school developed a tone and character which would place it more happily in a category with Cheltenham Ladies' College than with other high schools.[82] On the other hand the social background of the pupils was not so select as at

Cheltenham.[83] There are simply too many variables (nature of founda-tion, personality and values of the headmistress, scale of fees, size of school and so forth) to permit of any neat classification. But all these schools, along with the new colleges for women in the universities, have been regarded by historians of women's education as embodying or representing the reform impulse, and it is in this light that they will be considered here.

A standard assumption in the majority of texts on the history of women's education has been that the provision of these new kinds of schooling represented the achievement of feminists bent on widening opportunities available for women in public and professional life. These new schools, it is usually alleged, gave intellectual substance to women's education, heralding the end of the mid-Victorian obsession with pretty accomplishments, piano-playing, purse-netting and poor French. This standard interpretation has recently been challenged by two writers; by an American historian, Joyce Senders Pedersen, and in England by Sara Delamont.[84] Both of these writers have emphasised the pitfalls of automatically assuming that reforms in women's educa-tion were mainly the work of feminists. Committed feminists were very much a minority group in late-Victorian Britain. However vocal they may have been as a pressure group, however well-argued their case, it was unlikely that they would have gained sufficient support from the middle-class public to engineer reforms on the scale of those which actually took place. The Girls' Public Day School Company, for instance, became a thriving public concern — administered to some considerable extent by 'respectable' middle-class men. And as Pedersen has pointed out, it was highly unlikely that these men and the other social groups who supported new educational ventures for women would have done so had these ventures set out to challenge the con-ventions of family life, or even, to any substantial extent, to challenge conventions about acceptable 'womanly' behaviour or concepts of 'femininity'.

Pedersen's work has involved an analysis of the origin and structure of reforms in women's education, and a study of the values and aims of the individuals and social groups centrally connected with reform.[85] She argues that the period 1850-1900 saw the development of a new type of girls' school; much larger than the small, traditional seminaries, and with a formal commitment to academic achievement and merit-ocratic values. There were also important changes in the status of women teachers. In particular, the headmistresses of the new kind of girls' schools enjoyed a marked rise in social and professional status. Headmistresses like Miss Buss and Miss Beale were grand, remote, dignified public figures. They were very *unlike* the distressed-gentlewoman type of Lady Proprietress who ran a small school in her own household. The new headmistresses were well-paid, enjoyed comparative freedom from pressures and demands of individual parents, and evolved new standards of professional conduct and autonomy. At the same time, however, their position depended on the support of that section of the middle-class community who sought a new kind of education for their daughters. Support for the new schools and colleges, Pedersen argues, came above all from those professional groups and wealthy businessmen who aspired towards a new standard of 'gentility' which would differentiate them from the bulk of the middle class.[86] The system of social values espoused by this group involved the rejection of purely commercial utilitarian goals and the development of new codes of professional ethics and new forms of cultural idealism which affected their attitudes towards education. Pedersen holds that women's education was seen as important by this group because women were seen to enjoy the leisure which would enable them to pursue aesthetic and intellectual activities, and hence raise the standard of culture for the group as a whole. Sir Joshua Fitch, serving as Assistant Commissioner to the Schools' Inquiry Commission in the 1860s had argued that in a society where boys were expected to go into business, trade or the professions, women were the natural guardians of the nation's culture.[87] Pedersen shows that this view was expressed time and time again by middle-class exponents of the need for reforming women's education in the second half of the century.[88]

Reforms in girls' education then began to appear in a distinctly conservative light. The new schools and colleges, it may be argued, shared essentially the same kind of goals as their predecessors, aiming to turn out 'refined' ladies of leisure. There may indeed have been a revolt against superficial and showy 'accomplishments', a new emphasis on cultural and intellectual standards and achievement. But the new institutions were certainly not characterised by any attempt to challenge the sexual division of labour any more than they were by any other kind of social radicalism. The reformers rejected the idea that it was 'feminine' to be ignorant and waste one's time in trivial pursuits, and emphasised the desirability of educating women to be cultivated wives and mothers. They did not, on the whole, question the assumption that marriage would imply leisure because the middle-class woman was still expected to become economically dependent on her husband after marriage and to be able to employ domestic servants to service her household. The reformers *redefined* the Victorian concept of femininity: they did not (in the main) *reject* it.

Sara Delamont's work on the education of middle-class women in the nineteenth century has emphasised the contradictions inherent in the movement for reform.[89] Like Pedersen she points out that most middle-class parents wanted their daughters above all to grow into ladylike, marriageable young women. A reform movement which had aimed to challenge the sexual division of labour and to subvert conventional concepts of femininity could have had no chance of success in mid-Victorian society.[90] The pioneers of educational reform in this period, Delamont suggests, can be divided into two groups: the 'separatists' and the 'uncompromising'.[91] The 'separatists' aroused less opposition than the 'uncompromising' because they were content to see improvements in women's education without demanding that the results of these improvements be constantly measured against the standards currently used in male educational and academic circles. The 'uncompromising' group (of whom Emily Davies was the most famous example) insisted that girls should study the same subjects as men, and sit the same examinations: they were convinced that this was the only route towards equality. Women in this latter group, of course, were much more likely to be accused of unladylike behaviour, to be stigmatised as 'unfeminine', than were the separatists. But Delamont shows clearly that almost all of the reformers were to some extent trapped in a 'double-bind'. They were all torn between adherence to two sets of standards. On the one hand, sanctioned by a strong sense of propriety, were the standards of ladylike behaviour, the conventions of femininity. On the other, there were the standards of the male academic establishment. Neither the uncompromising nor the separatists were wholly able to ignore either of these orthodoxies, or the conflicts between them; conflicts which, albeit in a modified form, have persisted in women's education down to the present day.

In the pages that follow I want to look more closely at the character of the new schools and colleges, and to explore some of the ways in which their structure and curricula served to reinforce girls' learning about femininity. I do not want to argue that the new institutions functioned *primarily* to reinforce assumptions about the sexual division of labour and femininity; to succumb to any simple theory about education as 'social control'. A discussion of the conservative function of the institutions which historians have traditionally interpreted as embodying a distinctly 'progressive' or feminist ideology is intended partly to counterbalance these interpretations. To argue that the new high schools and colleges for women were in many ways conservative institutions is not to deny that they played a crucial role in the history of the feminist movement; the question of their contribution here will be taken up again in Chapter 5.

Perhaps one of the most striking features of the new schools and colleges for middle-class women established in the late-nineteenth century is the extent to which these institutions were sponsored by, organised by, patronised by and controlled by men. Those who have documented the history of particular institutions and of women's education as a whole have often referred to this rather obliquely, if at all, probably because it was taken for granted, or simply automatically accepted as a demonstration of generous paternalism. F.D. Maurice nobly taking up his sword on behalf of the distressed governess, Henry Sidgwick going without his summer holiday in order to be able to take the lease on number 74 Regent Street in Cambridge to house those young ladies who represented the beginnings of Newnham College: these actions are commonly mentioned in the standard histories and described as acts of chivalry. But however chivalrous or enlightened such forms of patronage may have been, the facts of power and control remain clear.

Queen's College, Harley Street, was governed almost entirely by men throughout the nineteenth century.[92] The Committee of Education (an offshoot of the Governesses' Benevolent Institution) which had originally sponsored the foundation of the College was a male committee. The Council appointed to govern the College consisted 'largely of absentee clerics and peers'.[93] Lectures were given by male visiting professors. Until 1931, successive principals were male. Women played an altogether subordinate role as junior 'tutors' and 'Lady Visitors'. The 'Lady Visitors' were older women who chaperoned pupils on a rota basis when they attended lectures. They had little formal power. They were allowed to 'make suggestions' in a locked suggestion book.[94] Many of the suggestions they made record their concern with social propriety. Elaine Kaye, the historian of Queen's, mentioned that in 1864 the greater part of one of their meetings was spent discussing whether or not they should suggest that the Council should rule the exclusion of daughters of retail traders.[95] Difficulties began very early in the history of the College because of a lack of communication between the male Committee of Education and the Lady Visitors. These two bodies never even met until 1874. Lack of communication – and the impotence of the female tutors – occasioned much bad feeling amongst the latter. Dorothea Beale, who had taught mathematics and Latin to younger girls in the College in the 1850s, resigned from her post in 1856 partly because she resented the fact that women were given so little responsibility for the interests of the girls they were teaching.[96]

Queen's College was unusual in the extent to which its government was dominated by men, although it was not the only case. Thomas Holloway, who founded and financed Royal Holloway College for Women in 1883 (in memory of his wife), stipulated plainly in his will that future trustees and governors of the College should be male.[97] And most colleges for women were sponsored and originally organised by committees on which men preponderated. Given the social and political powerlessness of women in the middle of the last century, given the fact that it was still regarded as unseemly for them to involve themselves in the male arena of public affairs, it was difficult, if not impossible, for women to organise public ventures *without* male support. The story of Bedford Ladies' College, founded one year after Queen's, in 1849, is instructive in this context.

Bedford College owes its foundation to Mrs Elizabeth Reid, a wealthy widow who developed a strong interest in schemes for elevating the moral and intellectual character of women in the 1840s. Little is known about any specific plans she may have had in respect of founding a college for women before 1849, but in the draft of a letter written later, in the 1860s, she alludes to having made 'several attempts' to interest people in such a scheme before eventually meeting with success.[98] An article later contributed by a friend of Mrs Reid's, Rachel Notcutt, to the *Bedford College Magazine* described the ploy which Mrs Reid ultimately resorted to, and which helped her launch her scheme. Mrs Reid evidently wrote a letter to a woman with some influence in London society, whom Margaret Tuke, the historian of Bedford College, thinks was almost certainly Lady Romilly; Notcutt recorded that this letter contained:

the startling announcement that half a dozen worthy gentlemen had met at breakfast at a friend's house and there had discussed the very unsatisfactory state of women's education. The letter went on to say that these worthy gentlemen, conscience-stricken at the advantages of education they had over their sisters, determined to see if something could not be done to mend matters.[99]

Lady Romilly was evidently suitably impressed, and fired with enthusiasm for the cause, although, as Notcutt continued:

> It soon appeared that these wealthy and conscience-stricken gentlemen were myths, conjured up by the writer of the aforesaid letter, Mrs Reid, who thought by this harmless device she could best introduce a scheme she had formed.[100]

Mrs Reid by all accounts was a woman with a particular abhorrence of publicity (Tuke writes of her 'almost morbid desire for self-effacement'),[101] but the episode does illuminate the difficulties women encountered in reconciling social propriety and their sense of what was fittingly feminine with the desire to take effective action in a public arena.

The problems encountered by the pioneers of Bedford College over the definition of a constitution further illustrate the kind of obstacles women met when trying to order their own affairs. Mindful of the position at Queen's, Mrs Reid determined that the government of Bedford College should from the beginning be entrusted mainly to women. A Ladies' Committee was 'entrusted with all arrangements which have reference to the comfort and convenience of the pupils', and a General Committee, on which ladies preponderated, was to direct 'the general and scholastic management' of the College.[102] However, Margaret Tuke points out that these early constitutional arrangements had subsequently to be altered because

> Experience during the provisional period seems to have shown that time was wasted in profitless discussion at Committee Meetings, many of the members being unversed in business or committee methods. Committee work, so familiar to women today, was a thing hardly known to those of 1849.[103]

A sub-committee was entrusted with the drawing up of a more workable scheme and the extent of female influence declined: Mrs Reid evidently regretted this, but accepted a new constitution as preferable to a break-down in proceedings. But reports of Board meetings from the period 1849-50 show that problems of defining responsibility for decision-making persisted, not least (the Report of 1850 alleges) because it was hard 'for ladies to deliberate and discuss freely in the presence of a large company of men'.[104]

It was extremely difficult for Mrs Reid to realise her vision of a college organised by, as well as for, women: convention made it much easier to provide for a Ladies' Committee to 'make suggestions' or exercise an indirect 'feminine influence' than to wield real power. However, the terms of the trust fund which Mrs Reid bequeathed 'for the promotion and improvement of female education' in 1860 (to come into operation after her death) stipulated that there should be at least three trustees, all of whom must be unmarried women, to administer the bequest.[105]

It is difficult for us today to realise just how radical any suggestion that women should be included on governing bodies was in the middle of the last century. Emily Davies, giving evidence before the Schools' Inquiry Commission in 1867-8 told the Commissioners that in her opinion:

> Where a school is for girls there ought to be some ladies on the governing board. In endowed schools generally the trustees or governors are all gentlemen, and the schools are apt to get neglected from their having so many other things to do. They do not give so much attention, I think, as ladies might.[106]

Mindful as she was of the fact that so many charitable endowments originally intended for the education of girls as well as boys had, in the hands of male administrators, been appropriated entirely for the use of boys, one must judge Emily Davies' observation here particularly tactful and well-phrased. But the Commissioners apparently had some misgivings over the idea of women on governing bodies. Mr Acland wondered whether a Ladies' Committee with advisory functions might be more fitting? Miss Davies thought not: she would prefer to see women represented on the governing boards themselves.[107] But those who shared her conviction had a long struggle ahead of them. In 1876, for instance, the Women's Education Union addressed a memorial to the Charity Commissioners, who had in 1874 taken over the powers of the Endowed School Commissioners (appointed to revise the administration of educational endowments and to extend or restore the benefits of these to girls).[108] The WEU wanted an assurance that women would be represented on the governing bodies of revised schemes. The Charity Commissioners' reply to a deputation sent in June 1876 was hardly encouraging. It argued that the question of women governors was 'surrounded with much practical difficulty' and that the Commissioners felt that they were unable to pledge themselves to any particular course – the most they could aim for was to 'assign influence' to women in the *management* of girls' schools.[109]

In the reform of girls' secondary schools, as much as in the area of higher education, we find that the lead was often taken by men, or that when women sought to implement changes they were heavily dependent on male support and patronage – which usually implied a fair amount of control. Cheltenham Ladies' College owed its foundation in 1853 to the efforts of four gentlemen (three with the title 'Reverend', and one doctor), who met to consider the best means of providing for the daughters of professional men in that town.[110] The idea that Worcester should have its own high school for girls came originally from the Reverend Canon Butler, in 1883, who summoned a meeting of 'representative churchmen and citizens of Worcester' (meaning prominent local business and professional men) to discuss the plan.[111] Joyce Pedersen points out that this was an extremely common pattern of events.[112] All over the country we find that the initiative for girls' schools at the local level was likely to have come from clergymen. Exeter's High School was founded under the auspices of Dr Temple; Truro High School by Dr Benson, then Archbishop-Elect of Canterbury. The Church Schools Company, as its name implies, was a clerical venture, founded in 1883 to emulate the example of the Girls' Public Day School Company in setting up 'improved' schools for girls.[113]

The GPDS Company was originally an offshoot of the 'National Union for the Education of Girls of all classes above the Elementary', a society established in 1871.[114] Its title was later shortened to 'The Women's Education Union'. The society owed its inspiration to the activities of two women in particular, Maria Grey and her sister Emily Shirreff. These women and other friends and supporters like Mary Gurney and Lady Henrietta Stanley were energetic in promoting and publicising the interests of the WEU (which continued in existence until 1882) and of the GPDS Company itself, formed in 1872. But the women leant heavily on the support of noblemen and distinguished clergymen. From the beginning Maria Grey realised the strategic advantages to be gained from such patronage. Lord Airlie, Lord Lyttelton, the Bishop of Exeter and the Dean of Westminster were recruited as Vice-Presidents of the WEU and Canon Blakesley of Norfolk gallantly offered to canvass more clerical support.[115] The first four Presidents of the GPDS Company were the Earl of Airlie (1872), Lord Aberdare (1881), the Earl Spencer (1896) and the Earl (later Marquess) of Crewe (1809). The first Council of 1872-3 comprised twelve men and six women. Successive Chairmen of Council from 1872 down to the 1960s were all male.[116]

Male patronage — particularly the support of those of high social status or some intellectual distinction — was crucial to the success of women's educational reform: women reformers themselves were usually aware of this and set out to court the patronage which would imbue their ventures with respectability in the eyes of the middle-class public. The Girls' Public Day School Company (later Trust) became an unimpeachably respectable organisation. It is of no small significance that Laurie Magnus, a sometime Vice-Chairman of the Council and the Trust's first historian composed the preface to his history in that most gentlemanly of gentlemen's retreats, The Athenaeum.[117] Gentlemen continued to sit in large numbers on the governing bodies of girls' schools and women's colleges, and on the platforms in the halls of these institutions on speechdays and special occasions. And professors and leading academics, of course, continued to be male.

These facts were certainly as important as, if not more important than, the more obvious forms of continuing discrimination against women in the educational world — such as Oxford and Cambridge refusing to admit women to full university membership until well into the twentieth century (the former admitting them in 1920, the latter holding out until 1947). Even in their own schools and colleges, women were likely to be presented with images of male authority, the structures of power and prestige which mirrored the realities of contemporary sexual politics. This might reinforce their learning about femininity through confirming their dependent status. The higher a girl pitched her aspirations to academic success, the more she was likely to feel that she was a trespasser in male preserves. Women students in Oxford or Cambridge at the turn of the century could not, of course, call themselves 'undergraduates'. Their status was anomalous — they were there on sufferance. Winifred Peck's descriptions of her student days at Oxford at this time convey clearly that she and her peers looked upon male academics 'reverently, from a distance', that their sense of their own insignificance, as females, their deference to the male intellect, was, if anything, confirmed by the experience of going to college.[118]

Some women found or made father figures of their male tutors. Some sought, perhaps, to confirm their own social and intellectual dependence through marrying men they might 'look up to' in these terms. Some undoubtedly learned to pursue strategic goals of their own through exaggerated forms of deference, or through flattering the male ego. M.V. Hughes related how, given the responsibility for organising a teacher-training course at Bedford College, London, at the turn of the century, she had been stumped by the problem of finding teaching in special subjects.[119] She hit upon the idea of persuading professors of various subjects to talk about teaching methodology. When they demurred (as they usually did) protesting that they knew little about the subject, she suggested that they might come and talk about the ways in which they considered their own students had been badly taught, adding persuasively that they might

> indeed talk about anything at all. It is the clash with a bigger mind that these girls want, especially with a man's, for they may be buried in girls' schools for years.[120]

As we have already seen, M.V. Hughes did believe in the intellectual inferiority of her own sex — hence she did not, apparently, feel herself too demeaned by this kind of 'feminine wile'.

It was extremely difficult for women, even when academically successful themselves, to challenge or even to relate to male authority on anything like equal terms. Margaret Murray, herself an eminent Egyptologist, described how women lecturers in University College, London, in the 1920s were not even able to go into the men's common room to drink coffee and discuss research with colleagues.[121] The sanctions were informal ones — the place was sacrosanct to male use, a kind of gentlemen's club. On one occasion Dr Murray ventured into this 'Lion's Den' as the guest of a sympathetic colleague. She chose a day when she thought few of the patriarchs would be present, but even so, remembered that:

> As I entered the room I encountered looks of shocked horror, changing to fury, from the die-hard anti-feminists present. But they rapidly buried themselves behind newspapers to shut out the dreadful sight.[122]

There was apparently a flaming row as soon as she left the room. The patriarchs won, and a 'feminist invasion' was accordingly averted. Of course, many Oxford and Cambridge colleges, even those that have recently begun to admit women students, persist in regarding the entry of women into public and academic life as a kind of sacrilegious indecency. There are still — even in the 1980s — common rooms and Combination Rooms which a woman cannot comfortably enter (unless she is a domestic servant).

66

Women were often as inhibited in challenging male authority (even where they perceived it as clearly in their interests to do so) as they were in entering the gentlemen's club. Again, one of Margaret Murray's anecdotes illustrates this well. She described how when University College needed to appoint a tutor to women students the selection committee drawn up for the purpose turned out to be all male.[123] The senior common room women were unhappy about the candidate who looked likely to be chosen and some felt it would be advisable to write to the Selection Committee suggesting that the women tutors be consulted on the matter. Others apparently felt this would appear unseemly. Margaret Murray eventually wrote to the Committee as an individual suggesting that the women be consulted. The Committee immediately accepted this as a sensible idea. 'This little incident', she commented, 'shows how strong the feeling was still amongst a certain type of woman, to be afraid to express an opinion which might offend the men.'[124]

Women were afraid of being labelled 'unfeminine', they were afraid of feeling shamed, they were afraid of ridicule. And as Sara Delamont and other writers have pointed out, most of the new High Schools and colleges for women in the second half of the nineteenth century reinforced these fears by being extraordinarily watchful over the behaviour of their pupils and students, extremely concerned to promote ladylike behaviour and to avoid any imputation of unseemliness.[125] Chaperones were insisted on. Girls' relationships with the other sex — even brothers — were carefully monitored. Some schools frowned upon certain kinds of sport and athletic activity as unladylike. In Cheltenham Ladies' College in the 1870s, girls were allowed to play lawn tennis if they wanted to, but more generally encouraged to take their exercise by going walking in the countryside or doing 'gentle calisthenics'.[126] Miss Beale frowned upon the idea of competitive games as unfeminine. At Worcester High School Miss Ottley allowed the younger girls to form a cricket club, but insisted that it was most unsuitable for girls over fourteen. An editorial in the School magazine stated that

> The Headmistress is anxious that it should be clearly understood that she utterly detests women's cricket.
>
> She considers it to be a game admirable for *little* girls and for all boys; exercising some of the best moral qualities as well as physical powers: but it is one of the things she would have girls lay aside

when they leave childhood behind and enter upon maidenhood. She earnestly desires that the 'note' of the Worcester High School should be delicate, womanly refinement, a high-toned courtesy, a gentle manner, a dignified bearing, which shall be as far removed from the loud, romping vulgarity of the hoyden, called 'the girl of the period' as from the mincing affectation of the 'fine lady' of the eighteenth century.[127]

Of course not all High Schools looked askance upon the idea of competitive sports or cricket, and the new 'public' schools for girls such as Wycombe Abbey or Roedean were enthusiastic about sport as a healthy antidote to feminine frailties or sentimentalities – a subject which will be returned to later.[128] But even those schools which advocated a certain amount of liberty *on* the playing field maintained a careful supervision of girls' social behaviour *off* it, particularly in matters of dress, deportment and decorum.

The same was true of the women's colleges in the universities. Reformers as uncompromising as Emily Davies and as compromising as Anne Jemima Clough were united in their anxieties to see their students dressed neatly and becomingly, fittingly chaperoned, observing proprieties and avoiding scandal. Miss Clough fussed about rumours that her young ladies were buttoning up their gloves in the street, and reputedly presented one student who had a *penchant* for clothes cut on severely utilitarian lines with an ostrich feather, anxious to add a softening touch to her attire.[129]

In many ways some of the early women's colleges continued the work of a middle-class family upbringing in sheltering girls from too much contact with the outside world and fostering 'feminine' behaviour. While colleges remained small, they were able to preserve an intimate, familial atmosphere – especially where principals deliberately set out to cultivate this. Anne Jemima Clough seems to have adopted a very 'maternal', protective attitude to her early students – however much certain of them resented it. Apparently she was constantly solicitous over health, diet, hours of sleep, exposure to draughts and fresh air.[130] Mary Paley Marshall's memories of her early days in 74 Regent Street (the first home of the first students of what was to become Newnham College) convey a strong impression of a cosy, family party; Henry Sidgwick playing the part of male provider, Miss Clough acting like a mother to the girls:

74 Regent Street had been taken for us by Mr Henry Sidgwick who

had spent his Long Vacation time and money in getting it ready. In a letter which he wrote in 1871 he says: 'I am not going to take any real holiday this Long, I have no money. The cares of a household being incumbent, I find myself estimating the expenses of Plate, linen etc.' So of course we wanted to be economical as well and my first recollections of Mr Sidgwick and Mr Marshall are the evenings when we sat round and sewed the household linen in Miss Clough's sitting-room.[131]

Although there were only five students originally, Mr Sidgwick had evidently found it difficult to keep them in order. Mrs Marshall quoted from a letter of his where he lamented that the women showed 'a strong impulse towards liberty' and would 'not submit to maternal government'.[132] There is no evidence, however, of any serious rebellion.

Winifred Peck's recollections of her student days in Oxford when Lady Margaret Hall was still in its infancy observe similarly that college life was like a 'small, homelike party of young ladies', gathered together in a household regulated very much along the lines 'of any well-ordered home of the period.'[133] Elizabeth Wordsworth, although much more of a scholar than Miss Clough, shared with this latter the aim of giving girls the chance of continuing their studies at a university level while safeguarding them from any danger to their religious faith and continuing their upbringing as young ladies.

Colleges of education aiming to attract middle- (or lower-middle) class girls who wished to train as teachers tended similarly to pride themselves on offering a secluded, family-like environment for their students. Bishop Otter College, Chichester, was founded in 1873 and aimed to attract 'ladies', rather than working-class girls, into teaching (although it evidently had problems in doing so).[134] Louisa Hubbard, who played a leading part in the foundation of the College, wanted it to remain small, with an intake of less than fifty students, in order to preserve the 'homely' atmosphere defined as suitable for fostering ladylike qualities. Giving evidence to the Cross Commission in 1886, Miss Trevor, the Principal of the College, emphasised that she needed to act like a mother to her girls.[135] When Charlotte Mason set up her 'House of Education' in Ambleside in 1892 (aiming to train girls from respectable backgrounds as superior nursery-governesses) she deliberately avoided calling her establishment 'a college'. 'Household life as a means of culture', she wrote, 'is much to be preferred to college life'.[136] The students (whom she referred to as 'her bairns') were minutely supervised and they followed an extremely rigid timetable in their studies. Essex Cholmondeley, a biographer of Charlotte Mason, observed that this had its uses: in their future posts the governesses would be expected to live in the constant company of their pupils – their training therefore 'prepared them to face with contentment this lack of personal freedom in term-time'.[137] A fittingly feminine dependence was thus confirmed.

Relationships between the principals and mistresses of the new women's colleges and their pupils were often extremely close. Most accounts of college life during the period contain accounts of long and frequent conversations with authority, solicitous enquiries from principals about family circumstances, the health and fortune of parents and brothers. The accounts are understandably nostalgic in tone and one suspects that the intimacy might at times have proved rather more claustrophobic than they suggest. Walking across the park regularly with a witty and accomplished conversationalist like Miss Wordsworth was no doubt pleasurable. But the obligation of sitting next to someone as reticent and austere as Mrs Sidgwick at dinner must have awed and exhausted many of the early Newnham students. Constance Maynard regularly invited her Westfield students to go touring round the country with her on a bicycle during the vacation. Her biographer, Constance Firth, who had been a student at Westfield, recorded that when her turn came she met Miss Maynard in Doncaster and they rode out in pouring rain. That night they took shelter in a cottage with but one spare room and one spare bed which they had to share. 'To go cycling with the Mistress of your college', Firth remarked, 'may be rather a fearful joy when you are very young.'[138]

As Pedersen has shown, the later nineteenth century did witness the development of a new type of girls' school – larger, moving away from the private-domestic model and committed to publicly recognised academic goals.[139] But many of the headmistresses of these new, large schools deeply regretted some of the implications of expansion – the loss of a family atmosphere, the advent of new kinds of formality and impersonality. Indeed, they sought ways of averting these changes. Alice Ottley began her teaching career with a marked distaste for the idea of high schools for girls because she felt individual character could only be developed in a small, intimate milieu.[140] As headmistress of Worcester High School she strove constantly to maintain close personal relationships with her pupils, against the odds which rising numbers implied.[141] Frances Buss remained a staunch believer in day schools for

70

girls because she believed that large boarding schools were likely to destroy family life.[142] Small boarding houses conducted like private households within the school (as in Cheltenham) might, she felt, mitigate these disadvantages to some extent. And if the large day school provided a social environment very different from that of the family, it was important to keep the school day short in order to safeguard the influences of family life. The majority of girls' high schools provided lessons only in the mornings: afternoons, it was felt, the girls should spend at home.[143] Most of the schools organised by the Girls' Public Day School Company did not introduce the principle of afternoon school until well into the present century.

The fact that headmistresses were sometimes divided in their own minds about the benefits of large and small schools, and that in their own careers they had often gained experience of very different types of school, might account for rather peculiarly contrasting elements in the ethos of girls' schools at the turn of the century. Women teachers undoubtedly found some difficulties in adjusting their behaviour from the forms appropriate in a small, private school to those more fitting in the new, large-scale and more formally organised institutions. Loelia Ponsonby remembers that when she was at Heathfield (a fashionable and High Church boarding school) during the first world war, the headmistress, Miss Wyatt, tried to form intimate relationships with all her charges:

> Every night she clasped each one of us – and we numbered over a
> hundred – to her bosom and, smelling heavily of lavender-water,
> placed a bristly kiss on our brow. This was the moment for whis-
> pered confidences. We were all very devoted to her.[144]

It was worth remembering that even the North London Collegiate School had started out as a small private venture, housed in the Buss family's own household. Miss Buss had adopted a very maternal role towards her charges, dismissing them one by one daily from her parlour with affectionate kisses.[145] As Josephine Kamm observed, rising numbers (the pupils had increased from 35 to 115 by December 1850) soon rendered such regular demonstrations of affection impractical.[146] However, throughout her long career Miss Buss's behaviour towards her pupils oscillated between dignified formality and sudden intimacy. She might preach from the platform, invoking the rule-book, but was equally likely to smother a girl with enveloping hugs and kisses.[147] The role-confusion stemmed on the one hand from ambivalence between the codes of behaviour appropriate to two kinds of school; on the other from a divided self-image. Headmistresses were increasingly aware of their dignity as figures of public importance, as Pedersen points out,[148] but from childhood they, too, had been schooled in 'feminine' behaviour. Somehow they had to reconcile the two.

On the whole the women who staffed the new schools and colleges for girls presented their pupils with conservative images of women's work and lives. They tended to be highly respectable women, exemplifying in their own lives the quintessentially 'feminine' virtues of selflessness and service, albeit in a comparatively 'public' arena rather than within the confines of family life. The huge majority of teachers in girls' high schools and colleges were unmarried. While feminism fell short of challenging the sexual division of labour this was almost bound to remain so. Full time, paid employment was still socially unacceptable for middle-class women after marriage. Women who sought personal autonomy and the stimulus of continued employment therefore sometimes chose to remain single. Frances Buss, Dorothea Beale, Constance Maynard and many others turned down offers of marriage. As Delamont has noted 'Celibacy was a common form of revolt against the traditional female sphere.'[149] It was inordinately difficult for women to separate their sexuality from what they had learned about 'femininity' — from associations of fragility, passivity and dependence. So they frequently denied both at the same time. But the celibate lifestyle of women teachers hardly commended them as role-models in the eyes of the majority of their pupils, and certainly helped to foster the illusion of there being a necessary choice, confronting all women, between career and marriage. Women were not generally allowed both.

Of course some women sought deliberately to gain support for educational reforms through emphasising their own respectability, by insisting that their programme aimed to restore to women not rights, but a consciousness of real feminine duties. Emily Shirreff and Maria Grey constantly asserted that their desire to see women better educated was motivated by a desire to see them more effectively carrying out their traditional obligations as wives, mothers, sisters and daughters. Addressing a meeting at the Albert Hall in 1872 Mrs Grey outlined her vision of reform in a way calculated to reassure antifeminists: a main object of her movement, she urged, was character-training, she wanted to see a girl brought to a proper understanding of

the relation in which she stood to the physical world around her; to her fellow-being, whether as members of her family, her country, or her race; to her God, the Father and supreme Lord; and to know and perform the duties which arose out of those relations.[150]

Similarly the Committee which governed the constitution of Manchester High School for Girls asserted that they aimed to fit the girls

for any future which may lie before them, so that they may become intelligent companions and associates for their brothers, meet helps and counsellors for their husbands, and wise guides and trainers for the minds of their children.[151]

These were aims which would certainly have been lauded by Sarah Ellis, or any other of the highly conservative writers who discussed on the subject of 'woman's sphere' from the 1840s onward: woman should be educated not for herself, but for the service of (largely male) others.[152]

Comparatively few women academics or educationists seem openly to have questioned the idea that women found their real selves in marriage. Even those who themselves remained unmarried sometimes encouraged their pupils to rate marital aims and domesticity high – even higher than intellectual goals. Blanche Athena Clough recorded that her aunt, Anne Jemima, 'attached great importance to home life, and was also decidedly an advocate for marriage', she 'by no means wished all women to take up professions'.[153] Winifred Peck remarked of Elizabeth Wordsworth that 'Probably to the end of her life she ranked a submission to God and a sense of duty to the family very high in the list of womanly virtues'.[154] Miss Wordsworth suggested that St Paul's words, 'Study to be quiet and do your own business' should adorn the mantelpiece in the dining hall in Lady Margaret Hall, as showing a remarkable insight into women's nature.[155] Peck also remembered that the principal made a habit of consoling students who had just missed achieving coveted academic honours by assuring them that it really didn't matter, for they were quite sure to get married, anyway.[156]

Given the fact that most women had deeply internalised the idea that femininity entailed self-sacrifice, that it was womanly to be modest, retiring and attentive to other's needs, it was not surprising that the majority of girls were either unambitious, and that those who *were* ambitious often felt embarrassed or guilty about being so. Victorian society was always likely to equate intellectual ambition in women with selfishness. Countless Victorian girls and young women must have been torn, like Florence Nightingale in her youth, between family obligations and their own inconveniently unfeminine intellectual restlessness and ambitions. When Florence Nightingale eventually found an outlet for her own ambitions, she found it at immense personal cost and her relationships with her family remained acutely painful and problematic all through her life.[157] It is also important to remember that Florence Nightingale's achievement could be countenanced by the Victorians, that she could become a 'heroine', because her work could be perceived, albeit distortedly, as fittingly feminine. The Victorians chose *not* to see the ruthless, ambitious, determined side of her personality and constructed instead an image of a gentle madonna of mercy, intent on succouring others.[158] Of course no young girl inspired by the popular image who modelled her behaviour on these sentimentalities could have survived even one day of Crimean conditions. But the persistence of the myth was important, and should remind us firstly, that women's achievements were only acceptable in certain 'feminine' areas like nursing. Secondly, sheer hard work, determination and ambitiousness — all the qualities which might be thought necessary to achieve *anything* of substance, were regarded as wholly unfeminine. Women's achievements, if they were to be acceptable to the Victorians, had to come about in an unrealistic, passive way.

A Victorian girl had learned from her childhood that worldly success was unfeminine, and in even in areas where women *might* achieve success, it was unfeminine to *seek* to earn it. It then becomes important to look at the lives and work of women academics and educationalists in order to try to determine the extent to which they might have acted as more acceptable positive role-models; the extent to which they may have inspired their students as examples of successful, strong women with a determined commitment to some kind of achievement in the chosen field of their endeavour.

We find, however, that many academic women had in their own lives experienced problems in coming to terms with their ambitions, ambitions which were not easily harmonised with the qualities they had learned to define as feminine. A very common resolution of the conflict was for women either consciously or unconsciously to seek to channel their ambition and their energies into the traditionally feminine area of service, either to God or to fellow mortals. This helped to mitigate any feelings of guilt they may have had over the desire to reduce or reject the claims of family life in order to pursue their own studies.

Constance Louisa Maynard, Dorothea Beale and Alice Ottley are examples of women who saw their own studies and careers very much in terms of service to God, a Divine Calling. They all stressed the importance of self-renunciation. Learning was not, for any of them, a form of self-development, it was a form of service. In an essay entitled 'Five Levels of Life' published in *Between College Terms* (1910) Constance Maynard outlined something of her philosophy.[159] Following Fichte, she suggested that there were five levels or planes of life on which one might live and act, five kinds of purpose or motive. The first and lowest she called 'Swimming with the stream', meaning a general acuteness, 'doing just what other people do because they do it.' The second level, she suggested, was

> the self-regarding life. Ambition is always nobler than the hunt for pleasure, because in ambition present self is sacrificed to future self, and that is a great deal better than no sacrifice at all. . . . But . . . self is still the centre and end of it all.[160]

The third level she called 'the Self-controlled Life,' which entailed the individual repressing his or her wants. Next came 'the Unselfish Life' — when one worked for something other than oneself — art, or some Institution like a school, college, hospital or orphanage. Finally came the most nearly perfect life, what Constance defined as 'the Life of the Will of God' — when the individual lived directly in accordance with his or her interpretation of a Divine Calling.

Constance Maynard's work as Mistress of Westfield College was to her, her calling, and she devoted her life to it. Both Dorothea Beale and Alice Ottley were equally inspired by a sense of Mission; both were moved by something very close to the conventual impulse. Both cherished visions of establishing a holy teaching order. Miss Beale felt a special affinity for St Hilda of Whitby, the sixth-century Abbess, scholar and teacher.[161] Alice Ottley was a founder member — and later Superior — of a society founded in 1872 called The Society of the Holy Name.[162] This association organised annual retreats for its membership, and dedicated itself to attempts to help teachers and governesses look upon their work as a high religious calling. The Worcester High School for Girls, like Cheltenham Ladies' College, abounded in religious iconography. White and blue — the colours of the Virgin — were chosen as school colours. The school badge featured a Madonna Lily, and Alice Ottley filled the school garden and regularly decorated the altar with these flowers.[163]

Another and perhaps larger group of women academics and educationalists chose to dedicate themselves equally zealously to an ideal of service, but this time to a more secular ideal. The two groups were not always distinct. Miss Beale, for instance, encouraged her ex-pupils to work amongst the poor; St Hilda's settlement in the East End of London was founded for this purpose.[164] It was really a question of emphasis. Both Oxford and Cambridge in the 1890s were full of women — often the wives of academics — with enthusiasm for social work, for settlements, housing reform, surveys of poverty and educational work amongst the poor. These women used their influence in academic circles to recruit young female students into new forms of social work. In Oxford, the young Eglantyne Jebb, then studying at Lady Margaret Hall, came under the influence of Mrs Toynbee, who inspired her with a sense of social need by taking her on a visit to a local Poor Law school. Mrs Toynbee encouraged her to follow up her degree with a course at Stockwell Training College in order that she might go and teach in an elementary school.[165] Later, when living in Cambridge, Eglantyne Jebb developed close friendships with Mrs Alfred Marshall, Mrs Neville Keynes and Mrs Arthur Rackham, three women strongly committed to social service. Her social survey of the Cambridge poor, entitled *The Other Cambridge* (published in 1906), owed much to the encouragement of these women.[166] Leah Manning, a student at Homerton Training College during the same period was also strongly influenced by Mrs Keynes, Mrs Rackham and their set, who encouraged her to take a first teaching post in a local elementary school.[167]

These community-minded, middle-class women seem to have exercised a strong influence as role models over a generation of young female university students. Their names feature more regularly, perhaps, and they are described more vividly in many personal reminiscences of student days than are most of the full-time women tutors and permanently employed staff of women's colleges. It is interesting to speculate why. To begin with, they were married (or widowed) and probably the majority of female students still found the vision of a married life more congenial than the celibate lifestyles of the majority of women academic careerists. The tendency, among some female academics, to reject fashionably feminine clothes as frivolous and to dress along rather severe or 'sensible' lines did not always commend them to their students. Winifred Seebohm, studying at Newnham in the 1880s, complained bitterly in her correspondence with family and friends about the sartorial standards of her tutors.

You *should* see Miss Gardner's get-up — droopy straw hat, shetland shawl thrown on without any grace, and big heel-less felt slippers in which she shuffles along. Then she evidently uses no mirror for her toilet, for this morning she came down with the ends of her hair sticking straight out like a cow's tail — she drags it back tight, twists it, and sticks one hair pin through. The style of dress here is certainly *not* elegant.[168]

Such recollections could be multiplied. Very few women dons (Jane Harrison at Newnham was a notable exception) gained any reputation for dressing well. In contrast, Mrs Toynbee was always 'elegant and diaphanous'.[169] And Mrs Marshall in her youth was gracefully Pre-Raphaelite. Winnie Seebohm wrote home enthusiastically about her:

But now I must tell you about Mrs Marshall, from whom I have had two lectures. She *is* a Princess Ida. She wears a flowing dark-green cloth robe with dark brown fur round the bottom (not on the very edge) — she has dark brown hair which goes back in a great wave and is very usefully pinned up behind — very deep set large eyes, a straight nose — a face that one likes to watch. Then she is enthusiastic and simple. She speaks fluently and earnestly with her head thrown back a little and her hands generally clasped or resting on the desk. . . . She looks at Political Economy from a philanthropic woman's point of view.[170]

This reminds one of the young Mary Arnold's (later Mrs Humphry Ward's) fascination with Mrs Mark Pattison, twenty years earlier:

It was in '68 or '69 that I remember my first sight of a college garden, lying cool and shaded between grey college walls, and on the green a figure that held me fascinated — a lady in a green brocade dress, with a belt and chatelaine of Russian silver, who was playing croquet . . . and seemed to me as I watched her a model of grace and vivacity.[171]

The two women, Emilia Pattison and Mary Paley Marshall were in many ways very unalike, but they shared the characteristics which so commended them to the younger women around them. They were both beautiful, well-dressed, intelligent. They both married men older and more eminent than themselves. They both channelled their considerable resources of energy and intellect into supporting their husbands' careers and persons. Mrs Pattison devotedly nursed her husband through the last two years of his life with no thought of self: 'If one life is to give way to the other', she wrote to a friend, 'I feel sure it should be mine; his is worth so much more – it represents much more of greater value to the world than mine.'[172] With equally commendable wifely loyalty, Mrs Marshall devoted long periods of her life to her husband's work. Her capacity for self-effacement was commended as 'truly feminine' by many contemporaries. G.M. Trevelyan, for instance, in his introduction to her volume of memoirs, recollected approvingly that Mrs Marshall always left the dining room to the men when they felt like any serious discussion of academic matters: and that 'the most ignorant Miss would not have pretended less than she to academic attainment.'[173] Both Mrs Pattison and Mrs Marshall turned, after their husbands' deaths, to social service. Mrs Pattison, who subsequently married Charles Dilke, took up the question of women's trade union organisation. Mrs Marshall became involved with Charity Organisation work.

Sara Delamont has argued that the reforms in women's education of the second half of the century created two new female roles, that of the celibate careerist, and that of the cultured, well-educated wife who was an intellectual partner to her husband.[174] Neither type was a wholly new phenomenon. Women in both these categories strove to reconcile what they had been taught about femininity with their intellect and energy as individuals. Both types of woman channelled their ambitions into the traditionally feminine areas of *service* – either to God, or to husband and family, or into social work – that remained essentially an extension of the kind of part-time, unpaid, non-professional charitable activity defined as appropriate for married women throughout the nineteenth century. Neither kind of lifestyle challenged the sexual division of labour, and so long as this persisted, girls approaching maturity would continue to be presented with a choice between marriage and career, between sexuality and intellect. The choice remained a crippling one.

3

◇-◇

Good wives and little mothers: educational provision for working-class girls

◇-◇

There was a strong current of opinion in mid-Victorian society which would hold the poor — through their attitudes, behaviour and domestic disorganisation — personally responsible for their own poverty. It followed that most reformers bent on tackling a whole variety of social ills channelled their energies into attempts to change behaviour rather than conditions. They sought to reform working-class lifestyles as a first means towards altering the environment in which working people lived; frequently looking towards *education* for solutions to poverty.

The educational policies devised by church and state in the second half of the nineteenth century aimed to 'civilise' the working class and to bring the structure and organisation of working-class family life into line with middle-class values and canons of 'respectability'. Middle-class reformers aimed to promote that sexual division of labour within the family which they regarded as proper to civilised society and in accordance with both divine intent and natural law. Fathers should be breadwinners, true heads of the household: mothers should stay at home. In 1843 Samuel Smiles had expressed what was essentially the dominant middle-class image of the undesirable effect industrialism had had on working-class family life:

> The factory system, however much it may have added to the wealth of the country, has had a most deleterious effect on the domestic conditions of the people. It has invaded the sanctuary of the home

and broken up family and social ties. It has taken the wife from the husband, and the children from their parents. Especially has its tendency been to lower the character of women. The performance of domestic duties is her proper office, – the management of her household, the rearing of her family, the economizing of the family means, the supplying of the family wants. But the factory takes her from all these duties. Homes become no longer homes. Children grow up uneducated and neglected. The finer affections become blunted. Woman is no more the gentle wife, companion and friend of man, but his fellow labourer and fellow drudge.[1]

Thirty years later Smiles confirmed this view even more vehemently:

Women can no more do men's special work in the world than men can do women's. And whenever woman has been withdrawn from her home and family to enter upon other work, the result has been socially disastrous.[2]

Even the French Revolution, Smiles hazarded, could be attributed to women's neglect of their true sphere:

The character of woman had become depraved. Conjugal fidelity was disregarded; maternity was held in reproach; family and home were alike corrupted. Domestic purity no longer bound society together. France was motherless; the children broke loose and the Revolution burst forth, 'amidst the yells and the fierce violence of women'.[3]

The home, then, he insisted, was 'the most influential school of civilisation', and 'one good mother' was 'worth a hundred schoolmasters'.[4] Virtuous women encouraged moral rectitude and paternal responsibilities in their husbands. The pages of Smiles' tracts, like those of most Victorian 'improving' literature, are replete with clichés and anecdotes about labouring men driven to the pub by wives who couldn't cook or have the evening meal ready by a welcoming fire when their husbands returned from work.[5] Women were equally held responsible for the character of their children. On this theme Samuel Smiles quoted from the report of a mid-nineteenth century school inspector, Mr Tufnell, who had declared that he was informed that

in a large factory, where many children were employed, the managers before they engaged a boy always enquired into the mother's character, and if that was satisfactory they were tolerably certain that her children would conduct themselves creditably. *No attention was paid to the character of the father*.[6]

In families where the father turned to drink, or had otherwise 'gone to the dogs', Smiles observed, where the mother was prudent and sensible, the family might still be kept together and the children make their way honourably in life. But where these roles were reversed, and it was the mother who turned out badly, the children stood little chance.[7]

Women were held to be uniquely responsible for working-class living standards through their administration of the family budget. 'The root of all domestic prosperity, the mainstay of all domestic comfort is *the wife*.'[8] This message is constantly hammered home throughout all of Smiles' writings and is a commonplace of Victorian literature on social problems. Poverty, it was repeatedly urged, could be cured through thrift and careful housekeeping. The inference usually drawn from this was that working-class women were poor cooks and improvident housekeepers. Lord Shaftesbury, for instance, had argued in the 1850s that he would like to see all working-class women being taught cookery, for he was certain, 'from experience of the working classes, that they (were) ten times more improvident and wasteful than the wealthier in the land'.[9] Matthew Arnold, reporting on elementary schools in the 1850s alleged that the daughters of the rural poor were lamentably ignorant of plain needlework:

> The importance to a poor family that the daughters should be skilful in plain needlework is obvious to all; yet their ignorance of it is something incredible. I heard the other day in a Lincolnshire village of a pauper family, in which were several daughters living at home; the family were actually in receipt of parochial relief; their debts were collected, and among them was found a considerable one to a dressmaker, who, it appeared, made all the clothes of the female part of the family.[10]

Things were no better, he claimed, in the towns. Harriet Martineau's article in *Household Words* had recently described the widespread ignorance of needlework and domestic skills amongst working-class wives in Birmingham, as well as providing information about the scheme of evening classes, organised by philanthropic ladies in the locality, to try to remedy the deficiency.[11]

If so much depended on women's domestic skills, and if working-class women were generally perceived to be so ill-equipped as wives, mothers and housekeepers, it followed in the minds of contemporaries that schooling might supply a remedy. And there was, of course, a further very important dimension to middle-class discussion over the desirability of domestic training for girls – a dimension supplied by the middle-class demand for domestic servants throughout the period. Domestic service constituted the largest single category of employment for women until well into the present century. It has been suggested that about one woman in three living in Victorian England probably served as a domestic servant at some point in her life, most commonly in the age range from around fifteen to twenty-five.[12] We have seen in chapter 1 that in some rural areas it was the common fate of almost every girl on reaching adolescence to 'go into service'. B.L. Hutchins calculated that of all girls between fourteen and eighteen years of age in 1911 registered in the Census as 'employed' 30.5 per cent had entered service (including hotel service, but excluding laundry and washing services). Taking the whole 'domestic' group together and including laundry and charing as well as service, the category accounted for 34.8 per cent of all the girls between fourteen and eighteen employed.[13]

Traditionally, charity schools had often been founded specifically with the aim of turning out well-trained servant girls. Various industrial schools, reformatories and orphanages continued to be conducted with the same purpose in mind right up to the first world war. A strong section of middle-class opinion believed that State elementary schools should also set out to train girls for service. There were perennial complaints about the supply of domestic servants: both about *quality* – girls were alleged to be ignorant and untrained – and about the *quantity* of recruits. It is noticeable that wherever new forms of employment opened up for working-class girls they were quick to take advantage of them – 'living in' domestic service was never a very popular occupation. The suggestion was often mooted that Board Schools should encourage their girl pupils to enter service as 'more fitting' or 'more natural' for young unmarried women than factory, shop or office (even though the girls themselves may have thought otherwise).[14] The National Association for the Promotion of House-wifery, organised by the wife of Lord Brabazon (later Earl of Meath) and other ladies, campaigned in the 1870s and 1880s to get domestic economy introduced into the Board School curriculum not only to train girls as future wives and mothers but also as an attempt to increase the supply of domestic servants.[15] Mary Headdon, on the Council of the Association, contemplated a system whereby the School Boards might farm out working-class girls to middle-class homes in the locality to gain an 'apprenticeship' in domestic service:

> there are many middle class families who would be glad to take into their homes young girls to be taught housework ... if such girls were under the supervision of School Boards until they had attained the age of, say seventeen, so that there should be some guarantee that they rendered their mistresses assistance and remained with them long enough to compensate them for the trouble of teaching.[16]

Doubtless the scheme, had it been implemented, would have relieved many of the anxieties of middle-class ladies suffering from the 'servant problem': nevertheless, one shrinks from imagining the kind of abuses such an officially-sanctioned system of slavery might have led to.

Another idea which appealed to Miss Headdon was one she put before the Cross Commission on Elementary Education in 1887. This was that three-year-old girls in the infant classes of Board Schools could be taught to lay tables and to make beds in time to music in order to learn how pleasurable housework might be. They would then be more likely to grow up enthusiastic about the prospect of going into service, instead of envisaging it gloomily as 'a life of drudgery and social degradation'.[17]

State policy — expressed through the statements of the Education Department in London — declared itself unwilling to countenance the use of elementary education as a training for domestic service. However, the Department was very responsive to the idea of modifying the curriculum to include domestic subjects to 'fit the girls for life'.[18] And textbooks and readers in domestic economy used in the 1890s and 1900s frequently extolled the advantage of service as a training for the working-class girl's future as mother of her own family. In a textbook written for domestic science teachers, for instance, Newsholme and Scott urged that:

> Teachers should, when possible, advise mothers to encourage their daughters to become good domestic servants in preference to entering upon indifferent callings which frequently entail late hours, injury to health and exposure to temptation.[19]

During and after the first world war, when girls flooded into munitions factories and other occupations in preference to domestic service, middle-class anxieties about 'the servant problem' increased. This produced a fresh crop of complaints in the correspondence columns of newspapers and periodicals from individuals who believed that elementary education should encourage girls to look upon housework as their 'natural vocation'.[20] The report of a Women's Advisory Committee set up to investigate 'the domestic service problem' for the Ministry of Reconstruction in 1919 declared that the Committee were strongly of the opinion that lack of training for domestic work lay at the root of the problem.[21] They recommended the provision of more facilities for training girls for two years after leaving school in domestic work, and suggested that the State, through the LEAs, should finance such training.[22] Only two members of the Committee (Lilian Harris and Dr Marion Phillips) ventured a protest here: both felt that the shortage of domestic servants stemmed from the fact that women shrank from the conditions of such servitude, the lack of freedom associated with 'living in', low wages and long hours of work. Neither could concur with the analysis that education alone could or ought to 'solve' this problem.[23]

Historians of women's education have, up until recent years, paid much more attention to the schooling of middle-class than of working-class girls. In generalising about provision for the latter, they have sometimes assumed erroneously that the education of the elementary schoolgirl was substantially the same as that of an elementary schoolboy. Dorothy Gardiner, in her *English Girlhood at School*, published in 1929, declared that after the Act of 1870, 'The destiny of the elementary schoolgirl (was) inseparable from that of the schoolboy'.[24] It is worth contrasting this view with that of the feminist writer Christina Bremner, whose survey *The Education of Girls and Women in Great Britain* appeared in 1897. This included an interesting section on the public elementary schools. Here, Bremner complained, girls were offered a curriculum heavily weighted by an emphasis on needlework and domestic subjects; their proficiency in arithmetic, history and geography tended to be seen as of less importance than that of the boys. The sight of small girls of eleven years or even younger learning cookery, housewifery and laundrywork was becoming common, 'as if little girls could not be too early pressed into a narrow mould'.[25]

In the rest of this chapter I want to look firstly at the evolution of the elementary school curriculum for girls, focusing on the development of domestic subjects, and locating this development in its changing social and ideological context. Secondly I want to survey some

general attitudes to the schooling of working-class girls, both 'official'
and popular. Finally, I shall extend this attempt to see schooling in
the context of wider contemporary attitudes to socialisation by looking
at the anxieties middle-class educationalists and social reformers
nurtured over the occupational experiences of young adolescent
working-class girls and some of the youth organisations and other
'educational' provisions they devised accordingly.

Needlework was regarded as an essential component of a girl's education. This seems to have been the case all over England in the early
nineteenth century. Charity schools and dame schools usually taught
knitting and sewing. Mary Smith, the daughter of a non-conformist
shoemaker who grew up in Cropredy, near Banbury in North Oxford-
shire, in the 1820s remembered that she had attended two dame
schools between the ages of four and eight or nine.[26] Her mother sent
her to the first school specifically to learn to knit and sew, and Mary
remembered that knitting and sewing occupied nearly the whole time
of the girls' day.[27] She further remembered ruefully that it was at the
age of around eight that she had developed a passionate love for books —
her mother resented this in a girl:

> It was indeed a very good school; thoroughness being the aim in the
> few things that were professed to be taught, as well as almost faultless
> discipline and good manners. A girl's education at that time consisted
> principally of needlework of various descriptions, from plain sewing
> to all manner of fancy work and embroidery, including muslin and net,
> on which we worked or flowered squares for the shoulders, veils,
> caps, collars and borders; likewise a multitude of things not in wear
> now, but then considered very necessary. Parents were prouder then
> of their daughters' pieces of needlework than of their scholarship.[28]

There is a pathos in the vision of young Mary, so avid for reading that
she recalled that she used to stay in at playtime to read Mangnall's
Questions, *The Pleasing Instructor*, and Goldsmith's *History of England*,
being compelled to spend endless days doing needlework:

> What long months I worked at it — and how I hated it — but it was
> all in vain! For long years Englishwomen's souls were almost as
> sorely crippled and cramped by the devices of the schoolroom as the
> Chinese women's feet by their shoes. I had to go on with this hateful
> employment.[29]

The only respite (aside from playtime) came in the form of special arithmetic lessons which her father arranged for her, arithmetic then being regarded as rather superfluous for girls. (Mary thought that this was particularly so in the Midlands; her later experience suggesting to her that arithmetic was much more thoroughly taught to girls in Scotland and the North of England.)

It is worth noting that schools in rural England seem to have prided themselves on their girls' achievements in fancy and ornamental needlework. Middle-class observers and educationalists later in the century were constantly critical of this as uneconomical and a waste of time. Matthew Arnold, lamenting upon the state of instruction in needlework in schools he was inspecting in the 1850s complained that:

> The parents also, in general, seldom have much value for plain
> needlework, nor do the mothers teach it at home to their daughters;
> the only kind of needlework which the parents admire, and which
> the children are anxious to practice, is crochet-work and ornamental
> needlework; this is comparatively useless, and managers and teachers
> should, in my opinion, utterly prohibit it in school.[30]

In 1862 the Revised Code made the teaching of needlework compulsory in schools which relied upon State support in the form of a grant from the Education Department in London. In most cases this probably only legitimised the existing curriculum, although the Department's stress on *plain* rather than fancy work was made very clear. M.K. Ashby recalls that in the school her father attended in Tysoe, rural Warwickshire, in the 1860s, the girls spent two afternoons per week sewing.[31] The boys spent this time doing more sums or dictation. In some areas girls seem to have spent as much as five afternoons a week on needlework — particularly in rural areas, and even in the early years of the present century.[32]

The occasions when male government inspectors visiting schools set out to judge the quality of girls' needlework gave rise to much embarrassment, amusement, and a copious fund of anecdotes usually centring on the idea of male ignorance about terminology ('yokes', 'gussets' and the various kinds of stitching used) or about the inspection of 'intimate garments'.[33] The London School Board found it necessary to appoint a 'Lady Needlework Examiner' in 1875 and soon after the Government also appointed a Directress of Needlework. E.M. Sneyd-Kynnersley, who recorded his experience as an HMI in the north-west of England in 1910 pointed out that:

In country schools there was not much fear of neglect (of needle-work teaching), for Mrs Squire and Mrs Rector kept vigilant eyes on this branch of education, and the subscribers to the school funds often got back part of the value of their money by sending their household sewing to be done in school.[34]

He alleged that in one school he had visited, maintained by a 'bountiful Earl',

the schoolroom had become the workroom of the Castle. There was a liberal display of household articles, and while the third class had sufficed to seam and hem them, it had been found necessary to employ the first class to mark them with coronets.[35]

Clara Grant, who taught in London elementary schools in the 1890s, suggested that one of the reasons why so much needlework was taught in rural schools in the 1860s and 1870s was because the children could be made to make and mend garments for the neighbouring gentlefolk.[36] She pointed out that even when teachers suggested that the girls might bring worn clothes from their own homes to practice on, many mothers felt it not quite right to do so. One mother had expressed the feeling of many when she demurred that she would 'not like to send my husband's stockings to school to mend, nor my old shifts'.[37] The local gentry seem to have been less sensitive on this score.

Clara Grant believed that some of the least imaginative teaching in the Board Schools of the 1890s went on in needlework classes, and wrote an amusing and satiric account of the pedagogical methods developed by Mrs Floyer, the first needlework examiner to be appointed by the London School Board.[38] Mrs Floyer's enthusiasm for needlework as the mainstay of the curriculum for girls seems to have been unbounded. She maintained that as well as acquiring the skill itself, girls in needlework lessons learned to practise cleanliness, obed-ience, caution, concentration and countless other virtues. She saw most other subjects of the curriculum as of secondary importance, Grant alleges, being mainly interested in them only insofar as they could be 'integrated' into the teaching of needlework. Spelling, Mrs Floyer mooted, could be learned by copying words such as 'herring-bone' or 'cross-stitch'; essay writing could be practised through writing out detailed descriptions of the execution of any complex stitch or pattern. The most disastrous effect of her ministry, Grant maintained, was the enthusiasm she inspired everywhere for the iniquitous 'needlework drill'. Whole classes of fity or sixty tiny infants would be expected to practise putting on thimbles (the 'Thimble Drill' or 'Knitting Pin Drill') without thread or wool, in unison, for an hour at a time, regularly. Eventually the LCC schools banished 'needle drill' from infant classes, but as late as 1911 manuals explaining the intricacies of the various 'drills' were still being published.

Various other kinds of protest were sometimes heard over the emphasis on and methods of teaching needlework in elementary schools. It was frequently alleged that over-fine work put an unwarranted and damaging strain on infant eyesight. This complaint was voiced so often that by the early years of this century the Board of Education's *Suggestions to Teachers* contained a warning against the practice of expecting young children to practise over-fine stitching.[39] A more radical objection to the teaching of the subject came from those who alleged that the sewing machine was rendering traditional skills obsolete. Anecdotes were passed around about male inspectors duped into admiring children's work as handwork when in reality it had been done by machine.[40] Emily Shirreff, as early as 1874, had contended that

> needlework is not of universal importance to women. Indeed, considered as a trade, it has been so far depreciated by the introduction of the sewing-machine that it becomes quite a secondary matter. Some people maintain that the use of the machine should be taught in schools — but why teach this to girls more than tailoring or shoemaking to boys?[41]

It is true that she was mainly concerned here with the curriculum for middle-class girls; but not entirely so, for she added acerbically that she could not easily see

> what educational advantage results to the girls (in elementary schools) from furnishing plain work to the ladies of the parish at a lower price than would be paid to a poor woman who depends for bread on her needle, or on the machine in which she has invested all her little savings.[42]

Such protests had little effect on official policy. A growing staff of women inspectors and needlework teachers and examiners all over the country had, of course, a strong vested interest in the subject. In a report on *The Work of the London School Board*, presented at the Paris Exhibition in 1900, Miss Loch, an LSB Examiner in Needlework stated firmly that

The argument which is often now advanced that the universal use of the sewing machine renders so much tuition in hand sewing unnecessary is not a sound one. The superiority of the hand-made garment over the cheaper machine-made article both as regards appearance and true economy is well known to all who have really studied the subject, and the homely arts of darning and mending save many a penny in a thrifty household.[43]

It is noticeable that the argument was rarely conducted in rational terms: the subject had assumed a *symbolic* importance. Proficiency with a needle implied femininity, it implied thrift. The Board of Education's *Suggestions for the Teaching of Needlework*, published in 1909, held that the subject appealed 'directly to the natural instincts of the girls'.[44] (It followed that the Mary Smiths of this world were, of course, unnatural beings.) In any case, the *Suggestions* maintained that

it should be looked upon as a matter of shame that any girl should reach woman's estate without a practical knowledge of what use she can make with her needle.[45]

The Board School curriculum originally contained little direct teaching in domestic subjects other than needlework. However, during the 1870s the arguments of those who believed it crucially necessary to supply this kind of training to girls in school, and the pressure from associations like the National Association for the Promotion of Housewifery began to take effect. The Education Department was in a position to influence the elementary school curriculum through the provision of grants made payable, under the Code of 1875, for scholars in the higher standards who passed examinations in no more than two subjects recognised by the Department as 'specific subjects'. The Code of 1878 made domestic economy a compulsory specific subject for girls. Between 1874 and 1882 the number of pupils studying domestic economy in the Board Schools rose from 844 to 59,812. Grants were first made available for teaching cookery in the Code of 1882, and for laundry work in 1890. In spite of various obstacles in the way of a speedy adoption of these subjects in some schools (the expense, for instance, of the necessary plant and equipment), the results of the grant being made available were quite impressive. According to a report on the progress of domestic economy teaching made to the Education Department in 1896, in 1882-3 7,597 girls from a total of 457 schools had qualified for the cookery grant: by 1895-6 these numbers had risen to 134,930 and 2,729 respectively.[46] Between 1891-2 and 1895-6 the number of girls attending recognised classes in laundry-work had similarly risen from 632 to 11,720: the number of schools offering these classes from 27 to 400 over the same period.[47]

The London School Board, by 1900, had managed to set up and equip a total of 168 'cookery centres', which were at that date supplying training for girls from 470 contributing schools.[48] Most of these centres were drawing teachers from the various domestic economy training colleges which had become established over the last twenty years or so. In London girls attended the cookery centres between ten and fourteen years of age. The more up-to-date centres at the turn of the century included facilities for laundry and other household arts as well as cookery — some contained rooms furnished and fitted along the lines of 'model' artisan or working-men's houses. In these, according to a description by the Domestic Economy Superintendent of the LSB in 1900,

> By careful arrangement of colours the children are taught that usefulness and art may be combined, and comfortable substitutes for cheap stuffed furniture are placed before their eyes. All the utensils provided in these centres are those used by the artisan class. A cottage stove is fixed in the kitchen, and the children cook daily the dinners for themselves and the teachers.[49]

Both this writer (Mrs E. Lord) and others interested in domestic teaching in Board Schools prided themselves on the progress which had been made over the last two decades; particularly in regard to having overcome what seems to have been a good deal of opposition, originally, from parents who considered they could better teach domestic skills to their daughters at home. Mrs Pillow (*sic.*) who compiled a special report on the progress of domestic economy work in schools for the Education Department in 1896-7 commented that in the 1880s,

> Extraordinary as it may seem in the face of the general ignorance on culinary matters, mothers frequently complained that their daughters 'wasted their time' in going to the cookery lessons.[50]

Similarly, Emily Briggs, superintendent of cookery for the London School Board, remarked that when cookery was first introduced into schools under the authority of the LSB, 'prejudice against it was almost insuperable, and parents put every possible obstacle in the way of their children attending the classes.'[51] Both writers argued that the lessons had gained in popularity over the last few years. However it is not difficult to imagine the kind of resentment some working women must have felt when their daughters were compelled to attend school to practise skills which they felt they could easily impart at home. Mothers who needed to go out to work in order to supplement the family income, and who would have welcomed the services of their daughters in the home in order to facilitate their doing so, probably felt particularly bitter about the situation.

During the first two decades of the twentieth century, discussion on the subject of the curriculum offered to girls in the elementary schools — and in girls' schools generally — ranged beyond narrowly educational circles. The obsession with Empire and 'national efficiency' in this period was bound up with a complex of anxieties about the quantity and quality of the population. Contemporary anxieties over 'physical deterioration' and national standards of health and fitness on the one hand, and over high infant mortality and low birth rates on the other, generated new and more powerful pressures from eugenists, the medical profession and a variety of other groups to increase the importance and widen the scope of domestic training in the elementary schools — as well as a movement to introduce these subjects into the secondary education of girls.[52]

The spectre of the 'physical deterioration' of the British people had its origin in late-Victorian social-Darwinistic ideas about evolution and social progress. Benjamin Kidd, Karl Pearson and other writers interested in eugenics and evolution helped to popularise a vision of history as a struggle between races in which only the 'fittest' or most 'efficient' peoples could be expected to survive.[53] These writers, centrally concerned with the questions of family size, class differences in the birth rate, child-rearing and infant survival, were drawn directly into late-nineteenth century discussions about 'the Woman Question'. Here they adopted a strongly conservative position: women, they argued, were the guardians of racial progress. It was women's responsibility to build homes and breed children. Low birth rates and a high infant mortality were testimony to the fact that they were shirking these responsibilities — too often for the sake of wage earning independence, or an emancipation which threatened 'social efficiency' and was inimical to the interests of the nation as a whole.[54]

Anxieties about 'national degeneracy' came to a head early this century following the recruiting experience of the Boer War. An alarming proportion (in Manchester, 8,000 out of 11,000) of volunteers in the larger cities had had to be rejected as unfit for active service. The nation panicked; and the British Government responded to the scare by setting up an Inter-Departmental Committee of Enquiry to investigate allegations about the 'physical deterioration' of the population. Urbanisation had often been depicted as socially menacing — were the towns indeed sucking the life-blood out of a once healthy, rural population and breeding a race of puny, consumptive slum dwellers?[55]

The Inter-Departmental Committee reported in 1904 and its conclusions were perhaps ultimately reassuring. The Commissioners pointed out that amongst the population as a whole standards of physical well-being were probably rising. At the same time, however, the Report drew public attention to the extremely *low* standards of living and physical fitness apparent in the congested central districts of larger towns and cities.[56]

In accounting for these conditions, the authors of the Report laid heavy emphasis on the habits and domestic organization of the inhabitants. Women, in particular, were blamed for their ignorance of household affairs, hygiene and nutrition; their diminished sense of maternal obligation and their wrongheaded notions of infant care. The entry 'Neglect of Home and Domestic Duties' occupies a commanding position in the index of the Report, heading 1½ columns of detailed references.[57] 'There is no lack of evidence of increasing carelessness and deficient sense of responsibility among the younger women of the present day', asserted the Committee. In some sections of the population, they alleged, standards of nutrition had significantly declined over the last ten years or so, owing to 'the growing consumption of tinned foods and its coincidence with the decrease of cookery at home.'[58] Almost all those who gave evidence before the Commissioners were inclined to blame the elementary school training, which they claimed emphasised the '3 Rs' for the low standards of domestic competence among women. 'Where the working woman's condition breaks down' insisted Mrs Mackenzie (the Secretary of the National Union of Women Workers) '. . . is that they have no home training, their time is spent in doing education which is not suitable for them.'[59]

In their final report, the Commissioners urged the need for 'Some great scheme of social education' which would aim 'to raise the standard of domestic competence' and to underline the importance of proper ideals of home life among young girls destined to become the wives and mothers of future generations.[60] They recommended that courses in cookery and household management, taught along simple and practical lines, should be seen as a vitally important part of the work of the Board Schools: a proper system of inspection should be instituted by the Board of Education to ensure this. The Committee felt that lessons in cookery and household management should as far as possible be made compulsory for the older girls, and that training of this kind was probably most effective when concentrated into the last year or so of school life. They felt that girls should drop certain other subjects in the curriculum in order to make room for household management at this stage. A further recommendation called for an extensive system of Continuation classes which would provide instruction in domestic subjects for girls who had already left school. For the moment – even if only as a temporary, 'emergency' measure – the Committee thought that attendance at these classes should be made obligatory, although girls in domestic service might be exempted.[61]

The Report of the Physical Deterioration Committee made an immediate impact at the Board of Education. A growing interest in the extent to which other countries provided domestic training for their younger female citizens had already encouraged Michael Sadler and Robert Morant to ask Alice Ravenhill, a lecturer in hygiene with the West Riding County Council, to report on domestic science teaching in the United States. Although this report had been ready in 1903, it had originally been decided to delay publication until similar information could be collected from various other countries, making it possible to issue a series of Special Reports on *School Training for the Home Duties of Women*. However, the publicity achieved by the Commissioners' Report in 1904 appears to have spurred the Board of Education to publish Alice Ravenhill's report straight away. It became available in 1905, the others in the series following in 1906 and 1908.[62] The pages of all these reports were riddled with alarming generalisations about the decay of homes and family life under the pressure of industrial conditions. Alice Ravenhill's was especially notable for its social-Darwinistic terminology and the urgency of its appeal to women as the guardians of 'racial efficiency' and progress. (She herself was an enthusiastic exponent of anti-feminist ideas with a strong interest in eugenics and a conviction that woman's 'Imperial Mission' lay in returning to the home.)[63]

With regard to what he judged to be the more urgent question of reviewing the state of domestic science teaching in Britain, Morant made arrangements, for the first time, for systematic and regular inspection of the teaching of domestic subjects both in the elementary schools and in the training of teachers. A staff of women inspectors were to be entrusted with this task. Meanwhile, a special 'on the spot' investigation into the way cookery was currently being taught in the public elementary schools had been organised under the direction of Maude Lawrence, the Chief Woman Inspector. And the *Suggestions for The Consideration of Teachers and Others Concerned in the Work of Public Elementary Schools*, published in 1905, alerted teachers to what the Board considered to be the nation's need. Girls must be provided with a thorough training in domestic duties, and must be taught 'to set a high value on the housewife's position', on the grounds that national efficiency must inevitably depend upon a strong tradition of home life.[64]

Maude Lawrence summarised the findings of this investigation in a Special Report, written in 1906 and published, with a rather lengthy prefatory memorandum by Morant, in the following year.[65] Over many parts of the country cookery teaching was deemed to be in a far from satisfactory state. Demonstration lessons were not properly followed up by practical sessions. In some areas inadequate resources, or the teachers' worries about losing money by cooking unsaleable food, rendered practical work extremely difficult. An inspector in the north of England mentioned one lesson 'On Roasting Meat' where it appears a solitary chop was prepared and cooked by eighteen girls.[66] One of the most frequently recurring criticisms voiced by inspectors was the tendency of teachers to concentrate on 'saleable' foods — girls were shown how to make toffee, buns and other popular sweetstuffs rather than the cheap, nutritious dishes they considered appropriate for artisan households. Morant admitted that much of what had hitherto passed for a 'training in cookery' in the elementary schools had constituted 'a serious waste of public money and a futile waste of time and teaching power'. The Board believed that the subject was one of prime importance to the national welfare and it was clear that new provisions were needed.[67]

Morant hoped that a series of new regulations for the teaching of domestic subjects contained in the Code of 1906 would effect a significant improvement; especially in conjunction with systematic inspection. These regulations had been designed to try to remedy some of the defects which had become most conspicuous under the old system. Courses were to be much more carefully structured in future; the interval elapsing between demonstration and related practical sessions was not to exceed eight days. 'Elaborate' cookery, fostered by advanced courses in the Training Schools, was to be discouraged: both the culinary apparatus used and the recipes taught should be of an essentially simple kind, adapted to the practical requirements of working-class homes.[68] The Board suggested that cookery teachers in the elementary schools should avoid any 'theoretical instruction as to the methods of cooking, or as to the principles of digestion beyond what (was) necessary for a general understanding of the subject.'[69] In this they went some way towards setting the seal of official disapproval on that movement which in recent years had aimed to 'upgrade' the teaching of domestic subjects by emphasising its 'scientific' basis. In the elementary schools 'domestic science' was to be made as *un*scientific as possible. This was in marked contrast to the Board's policy towards the teaching of the same subjects at the secondary level, a subject which I shall return to in the fifth chapter of this book.

Paralleling the movement to expand the teaching of domestic subjects was one to introduce lessons in childcare and infant management into the curriculum offered to working class girls. Again, this movement had its origin in early-twentieth century anxieties about social welfare: in particular, the high rates of infant mortality which prevailed in Britain at this time. An infant mortality rate averaging about 149 deaths per 1000 births through the nineteenth century had attracted little attention while the birth rate rose steeply, and while *general* death rates were also high. However, the rate of population growth had slowed down significantly during the last quarter of the century; the birth rate dropping from 35.5 per 1000 in 1871-5 to 29.3 in 1896-1900.[70] And the *general* death rate (or deaths per 1000 in the total population) had fallen between the 1860s and 1900 by about 15 per cent. In the meantime *infant* death rates in the 1890s remained as high as they had been in the 1860s.[71]

Contemporary discussion of high infant mortality rates was frequently couched in the rhetoric of the 'national efficiency' debate. Sir John Simon was widely quoted for having warned contemporaries that a high infant mortality rate denoted 'a prevalence of those causes and conditions which determine a degeneration of the race'.[72] There was much disagreement over what, exactly, these 'causes and conditions' were. Infant mortality rates varied widely between different areas of Britain. The higher rates were clearly correlated with overcrowded conditions of urban living, particularly in the mining and industrial areas of the Midlands and the North. But Dr George Newman, whose classic work *Infant Mortality – A Social Problem* was published in 1906 alleged that

> the problem of infant mortality is not one of sanitation alone, or housing, or indeed of poverty as such, but it is mainly a question of motherhood.
>
> Expressed bluntly, it is the ignorance and carelessness of mothers that directly causes a large proportion of the infant mortality which sweeps away every year, in England and Wales alone, 120,000 children under twelve months of age.[73]

Buttressing this argument with references to the findings of the Physical Deterioration Committee, Newman singled out the disinclination of young women to attend to domestic duties and their preference for work outside the home; their reluctance to breastfeed their babies and their ignorance of infant hygiene as major factors in the loss of infant lives.

The belief that the employment of married women outside the home entailed the sacrifice of infant lives had, of course, been widespread in the nineteenth century. Margaret Hewitt reviewed some of the evidence marshalled in support of this argument in her well-known work on *Wives and Mothers In Victorian Industry*, published in 1958. Sensitive to the bias of observers wholly hostile to the idea of women leaving the home, Hewitt exposed some of the more exaggerated claims of the Victorians. Even so, she remained impressed by data collected around the turn of the century by medical authorities like George Reid and George Newman, who both believed that an important and demonstrable connection did indeed exist between infantile mortality and women's employment. Hewitt's book tends ultimately towards a cautious acceptance of their viewpoint.[74]

The debate continued, becoming even more contentious, in the early years of this century. The 1904 Commissioners while noting the very obvious and close connection between infant mortality and insanitary conditions, had also suggested that 'the facts seem to point to a strong presumption that it (i.e. infant mortality) is also connected with the employment of mothers,

> although it was admitted that more research was needed. At the same time the Committee had asserted that they had no doubt that the employment of mothers in factories was bad for both mothers and children, and recorded their desire to see this 'diminished, if not altogether discontinued'.[75]

In November 1907 the Home Secretary instigated an inquiry, working with Medical Officers of Health 'of a number of representative industrial centres', to try to establish more clearly whether maternal employment did have any significant effect on infant mortality.[76] Apparently the evidence collected in response to this scheme of inquiry was never collated properly: certainly not in any published form.[77] However, some reports of local investigations survive, one of which had been carried out under the aegis of Dr John Robertson, Medical Officer of Health in Birmingham.[78] The results of this survey were interesting and became widely known for having established an inverse correlation between married women's employment and infant mortality in some of the poorest areas of Birmingham. It was reported that the chances of infant survival might be higher in families where the mother went out to work than in families (living in the same area) where she stayed at home. This might be directly attributable to the higher standards of nutrition an additional source of income in the family could purchase.

Robertson's report, published in 1910, achieved a good deal of publicity. In April 1910 the journal *Public Health* featured an editorial which declared that

> the importance of the industrial employment of married women as a factor in the causation of infantile mortality is a subject on which the current opinion has been gradually changing in recent years. Formerly it was almost universally held to be an etiological factor of preponderating importance; but the application of more precise methods of investigation has cast grave doubts on this view, and has called for a restatement of the whole question.[79]

Some authorities were decidedly reluctant to abandon the traditional equation between women's employment and a high rate of infant deaths, even though it proved virtually impossible to base this on any solid statistical evidence. Arthur Newsholme, who, as Medical Officer to the Local Government Board, was responsible for three major detailed reports on infant mortality between 1909 and 1914, refused to modify his viewpoint.[80] In all three reports prejudice and prior assumption jostle uneasily with the spirit of detached inquiry, Newsholme stubbornly insisting that working mothers were responsible for much loss of infant life; even when the empirical evidence collected by his own researches failed to support the hypothesis. Ultimately, Newsholme's opposition to women's employment in industry was grounded in a vision of social order premised upon a specific sexual division of labour:

97

the woman's sphere was domestic; a mother's place in the home. In his third report on infant mortality for the Local Government Board, for instance he asserted that

> in a wider sense *all* industrial occupation of women whether married or unmarried, may be regarded as to some extent inimical to home-making and child care. This is so even in the case of girls and their industrial employment should be associated with systematic training in domestic economy.[81]

But during the first decade of the present century, the focus of the debate over women's responsibility for infant mortality rates had shifted. A growing concern with the ignorance rather than the occupation of the mother became apparent. Newman's monograph had heralded the change. And Newman was in a powerful professional position – as Chief Medical Officer to the Board of Education, he stood in a good place to influence policy. Between 1910 and 1913 his official reports to the Board constantly reiterate his conviction that the ignorance and negligence of working-class women was a major – even *the* major cause of infant deaths in this country. 'After giving due weight to all and any influence contributing to the production of infant mortality', he announced to the Board of Education in 1914, 'it is impossible to arrive at any other conclusion . . . the principal operating influence is the ignorance of the mother',[82] and the remedy, he insisted, lay in *educating* schoolgirls and women for motherhood.

In 1910, Dr Christopher Addison introduced a bill into the House of Commons that would have required all public elementary schools to give instruction in infant care to girls over twelve years of age.[83] The bill was unsuccessful. Addison blamed the Board of Education for its demise.[84] But, as has already been shown, the Board was by this time very concerned with the whole question of the extent to which the elementary schoolgirl's curriculum should train her for a domestic role. Morant had already asked the Medical Department to draw up a memorandum on the teaching of infant care in the elementary schools. This memorandum was compiled by Dr Janet Campbell, one of the first three Medical Officers appointed to work under Newman's leadership. It was published in 1910, and circulated to local authorities in England and Wales with a prefatory note by Morant emphasising the importance of the subject. 'If girls and women could be taught how to take care of infants', he argued, 'we might hope to diminish not only the high rate of infant mortality, but also the large amount of unnecessary ill-health and physical suffering caused by neglect in infancy and childhood.' 'What is commonly called book-learning', he continued, 'has in past years been too much regarded as the supreme purpose of our elementary schools.' The elder girl pupils, particularly, might benefit from more domestic training. 'Few of these girls', Morant suggested, 'have mothers who are in a position to give them an efficient training in home management.' Instruction in infant care suited to girls of only twelve to fourteen years of age must admittedly be of a simple kind, but the Board were anxious to direct the attention of schools to the importance of providing it.[85]

The first section of the memorandum commented on the kind of arrangements already in practice in some schools. Short courses of perhaps half a dozen lessons given by nurses or visiting lecturers in hygiene were deemed to be inadequate. There were other schools which had devised schemes whereby girls were attached to 'home-making' centres either wholly or partially during their final year. Janet Campbell was more enthusiastic about experiments of this kind: with careful planning she thought local crèches or day nurseries might also be used to provide practical experience for the girls. The memorandum outlined some general principles to guide schools in the future. It was felt that infant care should be taught as part of an integrated course in hygiene and household management; and that the child-care classes should be postponed until as late as possible in the girl's school life — at least until the age of twelve, which would allow 'a sufficiently lengthy course, extending over say one or two years' to be devoted to the subject. Dr Campbell admitted that the practical difficulties in the way of obtaining a supply of live babies for regular classroom use were considerable: dolls would often have to be used, regrettably, since 'the frailty and helplessness of a baby appeals to these girls as perhaps nothing else can'.[86]

Pressure on the elementary schools to teach infant care to girls should be seen as part of the early twentieth century infant welfare movement, a movement often coloured, in its early phases, by the conviction that educational solutions to problems of infant well-being were more important than other kinds of remedy (such as more direct attacks upon poverty, bad housing and inadequate nutrition). However, by the end of the first world war several medical authorities had begun to challenge Newman's ideas about infant mortality on the grounds that his explanations consistently underemphasised the influence of poverty, overcrowding and other environmental factors.[87]

Infant mortality certainly declined spectacularly in Britain during the early decades of the present century, the rate falling from about 128 per 1,000 births between 1901 and 1910 to 53 per 1,000 on the eve of the second world war. But we still do not know precisely why this happened. The trend certainly *coincided* with the rise of the infant welfare movement, but this need not have been a simple relation of cause and effect. Some authorities believed the decline was related to autonomous epidemiological factors; such as an abatement of epidemics of zymotic diseases. Others contended that improvements in the supply of milk available for infant feeding were crucial. M.W. Beaver has recently argued in *Population Studies* that the sharp, impressive decline in infant mortality in England had its origin in the growing availability of pathogen-free milk, whether in liquid, condensed, or dried form, rather than in any general rise in living standards or improvements in midwifery or health visiting services.[88] However, one must remember that the majority of working-class mothers (Arthur Newsholme estimated about 80 per cent) had probably always breastfed their babies where at all possible, not least because it was the cheapest option available.[89] Condensed milk had several disadvantages as an infant foodstuff, and the separated sweetened and machine-skimmed varieties were particularly unsuitable in that they contained too much carbohydrate and insufficient fat.[90] However, the growing availability of *dried* milk products — distributed widely by infant welfare centres after about 1907-11 — was a trend enthusiastically commented on by contmporary authorities. By 1911 the Sheffield Dried Milk Depot claimed to have fed nearly 3,000 babies on cost-price Glaxo. In Manchester, it was reported that dried milk had significantly diminished the threat of the outbreaks of summer diarrhoea that had formerly proved so destructive of infant life.[91] A detailed report to the Local Government Board in 1918 was wholly enthusiastic about the properties of dried milk as an infant foodstuff.[92] Altogether, this apparently meant something of a revolution in the practice of safe artificial feeding.

The early years of the infant welfare movement witnessed the rapid growth of a whole variety of institutions: Milk Depots and *Gouttes de Lait* designed to improve the supply of uncontaminated milk; and 'educative' institutions — 'schools for mothers', infant 'welcomes' and health visiting networks which aimed to teach women to become better mothers. It remains extremely difficult to estimate the importance of education in preventing infant deaths, if only because 'educational factors' cannot easily be separated out from other influences at work.[93]

Infant Welfare Centres performed valuable information services, disseminating advice on care and feeding, and must be seen in the widest sense as 'educational' institutions. It seems very unlikely that lessons in 'mothercraft' supplied to girls of twelve and thirteen in the elementary schools were on anything like the same scale of importance. There is, as we have seen, plenty of evidence to suggest that girls in working-class families already received practice in bathing, dressing and otherwise caring for younger siblings at home. Women interviewed by Elizabeth Roberts, recollecting their childhood experiences in two north of England towns, Barrow and Lancaster, between 1890 and 1914, unanimously dismissed the kind of domestic training they had received at school as a waste of time. It was their apprenticeship in the home that they considered had provided the 'real' experience: lessons in home management provided in school seemed 'artificial' and of little value.[94]

The consensus of opinion amongst North country women interviewed by Elizabeth Roberts to the effect that they considered their domestic science lessons in school to have been 'unreal' and comparatively useless is interesting. Many contemporary exponents of the need for school training in home duties for girls were conscious of a nagging feeling that there was something artificial in the whole exercise. In a properly organised home, it was commonly argued, girls would indeed receive the best kind of training for their future through helping and observing their mothers. However, they were convinced that the 'disintegration' of working-class family life under new industrial and urban conditions made state intervention imperative. The state had to assume what should ideally be a parental role: schooling should remedy the deficiencies of the working-class home. Richard Johnson has commented upon this idea of the state acting *in loco parentis* in providing schooling in the writings of Kay Shuttleworth and others interested in educational provision in Victorian England.[95] Because it was popularly believed that the home was more important than the school in the upbringing of girls, the debate had particular relevance in respect of girls' education.

This becomes clear if we look at the problem of school attendance in late-nineteenth century England. Much of the evidence suggests that girls were likely to be kept away from school much more regularly and frequently than their brothers by mothers who needed their help with younger children and household chores. Mrs Layton, who grew up in Bethnal Green in the 1860s (before the Education Act), recollected that she and a sister had always stayed away from school on washing day to mind the babies. In the summer it was real sport, because so many people did their washing on the same day, and everybody had large families and generally kept the elder girls, and sometimes boys, at home to mind the little ones.[96]

During the last quarter of the century, when the School Boards were attempting to enforce attendance regulations, girls continued to stay away from school for rather different reasons than boys. Recent work by Anna Davin has shown clearly that double standards were applied by many authorities dealing with truancy in this period.[97] Amongst boys, 'truancy' was considered an offence; girls were more likely to be accused of 'absenteeism' than truancy; and their absences, particularly when explained in terms of having to care for younger siblings or support their mothers at home, were frequently accepted as facts of life. G.C.T. Bartley, writing in the *Journal of the Women's Education Union* as early as 1875 had remarked on this:

> Girls . . . suffer from this (poor attendance) more than boys; they are of use at home, are more handy in the household, and at a very tender age are trusted with the maternal duties of the family. Boys, however, are often sent to school, if only to be put out of the way. And more than this, the authorities of the School Boards are severer in the case of the boys absenting themselves from school than they are with girls. A sort of innate feeling, indeed, exists that school after all is more important to the boy than to the girl, so that if one must stay at home, it must be the girl.[98]

Further evidence of the tenacity of the belief that school was not always the best learning environment for girls comes from the Report and Minutes of Evidence collected by the Inter-Departmental Committee on Physical Deterioration in 1904. One idea which the Commissioners sounded out while collecting evidence for the Report was a suggestion that regulations for school attendance should be relaxed in the case of girls. They envisaged a scheme whereby parents might be encouraged to apply for permission to keep their daughters at home in the afternoons -- especially where the girls could be useful in caring for younger children, or would be able to help their mothers on baking days, or with the weekly family wash. It was suggested that school managers could be given authority to inspect the homes of those parents who applied to take advantage of this scheme: leave of absence could then be granted where the managers were satisfied that the girls would obtain a useful training in housewifery in a properly organised home.[99] Some of the witnesses interviewed by the Committee considered that there was much to recommend a scheme of this kind – Charles Booth's reaction, for instance, was favourable. However, those who did object to such proposals voiced their misgivings strongly. Sir John Gorst and Dr Eichholz expressed their conviction that such a scheme would all too easily degenerate into a system of child labour: Dr Eichholz remarked that he had had 'so much experience of the slavery of young girls in the homes of the poorer neighbourhoods' that although he recognised the need for domestic training for girls, he was convinced that it should be provided in the schools.[100] Faced with this kind of opinion, the Committee avoided making any clear recommendations on the subject of half-time attendance for girls in their final Report, although they did suggest that it was 'worth considering' whether a relaxation of attendance requirements could serve as a way of 'fostering the sense of domestic duties' in girls.[101]

However, the notion that schooling was encouraging the wrong kind of aspirations in girls, and undermining their attachment to home and appreciation of domestic duties, remained strong in many circles down to the first world war. As we have already seen, this generated support for an increasing emphasis on domestic training in the curriculum. But there were a few writers who still openly questioned the benefits of sending girls to school at all. The eugenist writers, W.C.D. and C.D. Whetham, for instance, believed educational reforms since 1870 were confronting women with a wrong ideal of life, leading them into competition with men for employment, astray from their mission as mothers and homemakers.[102] Catherine Whetham suggested in a book on *The Upbringing of Daughters* (1917) that schools were ideal places in which to educate boys, but daughters needed to be trained in the home. 'A few years ago', alleged the Whethams,

one of our Northern borough education authorities solemnly passed two instructions on the same day and at the same meeting. In the first it forbade the parents to keep elder girls at home and away from school in attendance on their mothers for the first two or three weeks following childbirth, threatening defaulters with the heaviest penalties of the law. In the second, it recommended the purchase of full-sized dolls and complete layettes as part of the school equipment in order to accustom the elder scholars to the care and protection of infant life.[103]

'Comment', they expostulated, 'is superfluous.'

Official attendance regulations could not eradicate the widespread assumption that schooling was anyway less important for girls than for boys. Magistrates and local authorities continued to look upon absenteeism amongst girls rather differently from truancy among boys, and to allow that there could be 'good' reasons for the former. And it is important to point out that even *in* school, girls could receive a variety of messages which would have reinforced any scepticism they had about the value of their own schooling. Any casual perusal of the kind of readers in domestic economy used in Board Schools at the turn of the century will show this. For instance, one reader published by Nelson for use in elementary schools in 1895 featured a story about a family of young children whose mother had recently died. The two girls (described in the text as 'dear little house mothers') resolved to leave school as soon as they could and take evening classes in domestic economy in order to keep house for their brother, who was thus enabled to stay on at school.[104] This is presented as wholly exemplary behaviour. Schooling, after all, mattered less to the *girls'* chances in life.

To conclude this chapter I shall look briefly at the origin of the Girls' Club Movement, Girls' Friendly Society, Girl Guides and other movements aiming to provide for the needs of adolescent girls, since the literature generated by the early exponents and organisers of these movements provides useful insights into middle-class attitudes to the socialisation of adolescent working-class girls during the period.

We have seen that the working-class girl would often gain her first experience of paid employment at a very early age. In Bethnal Green in the 1860s, Mrs Layton began to earn her own living when she was ten years old:

> I went to mind the baby of a person who kept a small general shop. My wages were 1/6 a week and my tea, and 2*d* a week for myself. I got to work at eight in the morning and left at eight at night, with the exception of two nights a week when I left at seven o'clock to attend a night school, one of a number started by Lord Shaftesbury, called Ragged Schools.[105]

During the last decades of the century school attendance regulations and complementary legislation restricting the employment of children modified patterns of early employment experience, but effected no overnight revolution. Large numbers of children attending elementary schools still took on a variety of part-time, casual jobs out of school hours — running errands, cleaning steps, minding children, hawking in the streets; or they were partially-exempted from school and continued in employment under the 'half-time' system. Even by 1914 some 40 per cent of children left school before the age of fourteen.

In an introduction to D.J. Collier's survey of *The Girl in Industry* (1918), B.L. Hutchins pointed out that 794,800, or 58.6 per cent of all adolescent girls between the ages of fourteen and eighteen were recorded by the 1911 census as being in full-time employment: of this number, as we have seen, 34.8 per cent were in some kind of domestic service (including hotel service, laundrywork and charing). In addition, 16 per cent were employed in the textile trades, and 19.2 per cent in the dress trades. Thus 'nearly 71 per cent of occupied girls were engaged in the occupations constantly associated with their sex and regarded as "womanly",' although most of the textile trades and much of the dress and laundry trades were by 1911 organised on factory lines. The remaining 29 per cent of young female workers were dispersed over clerical, artistic and other trades, and in miscellaneous factory industries.[106]

Middle-class anxieties about the employment and leisure activities of adolescent working-class girls stemmed from a variety of sources. It was argued that these girls were thrown too early upon the labour market, too early removed from the surveillance and protection of family or Board School Authorities. 'As soon as the discipline of school is removed', wrote Lily Montagu (an exponent of the need for clubs for girls), 'and the process of wage earning begins, girls are most seriously in need of training and protection. Their precocious self-dependence in itself menaces their proper development.'[107]

Regular wage packets were held partly responsible for 'precocious independence' amongst young girls, tempting many into extravagant taste in dress or unsuitable leisure-time occupations. It was claimed that girls were likely to fall amongst the wrong kinds of companions at work, become prey to idle chatter, addicted to the worst tastes in novel reading. Flirtatiousness would replace maidenly modesty and reserve, and ill-considered liaisons could only lead to early marriages and an improvident future.[108]

Those who advocated the establishment of clubs and associations for working girls usually emphasised their conviction that reform in this area would have far-reaching implications: adolescent girls were the mothers of tomorrow, and in raising their ideals and standards in life one was helping to improve the condition of the working class as a whole. Maud Stanley, in her manual on *Clubs for Working Girls* (published in 1890) argued this position strongly:

> We might almost say that the welfare of the work girl is at the root of the important questions now exercising the minds and thoughts of some of the best of our generation: the question, How are we to improve the lives of our working classes? . . . if we raise the workgirl, if we can make her conscious of her own great responsibilities both towards God and man, if we can show her that there are other objects in her life besides that of gaining her daily bread or getting as much amusement as possible out of her days, we shall then give her an influence over her sweetheart, her husband and her sons which will sensibly improve and raise her generation to be something higher than mere hewers of wood and drawers of water.[109]

Maude Stanley's views were reiterated by Lily Montagu. The Boys' Club movement, the latter added, could not succeed properly without a similar movement for girls: a girl's interest in the opposite sex during adolescence was paramount, her power of influence over her male associates strong. Boys could all too easily be led astray by a girl's flirtatiousness – it was a mistake to assume that the efforts of club leaders amongst one sex could achieve much without those of the other.[110] Mixed clubs, Miss Montagu emphasised, were not a good idea: they tended to encourage that 'precocious' interest in the opposite sex which most club leaders sought to play down. 'Generally speaking, the mixed clubs have failed because the girls will not be interested in the boys except as potential bridegrooms.'[111]

Certain kinds of work or work environment were judged to be particularly hazardous or unsuitable for young girls. Factory work, it was often claimed, could exert a very damaging influence on health, mind and morals.[112] Those who concerned themselves with the welfare of the working girl constantly complained about the low tone of conversation amongst workers on the factory floor, the coarse jests and vulgar talk which they feared was guaranteed to eliminate any trace of maidenly virtue amongst new workers. 'Old hands' in the factory were sometimes accused of leading the young astray: Miss Nunneley, a pioneer of 'Snowdrop Bands' (dedicated to preserve purity amongst working girls), alleged that in talking amongst factory girls in Birmingham and in Kettering she had been assured that most of the evil conversation carried on in the factories originates with the married women who still remain at work. In many cases these women, especially the younger ones, deliberately set themselves to corrupt the minds of the single girls.[113]

Another reason why factory work was considered hazardous was that much of it was sedentary and most tasks monotonous. Girls had little chance to let off steam; their senses were dulled and jaded by the working day and this produced a desire to escape, whetting the appetite for boisterous or lurid pleasures. 'It is only when we realise the monotony of the workshop life', suggested Lily Montagu, 'that we can understand why the craving for excitement is almost a necessary element in the working girl's composition.'[114] Similarly, fourteen years later in an essay on 'The Young Factory Girl' Emily Matthias insisted that

> Factory labour is repressive to a high degree. . . . No wonder that when the girls are 'let loose' they behave in what the general public may call an unseemly fashion. . . . Much of the immorality of which the factory girl is accused may be put down to sheer reaction. She is drugged with monotony and long hours of physical labour, and feels the need for a strong and sharp stimulus.[115]

Finally, factory work was often considered unsuitable for young girls because it offered no kind of training of relevance to the girl's future as wife and mother — indeed, it was commonly asserted that insofar as girls developed a liking for this kind of work, their inclination for domestic duties diminished. Hilda Martindale, reporting on what she deemed to be the lamentable reluctance amongst married women in the Potteries to relinquish their jobs on marriage, explained to the Inter-Departmental Commission on Physical Deterioration that

> At 13 years of age the majority of these women would have begun to work in a factory, to handle their own earnings, to mix with a large number of people with all the excitement and gossip of family life. They would thus, in most cases, grow up entirely ignorant of everything pertaining to domesticity. After marriage, therefore, it is hardly probable that they would willingly relinquish this life to undertake work in which they are in so large a measure ignorant, and which is robbed of all that is to them pleasant and exciting.[116]

These, then, are some of the reasons why factories were considered potentially dangerous environments for adolescent girls. Domestic service, of course, was widely regarded as a far safer and more fitting kind of employment for young women. However, even girls going into service were felt to need protection against a variety of dangerous influences which might come to bear on them once they had left the safety of the family home. Mrs Townsend, who founded the Girls' Friendly Society in 1874, had very much in mind the protection of the young girl from the country embarking into the difficult world of the city; going into service very often in an unknown household, with no real guarantee of the respectability and benevolence of her employers.[117]

The GFS was a highly conservative, Anglican religious association designed to promote friendship and social harmony across class boundaries; between mistress and maid. Upper-class Lady Associates were to adopt a protective, motherly role towards unmarried, working-girl members.[118] The idea caught on immediately and by 1885 there were 821 branches over England and Wales, the strength of the organisation being particularly apparent in rural areas, especially in the South. There were attempts to recruit girls in a variety of different situations: orphans in workhouses, factory girls in the large towns of the North — not always equally successful.[119] There is evidence to suggest that social distances between Lady Associates and millgirls in industrial areas were sometimes too wide: the girls were staunchly independent and resented patronage. Deference could be fostered much more readily in the countryside, especially in areas where domestic service constituted the only real opportunity for employment. In 1891 57 per cent of the total employed membership of the GFS were working as domestic servants.[120] Indeed, one of the most important aspects of GFS work was to improve the supply of domestic servants. This was achieved through a direct involvement in schemes for domestic training — a Department of Domestic Economy and Industrial Training was first created in 1881, and GFS lodges set out to train members in domestic work.[121] There was also the work of the Registry Department (established in 1878) which promoted and co-ordinated a network of District Registries, keeping up-to-date lists of 'good situations' and reliable girls in need of posts.[122] During and after the first world war the GFS took a leading part in schemes aiming to raise the social prestige of domestic service as a skilled occupation. The 'League of Skilled Housecraft', for instance, founded in 1922, which set out to examine girls all over the country and award certificates of competency in domestic subjects, was under GFS management.[123] Representatives from the Board of Education, Ministry of Labour and the London County Council served in an advisory capacity.

The GFS saw itself involved in a mission to 'purify' womanhood. The aim was to elevate, to fortify against, and protect girls from, 'temptation' – not to reclaim them once they had 'fallen'. Between 1879 and 1880 a serious internal dispute was provoked by the suggestion that a rule requiring chastity as a condition of membership should be revoked. The suggestion came from Associates who believed the Society should involve itself in reform working amongst girls who had already 'gone astray', leading them back, penitent, to the path of Christian womanhood. Mrs Townsend was obdurate in her conviction that such a 'compromise' would smirch the banner of purity: she was backed by the bishops, and the rules survived unchanged.[124]

Other societies defined their rules rather more leniently in an attempt to reach girls working in environments where they were felt to be particularly vulnerable. 'Snowdrop Bands,' popular around 1889-90, aimed to recruit factory girls in the towns of the Midlands and North of England. A member of a Snowdrop Band carried a card with a bunch of snowdrops on it – 'white flowers of a blameless life'. Round the border were printed the words 'Let thy mind's sweetness have its operation on thy body, clothes and habitation.' The promise printed on the back of the card read,

> We, the Members of the Snowdrop Band, sign our names to show that we have agreed that wherever we are, and in whatever company, we will, with God's help, earnestly try, both by our example and influence, to discourage all wrong conversation, light and immodest conduct and the reading of bad and foolish books.[125]

Miss Nunneley, an enthusiastic exponent of the work of these Bands, told a meeting of ladies involved in social work amongst women and girls in Birmingham in 1890 that the word 'try' in the 'promise' was crucial. It relieved the girls from the weight of a pledge, and thus,

> a member who is earnestly endeavouring to free herself from an evil habit is not made to feel that she has broken her word if she occasionally fails under pressure of temptation.[126]

The pioneers of the Snowdrop Bands were more interested in reaching young girls in factory towns than they were in domestic servants, although (in spite of their slightly more tolerant attitude to lapses in the girls' behaviour) it is doubtful whether they had any more success than the GFS in urban areas. Both organisations aimed to purify and exalt femininity, to persuade girls that the essence of womanhood lay in innocence, modesty, gentle devotion to duty and domestic tasks. Both feared that adolescent girls of the working class were too soon removed from the influence of family and school: they needed the restraining hand of adult authority, ideally the contact with 'cultured' benevolent ladies of the middle or upper class who could serve as models, as surrogate mothers, providing images of re- fined, feminine behaviour.

Initially, the impetus for the Girl Guide movement seems to have come from a different source altogether. According to the official histories of the movement, the inspiration came from below. It is alleged that when Baden-Powell turned up to inspect Boy Scouts at the first large official rally held at the Crystal Palace in 1909, he was embarrassed to come across a party of girls in khaki shirts calling them- selves 'girl scouts' and demanding inspection along with the boys.[127] Baden-Powell allegedly had serious misgivings over associating girls with the movement. 'Manliness' demanded a clear dissociation from anything female. He feared ridicule and the anger of 'respectable' matrons who would surely find the idea of girls marching in uniform quite unseemly.

Anxious to save scouting from the 'contamination' of feminine influence Baden-Powell insisted that the girls should form a separate movement, must adopt a different name (hence 'Girl Guides' rather than 'Girl Scouts'), different values and a more appropriately 'womanly' ethos. Notes on 'The Scheme for "Girl Guides",' published in the November 1909 issue of the *Headquarters Gazette* specified that:

> The training laid down by Boy Scouts, though it applies pretty generally to all boys, whether from Eton or from East Ham, does not apply equally to all girls, even when altered in details to suit the sex.
>
> With girls it has to be administered with great discrimination; you do not want to make tomboys of refined girls, yet you want to attract, and thus raise, the slum girl from the gutter. The main object is to give them *all* the ability to be better mothers and Guides to the next generation.[128]

In the case of the Scouts, Baden-Powell pointed out, the impetus for forming patrols had often come from the boys themselves, who had then persuaded local gentlemen to take command as their officers. With girls, he did not think this would do. It was presumably not 'ladylike' for the girls themselves to take the initiative – it was better, he thought, if the first step could be taken by ladies interested in the movement, who should form a committee, 'get hold of the right kind of young ladies to act as captains', then encourage the captains to set about recruitment.[129]

Baden-Powell then turned to his sister, Agnes, who agreed to take over the leadership of the Girl Guide movement. Agnes immediately set out to 'feminise' the movement and to direct it into what she regarded as respectable womanly channels. One of the first steps was the suppression of many of the patrol names chosen by the girls themselves – 'Wildcats', 'Foxes', 'Wolves' and 'Bears' were to adopt more suitable nomenclature and became 'roses', 'cornflowers', 'lilies-of-the-valley' and so forth.[130] A biographer of Lady Baden-Powell later remarked that

> this change of name and programme was not at first very popular
> with girls who had been Scouts. They had revelled in their Scouting
> and were rather lukewarm about being Guides. The Owls and Foxes
> kept their patrol cries, because as they explained Sunflowers and
> Pimpernels did not make any nice noises.[131]

Reports on the activities and progress of Guiding were published in the infinitely respectable woman's weekly magazine *Home Notes* during 1910 and 1911. Here Agnes regularly chided her readers against 'tomboyish' behaviour. In August 1910, for instance;

> I would like first of all to state that it (Guiding) is a feminine move-
> ment – a womanly scheme in the best sense of the word. There is
> no militarism in it – no idea of making girls into poor imitations of
> Boy Scouts.
> Education will be on such lines only as will make the girls better
> housewives, more capable in all womanly arts, from cooking,
> washing and sick nursing to the training and management of
> children. . . .[132]

At times Agnes's cloying emphasis on femininity became absurd. In August, 1910, we find her suggesting that,

> In order to look very nice on parade, Guides must remember how
> the lovely Venus, who was the Queen of Beauty, was evolved from

111

the foam on the top of the waves. She rose out of the sea a perfect beauty, with lovely fine seaweed-like golden silk for her hair and tiny shiny pink sea-shells for her nails, and that is why all Girl Guides polish their nails so well with chalk and flannel before parade, and get each other to smooth what the papers call their *coiffure*.[133]

During the War, Olave Baden-Powell (née St Clair Soames), who had married Robert in 1912, began to channel her abundant energies into the organisation of the Guide movement. Agnes was pushed into the background, although she retained a nominal Presidency until 1920. Olave was appointed Chief Commissioner in 1916, and eighteen months later took the title of 'World Chief Guide'. Lady Baden-Powell's outlook was breezy and self-consciously 'modern'. She clearly regarded Agnes as an old fuddy-duddy, 'thoroughly Victorian in outlook'.[134] While conceding that some caution had been necessary in 1909 to convince mothers of the 'respectability' of Guiding as a movement she believed a more adventurous programme was now called for. Girls were called upon to become more resourceful and self-reliant in order that they would grow up fitting 'pals' and comrades to their husbands. Warnings against tomboyishness still appeared in the Official Handbook, but they were milder in tone. Even so, the stress on 'womanly arts' and homekeeping as the loftiest goals of a girl's existence remained. The tone is best summed up in a passage from the 1918 edition of the handbook, where B-P reminds his readers:

> as I have said before, success in her professional career is neither the end and aim nor the greatest joy of the girl's life. She has still before her her reward, all the sweeter when it has been won by hard work, the glorious reward of having a home of her own, the shrine of her life, a man after her own heart to share it as her pal and protector (for however independent and self-reliant she may have felt in her time there comes a joy in snuggling down under the care of a strong, loving right arm).[135]

Guide leaders commonly asserted that one of the main aims of their movement was to develop habits of self-reliance and independence in young girls. However, there was a marked ambivalence here. In 1910 Agnes Baden-Powell had argued that a movement like Guiding was vitally needed among working-class girls — 'the girls of the factories and of the alleys of our great cities' — who otherwise escaped totally from any kind of restraining, adult influence immediately they left the elementary schools.[136] Guiding, like the Girls' Club Movement, Snowdrop Bands, GFS and similar organisations aimed to fill the gap, to supply that benevolent, protective adult authority which it was believed a young girl needed once she had shaken free of the controlling influence of family and school. Too much independence amongst young girls was definitely considered a dangerous thing. It is significant that in most of the literature expounding the need for clubs and societies among adolescent girls the working girl's independence is perceived as 'precocity'. Wage-earning is believed to buy them a premature and socially undesirable independence. Further there is a strong assumption (which one meets over and over again in the literature) that financial independence and sexual precocity go hand in hand — wage-earning girls were constantly accused of taking what many reformers deemed to be an unhealthily premature interest in the opposite sex. During the first world war such anxieties seem to have increased. A volume edited by J.J. Findlay (Professor of Education at Manchester Universtiy) on *The Young Wage Earner* (in 1918) contained an essay by James Shelley suggesting that the drift of young women into munitions and other factories had had alarming social consequences.[137] The home was no longer the controlling factor in the socialisation of adolescent girls; they escaped too early into the labour market, lured by abnormally high salaries, and this had the effect of distorting their values and destroying their education in domestic life. The popular press had, of course, delighted in copy dwelling on the extravagant spending habits, luxurious attire and 'advanced' behaviour of office girls and munition workers throughout the war years.

Lady Baden-Powell enthusiastically latched on to these denunciations in the popular press. Writing about how she had become a Commissioner, in *Training Girls as Guides* (1917), she quoted approvingly from a weekly periodical which had recently featured an article entitled 'Our Brazen Flappers'. 'The Flapper', she explained, was an unprotected girl, 'a mere butterfly enjoying her escape from the chrysalis of childhood.'

She means no harm by her frivolity at first, but she soon grows wise in exploiting herself. One finds her aiding nature by eyebrow pencil and lip-salve, powder-puff and rouge-pot, at an age when such things should not exist for her. Sex problems present themselves far too early in life, and what intellect she has is used but in one direction — to capture the eye of the male.

Familiarity with freedom is apt to make a girl blasée. When she has learnt the ABC of sin it is but a step towards the first primer of vice.[138]

Lady Baden-Powell then embarked upon a catalogue of what she considered were the outstanding social ills of the time, dredging up all the clichés of nineteenth-century social reform literature and presenting them in the style of twentieth-century sensational journalism. Blame for road accidents, intemperance, the squalor of city tenements and high infant mortality rates, she asserted, could often be laid fair and square on the heads of incompetent housewives.[139] Girls needed a more efficient training in domestic work, otherwise the country would continue to suffer from miseries inflicted by careless mothers and incompetent domestic servants. The schools had failed to take sufficient notice of this need up to the present time. The secondary schools, Lady B-P insisted, were even more culpable than the elementary schools in this respect.[140] They put too much emphasis on academic subjects and work for the Oxford and Cambridge Locals — the girls were not given enough training for their future role in the home. Until this state of affairs might be remedied, Guide leaders were left with a vitally important task on their hands. Girls had to be made into 'efficient women citizens, good home-keepers and mothers'. Ultimately Guiding, the GFS and other organisations for adolescent girls, as much as changes in the elementary school curriculum in the period, were designed to teach girls about femininity.

4

Adolescent girlhood: autonomy versus dependence

Adolescence, it is sometimes claimed, was first 'discovered' in the nineteenth century. As industrial society came to subject children and the young to ever longer periods of tutelage and formal schooling, the transition from childhood to a generally recognised adult status became more drawn out and complex.[1] A proliferation of discussion and writing about 'youth' from around the 1890s onwards testifies to the increasingly common assumption that *adolescence* as a phase posed developmental problems, while *adolescents* as a group might well constitute something of a social problem. It was in this context that G. Stanley Hall compiled and published his mammoth tract on the 'biological psychology' of the young, *Adolescence*, a work dauntingly subtitled *Its Psychology, and its Relation to Physiology, Anthropology, Sociology, Sex, Crime, Religion and Education*.[2] This work first appeared in the USA in 1904, and was widely read on both sides of the Atlantic. This century has seen a steady stream of literature published focusing on the problems of youth and adolescence, considered from a variety of intellectual viewpoints. Alongside the works of social and developmental psychologists there have been numerous studies of juvenile employment and delinquency, studies of juvenile leisure activities (which proliferated particularly around the 1940s and 1950s) and more recently, a number of works addressing themselves to a discussion of 'youth culture' generally.[3]

Over the last couple of decades social historians, too, have developed an interest in the history of childhood and adolescence. Philippe Ariès' celebrated and pioneer work *Centuries of Childhood* first appeared in

1960;[4] Ive Pinchbeck and Margaret Hewitt's two-volume history *Children in English Society* in 1969 and 1973.[5] The historiography of adolescence is more recent still, only really beginning to emerge over the last ten years: John Gillis' *Youth and History* was published in 1974, John Springhall's *Youth, Empire and Society* in 1977, and Joseph Kett's *Rites of Passage, Adolescence in America, 1790 to the Present* in the same year.[6]

Few of these works pay much (if indeed any) attention to girls. John Gillis admitted in the preface to *Youth and History* that his main concern in the book was with male youth: his chapter on the discovery of adolescence is significantly subtitled 'Boys will be boys'. John Springhall's study of youth organisations focuses exclusively on boys. Historians seem all too easily to accept the assumption one comes across time and time again in the literature on adolescence – the category 'Youth' is implicitly understood to refer primarily to boys, or even to the male sex solely.

Many of even the most up-to-date sociological and ethnographical studies of youth culture either omit reference to girls altogether, or refer to them cursorily or dismissively in passing. In a recent essay on 'Girls and Subcultures' Angela McRobbie and Jenny Garber have discussed some of the problems this raises.[7] Does the dismissive treatment of girls in the literature on youth culture merely reflect the bias of male researchers or does it reflect the fact that girls do not generally participate in the same activities as boys? And, again, if girls do share in youth culture, what sort of roles do they play?

The historian interested in adolescent girlhood is faced with similar kinds of problems in interpreting sources. Much of the general literature on adolescents and their activities which has come down to us from the period c.1890-1920 was written by middle-class club leaders, clergymen, social and welfare workers of various kinds. Again there is a heavy concentration on the male sex – comparatively few works concern themselves primarily with girls. References to girls are characteristically value-laden and stereotyped. The kind of reference which McRobbie and Garber cite from T. Fyvel's study of Teddy Boys as typical of the recent literature (the 'dumb, passive teenage girls, crudely painted') comes close to the kind of reference common in equivalent accounts fifty or sixty years ago.[8] Working-class girls are often dismissed in a few stock phrases as painted, pleasure-seeking flirts with vulgar tastes and cheap morals. Lily Montagu, who contributed a chapter entitled 'The Girl in the Background' to E.J. Urwick's collection,

116

Studies of Boy Life in Our Cities (compiled for the Toynbee Trust in 1904), presented a picture of city streets crowded by working girls with a 'dangerous craving for excitement'. Their sensibilities coarsened by addiction to the reading of 'mawkish novelettes', they were hot in pursuit of romance and, she suggested, constituted a formidable danger to the moral uprightness of the nation's boyhood.[9] Social work was crucially necessary not so much for the girls' own benefit, but more importantly to 'refine' their instincts in order that they should come to exert an 'elevating' influence on the young men they sought to partner.

Alongside the problems of locating evidence and adjusting for the biases of class and gender inherent in so much of the source material there are also certain conceptual problems which confront anyone interested in adolescent girlhood. There is, as has already been suggested, room for considerable discussion over the extent to which 'adolescence' represents a developmental stage with fairly distinct biological or psychological characteristics and the extent to which it represents a social construction, a phase in growth to which certain societies in certain historical periods have attributed particular meanings. Social psychologists in recent decades have tended to present adolescence as a phase in which the growing individual undergoes an often confusing search for personal and social identity, for the mature self. But the concept of 'maturity' of mind or behaviour cannot be defined in anything other than a heavily value-laden way. It can carry vastly different connotations, for instance, depending on whether it is used by someone inclined to accept the basic features of the existing social order as normal, natural and desirable, or by someone who questions these arrangements.

This becomes particularly important when we consider the differences between social definitions of mature behaviour in men and women respectively. A writer who accepts the sexual division of labour which ascribes the major 'breadwinning' role to the adult male and an almost exclusively child-rearing role to his wife will clearly tend to define male and female 'maturity' in very different ways. Maturity for the male sex will be judged in terms of a boy's ability to make workable occupational choices and to achieve economic independence – his ability to 'hold down a steady job' or 'keep a family in reasonable comfort'. For girls, on the other hand, 'maturity' is likely to be defined in terms of accepting economic *dependence* on a husband's pay-packet and the equation of her personal goals in life with maternity. It may be (and frequently has been) insisted that these divergent criteria do not

117

necessarily imply inequality (the different-but-equal argument), but what we have here is clearly a double-standard. Many of those forms of behaviour which society would deem 'adolescent' or 'immature' for the male sex will tend to be seen as appropriate for women at any age. Or, to express the same idea slightly differently, women are likely to be seen as permanently rather immature or childish.

Leta Hollingworth, whose well-known text *The Psychology of the Adolescent* was published in 1930, realised something of this when she wrote.

> The adequate adult is able, in the first place, to sustain himself or herself physically. This means economic competence. He is in condition to wait upon himself or to pay directly for the services of others. It is in this fundamental respect that women have had and still have the greatest difficulty in meeting the conditions of adulthood. Because of their part in reproduction, women have been dependent on men for subsistence instead of being themselves in direct contact with the means of supply. Thus, childishness must be expected more commonly in women than in men, for fewer women have been able to achieve self-sustenance by direct effort.[10]

G. Stanley Hall significantly argued that women never really outgrew their adolescence — psychologically and emotionally they could best be understood as having had their growth arrested in the adolescent phase.[11]

I should like to suggest that there are two angles from which we can usefully consider 'adolescence' in relation to women's experience in our culture. To begin with, a society which defines maturity for men in terms of economic and occupational independence and actively discourages women from achieving economic independence *is* effectively condemning women to a permanently 'adolescent' state. Many women, particularly those who do not find complete personal fulfillment in motherhood, together with those who feel a profound loss of self when their children grow up and are no longer dependent on them, experience a protracted 'identity' crisis which may never be satisfactorily resolved. This has provided subject matter for countless novels by women writers. In recent decades, particularly, the plight of the young middle-aged woman whose energies are no longer fully demanded by her family and who is consequently forced into an often very painful search for identity has been explored by novelists such as Doris Lessing and Penelope Mortimer.[12]

It might be argued, however, that these 'psychological' problems, the loss of self-respect and problems of identity experienced by women who have always been supported by someone else, are frustrations which have commonly been experienced by many more women in the middle class than further down the social scale. In exploring the lives of working-class girls and women, particularly in the early decades of the current century, it is tempting to suggest that far from being condemned to 'permanent adolescence', many of these women never experienced anything resembling a state of adolescence at all. As children, as soon as they could be considered remotely competent, they would have been expected to take on household duties and encouraged to see themselves as 'little mothers' ministering to the needs of the family. Girls were much less likely than their brothers to have been allowed a period of legitimate freedom, however transitory, removed from adult surveillance and unencumbered by responsibility for domestic chores. Seen in this light, girls enjoyed a shorter period of childhood than boys. And if adolescence is identified as a transitional phase between childhood and the assumption of 'adult' tasks, a hiatus institutionalised to some extent as a period of liberty and choice, then adolescence for girls had relatively little meaning. Indeed, this might be argued to have been the case not merely with girls growing up in working-class families, but with girls almost everywhere.

Much of the debate over and social concern with 'adolescence' over the last century can best be understood as a concern with questions of autonomy and dependence. John Gillis has argued that adolescence was 'discovered' by the European middle class and that in England this discovery was intimately related to the reform of the public schools and the rise of secondary education from the mid-nineteenth century onwards.[13] Young people who enjoyed an extended period of schooling were being subjected to a period of extended dependency upon adults, a longer period during which their behaviour was likely to be restricted by parental and institutional controls. This was, in the first place, essentially a middle-class phenomenon. Gillis argues that in consequence, middle-class observers came increasingly to look upon the experience of working-class youth as problematic. Working-class youngsters, it was feared, were inadequately disciplined at home, and when whatever schooling they were given ended, generally in the early teens, they were seen as being precipitated into a dangerous and precocious independence. The movement to 'organise' youth, Gillis maintains, can best be understood as stemming from these anxieties: Boys' Clubs,

Brigades, Church Groups and Scouting were all intended to restore adult authority; to guard against what was perceived to be the excessive independence of the young.[14]

Gillis's argument is convincing, although unfortunately, as mentioned above, he does not make room in his interpretation for any consideration of the female sex. Middle-class girls were subjected to infinitely more restrictions on their independence than were their brothers. Middle-class boys were sent away to public schools to prepare them for an independent life. Prolonged schooling may have entailed a longer period of financial dependence on a father's purse, but this was temporary. The ostensible aim of the boys' schools was to provide a training in self-reliance, and to inculcate 'manly' virtues of emotional independence, the 'stiff upper lip' and so forth. Not only were middle-class girls much less likely to be sent to school than their brothers, but as we have seen, when they *were* schooled, they tended to be sent to schools which replicated the family model, and provided the 'homely atmosphere' felt conducive to a training in feminine virtues and a womanly dependence.[15]

I have suggested that the late-nineteenth century changes in provision for the education of middle-class girls were by no means as radical as has sometimes been assumed. The new girls' high schools and women's colleges were in some ways conservative institutions: certainly not seminaries of feminist consciousness committed to any comprehensive scheme of social change. If they offered their pupils a vision of independence, it was a limited one; in that girls still learned that careers for women had generally to be bought at the high personal cost of remaining celibate. No doubt many teachers in the new educational institutions for women still saw the encouragement they held out to their pupils to prepare themselves for self-support in terms similar to those they used when attempting to 'sell' the policy to middle-class parents: it was prudent for a girl to contemplate some means of self-support as a form of insurance against the possibility of her being unfortunate enough not to make an acceptable marriage.

Limited though the vision of 'independence' offered to girls by the new institutions was, and in spite of the fidelity with which, on the whole, these new schools and colleges transmitted the values of 'respectable' middle-class society, the new educational provisions for women were still viewed from a number of quarters as socially threatening. The attempt to provide *higher* education for women particularly aroused immense opposition from clerical and medical quarters.[16]

Anglican clerics in Oxford and Cambridge, already gloomily contemplating the declining power of the church in universities, saw the 'invasion' of their hallowed male precincts by women as the final desecration. Clergymen such as Christopher Wordsworth and J.W. Burgon preached zealously against any notion of equality in education, insisting that the notion of 'separate spheres' for men and women had been Divinely Ordained.[17] At the same time voices were raised from the Medical Profession urging dire warnings about the constitutional overstrain and physiological damage which it was predicted women would inflict upon themselves if they foolishly embarked on courses of advanced intellectual work.[18] Evolutionary theorists, social-Darwinists and eugenists propounded still more theories about the social and biological inadvisability of women deserting their 'responsibilities to the race' by selfishly developing their own intellects at the expense of reproduction.[19]

Some of these ideas will be discussed in more detail in the next chapter. Here I want to examine the theory of one particular writer who concerned himself with the nature of female adolescence and its educational consequences, namely G. Stanley Hall. I have chosen to devote space to this American writer in a book concerned with English social history for a number of reasons. To begin with, Hall's writings on female adolescence formed part of his massive two-volume work on adolescence generally, which, as pointed out at the beginning of this chapter, constituted a landmark in the history of ideas on the subject and was extremely widely read in both England and America. Both at the time of publication and subsequently, the book aroused fury among feminists. M. Carey Thomas's reaction, as President of Bryn Mawr College in the United States, has often been quoted. Addressing the Association of Collegiate Alumnae in 1907 she declared that although she had spent the thirty years between 1874 and 1904 reading every book on women that she could obtain, in any language, she 'had never chanced again upon a book that seemed to me to so degrade me in my womanhood as the seventh and seventeenth chapters on women and women's education of President Stanley Hall's *Adolescence*.' At the time, she recalled, she had been terror-struck, 'lest I, and every other woman with me, were doomed to live as pathological invalids in a universe merciless to women as a sex.' However since then, she claimed, she with other women had come to realise that 'it is not we, but the man who believes such things about us who is himself pathological, blinded by neurotic mists of sex.'[20]

In the pages that follow I shall suggest that Stanley Hall's theories could arouse such a strong response because of the very comprehensiveness of his attack on feminism; the carefully deliberate and systematic way in which he attempted to refute the possibilities of female autonomy, be they at an economic, physical or even at a psychological level. Both Hall's writings and indeed his whole personality can still offer us fascinating insights into the nature and psychology of patriarchy.

Adolescence, Hall maintained, had very different meanings for the two sexes.[21] For the boy, it was a time of ambition, growth and challenge. For the girl, it was a time of instability; a dangerous phase when she needed special protection from society. During adolescence, boys grew towards self-knowledge. Girls, on the other hand, could never really attain self-knowledge. They could never hope to understand much of themselves or the motives for their conduct, for their lives were ruled by 'deep unconscious instincts', and a girl's self-consciousness was only 'the reflected knowledge others have of her'. Women, Hall insisted, never really outgrew their adolescence, and this constituted their charm, their eternal womanliness.[22]

Hall's work is not easy to read. *Adolescence* is a work formidable both in style and content. Vast edifices of speculative theory jostle together with catalogues of obscure references, all in a style ponderous, pretentious and rhetorical. The sections on women are especially florid. In talking about motherhood Hall tends to adopt a mawkishly reverential tone.[23] But his descriptions of adolescent girls are generally couched in a particularly glutinous, leery prose. Young girls are variously referred to as 'buds', *backfisch*, 'missies' or 'coy maidens'. It is impossible to avoid quoting at length in order to convey the full impression; the passage that follows is from a chapter entitled 'The Budding Girl', in *Educational Problems* (published in 1911).

Backfisch is a colloquial German term for a girl in the very earliest teens, and I use it here because I know of none in English or any other language so expressive, and because the age is as unique as the name. It is better than the French *'tendron'* or the English 'bud'. It means a fresh fish, just caught but unbaked, though fit and ready for the process. The naivete of instinctive unconscious childhood, like the glinting sheen of sea hues, is still upon the *Backfisch*. Save for a little mechanical drill, and breaking in to a few of the most rudimentary conventionalities of learning and conduct, her real nature is wild with a charming gamey flavour. She is unspoiled by any of the recipes given in the cook books of pedagogy and society, for making human nature more appetizing to their highly artificial tastes. Girls with hair demurely braided down their backs, and skirts just beginning to lengthen toward their ankles are buds that should not blossom for some time, but should be kept as long as possible in the green stage; or, to change from a floral to a faunal trope, they are only squabs and not yet doves, maturing pupae and not yet butterflies, and this calf or filly stage should be prolonged by every artifice.[24]

Adolescent girls were according to Hall recognisable by their clothes-consciousness, whimsicality, unconscious flirtatiousness, fads, fickleness, weepiness, giggling, coquetry, passion for secrecy and, above all, by their strong distaste for study.[25] This last attribute he claimed to be both natural and beneficial, for one of the most crucial requirements of the growing girl was rest and protection from the stress of too much brainwork.[26]

At this point Hall marshalled together all the testimony he could find from doctors who believed that puberty involved special hazards for the female sex. Views of this kind were generally bound up with the conviction that human physiology was governed by a fixed sum of energy. It was alleged that during puberty the growing girl needed to conserve all her energies in order to establish a regular menstrual cycle. If she spent too much of her energy on intellectual work, the argument ran, her menstrual cycle might fail to establish itself and there was a serious risk of permanent damage to the reproductive system.[27]

Hall fully subscribed to such ideas about the physiological vulnerability of the adolescent female. Girls needed to be protected from the rigours of serious study, he contended, until they had crossed 'the Rubicon of Menstruation'.[28] Some girls might undoubtedly resent being incapacitated in this way, but equally many, he reassured the reader, would derive great pleasure from being thus 'taken in hand, managed and commanded'. Using language highly revealing of the workings of his less conscious mind, Hall asserted that girls should be gently urged to retreat from academic work, to 'lie fallow' for a while, and let 'Lord Nature do his magnificent work of inflorescence'.[29]

Any idea of equality between the sexes, together with all schemes for co-education were peremptorily dismissed by Stanley Hall as mere 'cant', 'flying in the face of common sense'.[30] The process of evolution, he asserted, involved a movement towards greater differentiation between the sexes. Co-education would thwart progress. Boys might become 'feminised'. Girls would be presented with false goals in life. Hall was also anxious lest girls should lose their respect for the male sex if they had too much contact with 'callow, unripe youths' of their own age.[31]

Ambition in women represented a substitute for maternal fulfilment, Hall maintained. The intellectual woman who did not find her supreme interest in marriage and motherhood was sick, sterile, likely to become a crabbed degenerate; 'the apotheosis of selfishness from the standpoint of very biological ethics'.[32] It was criminal that women's colleges should be staffed by such degenerates. Hall predicted a gloomy future for the human race if current trends in educational provision for women were not reversed.[33] Since women could not be 'objective' in defining their real interests, he urged upon his male colleagues the necessity for advancing the study of feminine psychology. Women, he asserted,

> must be studied objectively and laboriously as we study children, and partly by men, because their sex must of necessity always remain objective and incommensurate with regard to women, and therefore more or less theoretical.[34]

In *Youth: Its Regimen and Hygiene* (1906) Hall elaborated his own ideal scheme of education for the adolescent girl. Girls between the ages of twelve or thirteen and the early twenties might most appropriately be sent to institutions secluded 'in the country in the midst of hills'.[35] There should be an over-riding concern with health: food, sleep, and gentle non-competitive exercise. Dancing was important, especially the minuet, which gave poise. Manners and grace were crucial: tact and taste were much more important than brains in women:

> Another principle should be to broaden by retarding: to keep the purely mental back and by every method to bring the intuitions to the front; appeals to tact and taste should be incessant. . . . Bookishness is probably a bad sign in a girl; it suggests artificiality, pedantry, the lugging of dead knowledge.[36]

The details of the perfect curriculum Hall envisaged echo, fairly predictably, the kind of intellectual diet offered in the traditional early-nineteenth century 'Seminary for Young Ladies'. Religion, he contended, should be considered as important for girls as was politics for boys. Mathematics didn't matter. It should be taught 'only in its rudiments', and those who showed special taste or talent for it should be sent off to what Hall rather menacingly refers to as 'agamic' or 'agenic' schools. Botany was useful but the difficult Latin names should be left out. Chemistry wasn't important: 'The average girl has little love of sozzling and mussing with the elements.'[37] Literature was useful as a vehicle for teaching refinement. Perhaps the most important subject in the curriculum was 'Domesticity', which should be taught using buildings to replicate an ideal home, and using 'laboratory methods'. Child study was vital, and the girl's final year of schooling should involve a comprehensive, culminating course in what Hall dubbed 'maternity', although he added that 'in its largest sense maternity might be the heart of all the higher training of young women'.[38]

What this essentially constitutes is of course an education for dependence on the male. Hall makes this quite explicit:

> I insist that the cardinal defect in the woman's college (he means
> here the new 'academic' foundations in America and England) . . .
> is that it is based upon the assumption, implied and often expressed,
> if not almost universally acknowledged, that girls should primarily
> be trained to independence and self-support, and that matrimony
> and motherhood, if it come, will take care of itself.[39]

This 'manifesto' was to be echoed approvingly over the next few years by a number of those who believed that 'feminist influence' on women's education was spoiling girls for marriage and maternity. Truby King, for instance, who pioneered the 'Mothercraft' movement first in New Zealand and later in England, repeatedly quoted Stanley Hall's words here, identifying himself wholeheartedly with this viewpoint.[40]

One cannot conclude this account of Hall's educational vision for women without mentioning what was perhaps its most original feature. This was the explicit provision he envisaged for teaching the girls to submit to the beneficial influence of patriarchal authority. Within each department of his educational household Hall suggested (and once again I cannot avoid the temptation to quote in full),

> There should be at least one healthful, wise, large-souled, honourable, married and attractive man, and if possible, several of them.
> His very presence in an institution for young women gives poise,
> polarizes the soul, and gives wholesome but long-circuited tension at
> root no doubt sexual, but all unconsciously so. This mentor should

not be more father than brother, though he should combine the best of each, but should add another element. He need not be a doctor, a clergyman, or even a great scholar, but should be accessible for confidential conferences even though intimate. He should know the soul of the adolescent girl and how to prescribe, he should be wise and fruitful in advice, but especially should be to all a source of contagion and inspiration for poise and courage even though religious or medical problem be involved. But even if he lack all these latter qualities, though he be so poised that impulsive girls can turn their hearts inside out in his presence and perhaps even weep on his shoulder, the presence of such a being . . . would be the centre of an atmosphere most wholesomely tonic.[41]

The implication of this, as with Hall's earlier premise that man should be not only 'woman's protector and provider, but also her priest' is abundantly clear.[42] It was his profound conviction that women should be wholly dependent on man: economically, as wife, physically, as patient; intellectually, as pupil; emotionally and psychologically, whether in the priest's confessional or on the analyst's couch. To him the law of patriarchy was a law of nature, a law of 'biological ethics', and a structure of profound social importance.

Stanley Hall's theories about women can supply fascinating insights into the nature of nineteenth-century patriarchal attitudes. One has to inquire first about the extent to which they derived from or were related to conflict at work in his own mind. There then remains the question (especially in view of the favourable reception which his theories were given in many quarters) of how typical his particular cast of mind and personal psychological dilemmas were.

In *The Psychologist as Prophet* (1972) Hall's most recent biographer, Dorothy Ross, has argued that Hall's theories about adolescence can indeed best be understood as a response to a set of personal conflicts triggered off by childhood experience.[43] The following summary is taken from her work. As a boy, Hall apparently enjoyed a very close, affectionate relationship with his mother. His father was evidently a stern, violent-tempered man and the relationship between the parents was one of fierce conflict. Although Hall himself later idealised his mother as a pure, ideal, maternal woman his feeling for her does not seem to have been so simple. Ross suggests that:

His latter, complex feelings towards women suggest that his feelings towards his mother were neither so pure nor so unwavering when he had to go beyond the fundamental matrix of dependency and trust. Even at the end of his life, he liked to imagine his mother emotionally unfulfilled in her marriage, and he was astonished to discover through a cache of letters, that she had shared a warm and intimate relationship with her husband.[44]

Hall's adolescence was marred by strong feelings of guilt: loving and jealous of his mother, he felt hatred for his father rendered more difficult by anxieties about his own sexual identity, the fear that he could not measure up to the 'manliness' of his father.

Later, as a student in Europe, Hall evidently met and developed an attraction for a young woman called Cornelia Fisher. The relationship was an uneasy one. In 1878 Hall wrote a romantic story entitled *A Leap Year Romance* which transparently featured himself in the role of the hero, whilst the heroine was based on Cornelia. The hero, an introverted Professor, strongly believed that women should be dependent on men. The young woman he was attracted by strongly disagreed: they parted. Later the young woman came to see the error of her ways and to appreciate that womanliness meant submission. As she repented, and stood on the verge of entering a nunnery, the young man rushed to claim her.

In discoursing on the theme of ideal womanhood the Professor in this tale becomes greatly excited by the subject of what he perceived to be the need for women's total surrender, associated with quasi-religious feelings of dependence and sacrifice. One cannot escape the inference that Hall himself derived pleasure from masochistic fantasies. Ross concludes:

It is not difficult to see in the desire for dependence and self-sacrifice, the religious sentiments and 'aesthetic susceptibilities' Hall ascribed to the female nature, feelings he powerfully felt. Victorian culture had assigned these characteristics pre-eminently to woman's sphere. On a personal level, Hall evidently experienced severe conflicts over his identification with his father and a substantial desire to follow his mother. Hence, to secure his masculine identity, he had to try to repress or disown powerful feelings of dependence and a latent feminine identification. Hall's desire to reduce his female partner to complete submission reflected his need to keep these 'feminine' desires within himself under control.[45]

She suggests further that Hall's later enthusiasm for evolutionary biology, with its vision of nature as an omnipotent, overwhelming force can partially be explained in terms of the imaginative scope it afforded for his ambivalent needs for both power and submission. Hall had evidently been strongly influenced by his reading of Professor A.H. Drummond's Lowell Lectures on *The Ascent of Man*, which were published in 1894. Drummond presented the evolutionary process as governed by the growth of altruism, as well as by the struggle for survival. In particular, he saw the development of altruism in women in the shape of 'maternal instinct' as crucial to human progress. The human mother, he argued, constituted the 'highest product' of evolution. Self-sacrifice in women was 'a biological duty', and women represented the natural guardians of evolutionary ethics.[46] Drummond's religiose, lengthy purple passages celebrating the self-sacrificial characteristics of motherhood would have had a particular appeal for Hall.

Ross contends that Hall developed his theory of adolescence as a creative solution to his own ambivalence over the adult, masculine role as defined by the society in which he grew up. He conceived of adolescence for boys as a passionate stage in life during which they were licensed to experience and display those qualities — idealism, emotionalism and instability which were defined by their culture as 'feminine' qualities.[47] Hall's ideas about *female* adolescence reveal his own profoundly ambiguous feelings most acutely.

This brings us back to the question of just how typical of late-Victorian society the kind of psychological conflicts and ambivalences afflicting Hall were. It is worth drawing attention to a recent essay by Carol Christ, entitled 'Victorian Masculinity and the Angel in the House', which suggests a number of insights into the problem.[48] Carol Christ has argued that the kind of literary ideals of femininity which were elaborated in the Victorian period by writers such as Ruskin, Coventry Patmore and Tennyson can best be understood as reflecting the deep ambivalence many male writers felt about their own gender identity and hence their sexuality. Like Dorothy Ross she suggests that this tension in large measure derived from the very stringent definitions of and differentiations between sex roles in Victorian society.[49] An over-simplified conception of gender distinctions, a rigid insistence on labelling some forms of behaviour 'masculine' and others 'feminine', reproduces its own distortions.

Both *Adolescence* and a shorter version of the text which Stanley Hall published under the title *Youth: Its Regimen & Hygiene* (1906) were widely read in America and Europe. Hall's theories about adolescent girlhood certainly appealed to patriarchally inclined biologists and medical men, but also, as Dorothy Ross points out, to certain groups of women.[50] In America, many women active in such movements as the Child Study and Social Hygiene movements and also the National Congress of Mothers tended to respond favourably to his ideas. Women like this were in the main more publicly active than the average middle-class wife confined in a domestic milieu, but less radical than some of the suffragists and feminists. They were keen to widen women's activities but not to challenge the basic features of the sexual division of labour; claiming instead a more active role for women *within* her 'traditional' sphere.

In England, a group of women who had been inspired by Hall's ideas at the International Conference on Education at the World's Fair in Chicago in 1893 founded local Child Study groups which were federated into the British Child Study Association in 1898. This Association published a journal entitled *The Paidologist*. In 1908 the group amalgamated with the Childhood Society, originally founded in 1896 under the presidency of Sir Douglas Galton. The newly amalgamated society retitled itself as The Child Study Society with a journal called *Child Study*. First Sir Edward Brabrook, and later Sir James Crichton Browne became President.[51]

Both *The Paidologist* and *Child Study* published a number of articles elaborating upon Hall's views on female adolescence. Volume VII of *The Paidologist*, for instance, featured an article by M.E. Findlay on *The Education of Girls*.[52] She argued that girls denied adequate rest during puberty were likely to suffer from amenorrhoea, chlorosis and hysteria. They should be barred from access to public examinations between the ages of twelve and eighteen and should regularly take time off from school during menstruation. Ideally, she ventured, girls would be better staying at home altogether rather than being sent to school in their 'teens. This would enable them to develop more interest in domesticity and to profit from intimate personal relationships with their mothers. Mary Scharlieb, a gynaecologist with deeply conservative views about the role of women, contributed articles to *Child Study* in which she fully endorsed many of Hall's tenets about the nature of female adolescence.[53] Girls needed to be protected not only from intellectual strain at puberty, but also, she contended, from the unhealthy effects of too much physical exercise. The new fashion for athletics and vigorous recreation in many girls' schools had gone too far:

Doctors and schoolmistresses observe that excessive devotion to athletics and gymnastics tends to produce what may perhaps be called the 'neuter' type of girl. Her figure, instead of developing to full feminine grace, remains childish, or at most tends to resemble that of a half-grown lad, she is flat-chested, with a badly developed bust, her hips are narrow, and in too many instances there is a corresponding failure in function. When these girls marry they too often fail to become mothers, and it appears to be probable that even when blessed with children they are less well-fitted for the duties of maternity than are their more feminine sisters.[54]

Hall's views were also quoted approvingly by Sir T.S. Clouston, who had twenty years earlier expounded alarming ideas about the dangers of educating women in two lectures published under the title *Female Education from a Medical Point of View* (1882).[55] Clouston found Hall's style somewhat 'paralysing' to the general reader but was himself substantially in agreement with the main features of the argument.[56] His colleague, Sir James Crichton Browne, President of the Child Study Society and another eminent medical man, similarly inclined to the opinion that women who devoted their adolescence to hard study were in some way incapacitating themselves for motherhood.[57]

J.W. Slaughter's study *The Adolescent* (1911), which set out to bring Hall's theories before a wider audience of teachers and youth workers in England (and was dedicated to his mentor), adopted a rather more liberal stance towards the education of the adolescent girl.[58] Slaughter admitted that social definitions of women's physical and mental capacities were continually changing, and that women might well come to play an important role in public and economic life. However, he still considered that a girl's education should be 'adjusted to the central fact of a woman's life, that of motherhood.' Further, he had doubts about the wisdom of allowing woman to determine her own future in the educational sphere: 'She, herself, is not at present entirely qualified to pass judgement as conditions impose upon her vision a distortion of features.'[59]

Slaughter's position appears surprisingly moderate when compared with that adopted by one of Hall's personal pupils in Massachusetts, Phyllis Blanchard, who applied herself under his direction to a particular study of the social psychology of adolescent girlhood (before going on to establish herself as a fairly distinguished clinical psychologist). Blanchard's book, *The Care of the Adolescent Girl*, was published in

England in 1921 with two prefaces: one contributed by Mary Scharlieb, the other by Hall himself.[60] Mary Scharlieb introduced the book guardedly as a valuable but controversial contribution to the subject. Hall's preface was straightforwardly enthusiastic. He judged the book important, he insisted pugnaciously, precisely because it strongly contested the feminist demand for girls to receive the same treatment as adolescent boys. The author restated his own long-standing conviction that women found it difficult to know their own minds:

> It is probably far harder for woman to achieve true self-knowledge than for man to do so. She is more prone either to over or to underestimate herself, or to take flight from reality, or to misconceive what she really wants.[61]

Blanchard's descriptions of adolescent girlhood (an obsession with clothes and looks, fits of giggling, fads, whimsicalities and so forth) followed Hall's own, but her interpretation as a whole put much more emphasis on sexuality and theories about the sublimation of the libido deriving from her reading of Freud, Jung and Adler.

Blanchard's main argument was that the psychology of adolescent girlhood had to be seen as a conflict between the girl and her own 'femininity': a refusal to be reconciled to the feminine role was common in girls at puberty

> For the physical pains of menstruation and the accompanying mental depression are bitterly resented, and at one time or another almost every girl had been heard to exclaim in passionate protest, her desire to be a man.[62]

This struggle Blanchard interpreted as a conflict between 'egoism' and 'submission to racial instincts'. Submission and self-sacrifice she defined as the essence of 'true femininity', contending that: 'The masochistic sacrifice of self is a fundamental concomitant of the sex life of womanhood.'[63] This stance had decided implications for the way she viewed feminism. Feminist theory, she insisted, represented a colossal 'masculine protest'; a pathology, or 'in Adlerian terms', 'a fictitious power goal of the wholly neurotic'.[64]

It is difficult to know how widely read Blanchard's book was. Its circulation may have been limited because it is now difficult to get hold of. However, the book was referred to by several of the more popular writers on adolescent girlhood in the 1920s and 1930s. E. Saywell's text, *The Growing Girl*, for instance, published by Methuen in 1922 (with a preface by the psychologist Hugh Crichton Miller), was written in a simple direct style and aimed at a wide audience of teachers and youth-workers in regular contact with young girls.[65] Saywell reiterated Blanchard's contention that girls frequently found adolescence difficult because they resented the sacrifice of ambition, individualism and freedom. She concluded that workers among adolescent girls should set out to provide counselling and 'the sympathetic advice' that was needed to help them understand that women only reached their full stature through self-sacrifice and renunciation of personal goals.[66] Even in childhood, Saywell insisted, it was only the 'abnormal girl' who showed no signs of this 'essentially maternal' impulse; only the abnormal girl who enjoyed 'tomboyish pursuits' or showed 'an unusual fondness for books'. Generally, adolescence 'corrected' such deviancy.[67]

Other writers, such as Mary Scharlieb and A.B. Barnard, expressed similar views about the nature of 'tomboyish' or 'bookish' behaviour in girls.[68] A.B. Barnard's *The Girl's Book About Herself*, written in 1912, was fairly representative of a whole genre of encyclopaedias, compendia and advice manuals addressed to girls which were published at the turn of the century. Many of these adopted a cloyingly sentimental style, or a tone of insinuating intimacy between author and reader. Barnard referred to the adolescent girl with 'tomboyish' inclinations who chafed at the restrictions of 'feminine' behaviour as 'a rosebud set with little wilful thorns'.[69] While some attention to serious study was commendable in young girls, the writer was at pains to emphasise the dangers of 'excessive devotion to books'. Growing girls should take care not to tax their brains, and often needed persuading to 'put away the trigonometry and do some needlework'.[70]

In sum we can point to a growing consensus early this century amongst a wide range of groups — medical authorities, evolutionary thinkers, social psychologists and others — all of whom were keen to argue that adolescence constituted a period of extreme difficulty for girls. Special forms of provision and protection were envisaged as being necessary to protect the interests both of individuals and of the race. These views made their imprint on educational discussion in government circles. In 1923, for instance, the Board of Education published a *Report of* (its) *Consultative Committee on the Differentiation of the Curriculum for Boys and Girls Respectively in Secondary Schools*, which gave detailed consideration to the 'strains' schooling allegedly imposed upon growing girls.[71]

The introduction to this report summarised the history of girls' education over the last hundred years. Up until the mid-nineteenth century, it was contended, girls had been educated very differently from boys. Late-Victorian feminists had argued the case for equality and demanded that girls should follow the same kind of curriculum as boys. Perhaps the time had now come, the Committee suggested, to review things once again; this time recognising that boys and girls were very different, and would have different roles to play as adults in the society they grew up in. Equality, they ventured (harking back to Tennyson's *Princess*) did not need to mean identity. In the recent past, perhaps 'old and delicate graces' had regrettably been sacrificed upon 'the austere altar of sex equality'.[72]

The Committee had set out to collect evidence on sex differences in cognitive ability, temperament and physiology; consulting educational psychologists, doctors and teachers. Their conclusions – like the Report as a whole – were ambiguous and evasive in tone. There was a marked discrepancy between the findings of educational psychologists such as E.L. Thorndike and Cyril Burt, whose experiments had yielded little or no support for any theory of sex differences in intellectual ability, and the weight of teachers' impressions and testimonies, all arguing in favour of clear differences in ability and aptitude between boys and girls. Girls were consistently perceived by their teachers as being more imitative, conscientious, retentive and intuitive than boys. Boys were allegedly superior in logic, ingenuity, abstract and analytical reasoning. The Consultative Committee elected to reconcile the divergencies between the findings of educational psychology and the empirical observations of teachers by emphasising the importance of physiological and emotional differences between the sexes.

Adolescent girls, the Report suggested, had less energy than adolescent boys. This was partly because their blood was lower in specific gravity, carrying less haemoglobin than did boys' blood after puberty.[73] Further, menstruation posed problems: 'the periodic disturbances to which girls and women are constitutionally subject, condemn many of them to a recurring if temporary diminution of general mental efficiency'.[74] The calcium metabolism in females was believed to become unstable with the onset of puberty: a deficiency in calcium, it was mooted, might be considered at least partly responsible for the 'greater nervous excitability of the female sex'.[75] For these reasons, and others which the Committee admitted were not yet perfectly accessible to science, but apparently connected with the relation between hormones

133

and the glandular or nervous system, girls were 'not so strong physically as boys, and (were) more highly strung and liable to nervous strain'.[76] Menstrual problems were 'most intense and pervasive' during the years of school life. This probably accounted for the fact that girls were 'far more liable to neurotic disturbances and mental breakdown from overwork' than were their male counterparts. The Committee concluded:

> We are inclined to think that the predisposition of girls to nervous adolescence, is one of the most important factors in the problem of female education . . . there should be a well-defined difference in the extent of the demands made on boys and girls at school.[77]

Janet Campbell, the Chief Woman Medical Advisor to the Board of Education and a member of the Committee, had long since been an advocate of the need to protect girls from too much schoolwork at puberty. In a paper presented to the Association of University Women Teachers in 1908 she had argued that as soon as a girl reached the age of thirteen or fourteen, studies should be relaxed:

> As regards mental work, great care should be taken to avoid any undue strain. Lessons requiring much concentration and therefore using up a great deal of brain energy, Mathematics, for instance, should not be pushed. With some girls it is well to discontinue one or more subjects for a time if they begin to show signs of fatigue, and the subsequent progress will fully justify this action. Such subjects as cookery, embroidery or the handicrafts may well be introduced into the curriculum as they cause comparatively little mental strain.[78]

Janet Campbell had contended that all public examinations were best avoided for girls below the age of seventeen or eighteen. The recommendations put forward by the Consultative Committee in 1923 did not go quite this far, although they strongly urged the advisability of girls sitting School Certificate examinations on average a year later than boys.[79] A number of allied suggestions were formulated at the same time to protect girls against 'overstrain'. Most of the high schools for girls founded in the last quarter of the previous century, it was pointed out, had only provided morning lessons for pupils. Afternoons had been left free for the girls to involve themselves in home duties and social life. The newer municipal secondary schools for girls, on the other hand, had tended to require the same hours of attendance from girls as from boys. The Consultative Committee suggested that shorter hours would be more beneficial for girls. Every effort should be made to discourage schools from fostering unnecessary competitiveness, whether academic or sporting, amongst girls. And steps should be taken to reduce the amount of homework expected from female pupils 'especially in view of the fact that most girls are expected to do a certain amount of household work in the home.'[80]

Those who were most anxious about the damaging effects which they believed intellectual effort would inflict upon adolescent girls were obviously most concerned with that minority of middle-class girls who attended academically oriented secondary schools and institutes of higher education. Paul Atkinson has in a recent essay analysed the response of headmistresses in late nineteenth-century girls' schools faced with allegations from the medical profession and elsewhere to the effect that rigorous study involved serious health hazards for their pupils.[81] A common pattern of response was for headmistresses to insure themselves by paying particular attention to the health of the girls in their charge. School medical officers – generally women – were appointed, who would carry out regular and thorough physical examinations. Record cards would be kept on file, registering in minute detail the progress of growth, state of health and medical history of each individual girl.[82]

Some of the women physicians with experience of school medical work wrote manuals of advice on the health of adolescent girls. Catherine Chisholme, who worked as Medical Inspector to Manchester High School for Girls early this century compiled a textbook on *The Medical Inspection of Girls in Secondary Schools* published in 1914.[83] Sara Burstall, then headmistress of the School, contributed a preface in which she warned her readers that girls had a tendency to suffer from over-ambition, to be anxious to excel, and to work too hard. It was important to keep check on this, for the sake of the girls' own health and also in the interests of national efficiency and the race.[84] Chisholme's text is robustly common-sensical in tone. 'Many erroneous ideas are held on the subject of the health of girls in adolescence', she declared, there was no need to be too protective. Menstrual disturbances were rare and should be regarded as pathological – 'never as an inevitable condition of feminine life'. In the case of the average girl:

The onset of menstruation ought to make little if any difference to her daily life. She ought to be working well and playing well, but doing neither so vigorously or unwisely as to have to knock off at the time of her monthly period.[85]

Alice Burn, an Assistant School Medical Officer at Cheltenham, who had earlier worked at Wycombe Abbey, tendered advice in a similar vein.[86] Provided that girls did away with corsets, exercised sensibly and gained a healthy knowledge of and respect for their own bodies, their well-being during adolescence should give no cause for alarm.

During the 1880s there was rising concern in some educational and medical circles about whether the curriculum in Board Schools was overloaded and responsible for strain and 'overpressure' on working-class pupils.[87] However, those involved in this controversy were not especially concerned with sexual differences in physiology. The debate over the effects of strain — whether intellectual or physical — on the constitution of the adolescent girl focused, in the main, on the education of the middle-class girl. It is noteworthy that doctors rarely if ever seem to have concerned themselves with the effects of long hours of household drudgery on the menstrual cycle of young female domestic servants.[88]

The first world war, it is true, generated some public concern over the health of young female factory workers, particularly in the munitions industry. In 1918 D.J. Collier published a report entitled *The Girl in Industry*, which set out to look at 'the biological effects of early employment, or, in other words, the reaction on the woman and her offspring of industrial employment in the adolescent years'.[89] This carried a foreword by B.L. Hutchins, who referred to Stanley Hall's work. Although the report drew attention to the damaging effects of fatigue on adolescent girls in industry in a somewhat generalised fashion, it admitted the impossibility of collecting any significant data at that time, and was reduced instead to arguing the case for further, more extensive research.

A large body of literature giving advice on health to women and girls appeared in the early decades of the present century. Much of this was characterised by a strident, imperialist vocabulary, urging women to regard the preservation of their own health as a moral duty, a duty they owed 'to the Empire and the Race'. The tone of this literature, with its quasi-military call upon women to disciplined exercise and 'to sit up straight', its unwavering insistence upon health as the moral responsibility of the individual, often contrasts strangely with the formulations of doctors and other authorities anxious about overstraining the delicate female constitution. The literature anticipates the kind of approach adopted by the Women's League of Health and Beauty in the 1930s. The best examples of the genre before the first world war are probably the books compiled by Dr Elizabeth Sloan Chesser, a lecturer in hygiene with the Women's Imperial Health Association, and a writer keenly interested in eugenics and questions of girls' education as preparation for motherhood.[90] Sloan Chesser's manuals all laid heavy emphasis on the idea of physical health as a product of 'mental and moral hygiene'. In *Physiology & Hygiene for Girls' Schools and Colleges*, published in 1914, she declared that:

> Good health is very largely dependent upon hygiene, especially if the term includes mental hygiene as well as personal and home hygiene. . . . Every girl should regard it as a duty to maintain her health at the highest possible level. . . . Every girl can determine to cultivate good physical and mental habits, which will have far-reaching effects upon health and character.[91]

Sloan Chesser went on writing books on women's health through the inter-war period. By the 1930s, her insistence on equating illness with moral weakness had become even more unwavering. In *Vitality*, published in 1935, she declared:

> If we are ill, it is probably our own fault. Even if we are not personally to blame, illness is a disgrace to somebody, because it indicates physiological sins past or present.[92]

Mary Humphreys, whose *Personal Hygiene for Girls* was published in 1913, similarly insisted upon health as a moral and patriotic duty:

> Neglect of health is a particularly selfish and absolutely unpardonable offence. Let it be one which you never lay upon your conscience. *Keep well* for your own sake, for the sake of the nation which looks to its youth for the regeneration of its general health.[93]

Humphreys relentlessly hectored her readers with exhortations to stand firm, to avoid 'slackness' in all areas of life:

> *Careless indifference*, (she threatened), which leads to *worthlessness*, is shown by the slipshod, *untidy dress*, the *lagging step*, the *dull eye* and *heavy countenance* of the girl who cares nothing about the duty she owes to herself and the world. But the other kind of person, the kind that *you* are going to be, has an *upright carriage*, which denotes *uprightness of character, a firm and ready step*, proving *steadiness* and *stability of mind*, a bright, *cheerful face*, with a clear outlooking

eye, showing the mind at peace with all below, the heart whose love is innocent.[94] (the italics are all hers)

The bracing tone and the call upon the individual to make herself responsible, through clean thoughts and self-discipline, for both her own health and her country's welfare closely resemble the advice on health meted out to adolescent boys in Baden Powell's handbooks on scouting. Lady Baden-Powell's addresses to guides and guide leaders have a similar content. Lady Baden-Powell's approach to the 'problem' of adolescence in girls was based on a clear assumption that girls, like boys, suffered from restlessness deriving from a 'surplus' of energy at this stage. Denied safe outlet, this surplus energy could too easily channel itself into destructive or socially unacceptable behaviour.[95] The view contrasts sharply with the ideas of those medical and other authorities obsessed with 'conserving' the energy of adolescent girls.

This contradiction to some extent relates to social class. Middle-class girls were more likely to be defined as having limited energies and to be in need of rest. Working-class girls were more likely to be perceived as precociously independent, bursting with energies whose discharge called for careful supervision, lest they manifest themselves in the wrong kind of behaviour. And the contradictions go further. Doctors often registered alarm over what they saw to be the consequences of *middle-class* girls taking their health into their own hands. On the other hand, amid public alarm over 'physical deterioration' and high infant mortality rates early this century, social and medical workers strove to impress upon *working-class* girls and women the duty of taking full responsibility not only for their own health but for that of the whole family. The behaviour of middle-class girls was likely to be defined as problematic when they sought to pursue goals *outside* marriage and family life. Working-class girls, on the other hand, were criticised for a narrow obsession with courtship and marriage. Middle-class girls could be seen to have problems *because* they were adolescents; working-class girls because they grew up too soon. The paradoxes are endless. But above all, and whatever her social class, the growing girl tended to be seen as a problem when and where she showed signs of cherishing anything resembling autonomy.

5

◇◦◇

Feminist perspectives and responses

◇◦◇

Definitions of Feminism

Industrialism   sharpened the sexual division of labour in nineteenth-century England; patterns of urban development sharpened the separation between home and workplace. The ideology of family life associated with these changes was premised upon the assumption of 'separate spheres': the man's sphere the world of work, commerce and professional endeavour; the woman's sphere the home. Nineteenth-century feminists struggled against the restrictions imposed upon their behaviour by exponents of this theory of separate spheres; this led them to criticise certain aspects of the sexual division of labour and some of the conventions surrounding 'femininity'. But these criticisms were limited. Victorian feminists in the main sought wider opportunities for women – particularly unmarried women – outside the home. They sought to enlarge women's sphere of autonomy in some areas of private and public life. But the changes envisaged by the majority fell far short of the kind of radical restructuring of family roles and relationship considered essential by the feminist movement today.

Anyone writing about feminist ideas in the last century confronts tricky problems of definition. The assumption that all those who sought changes in women's education can be classified as 'feminist' can be (as I have suggested earlier in this volume) quite misleading. Some of those who pleaded for 'a better education' for women in the period defended their plea on highly conservative grounds. Emily Shirreff, for instance, expressed sentiments very close to those of Ruskin when she argued that middle-class girls should be educated to perfection precisely because as married women they would be secluded from the world and as guardians of the home could help to elevate and purify man's instincts: 'The moral lesson to be taught to the young girl', she had written in *Intellectual Education and its Influence on the Character and Happiness of Women* (1858),

> is that she should value among the highest privileges that exemption from coarse experience and degrading temptation which is ensured to her by her position in society, and which allows her to remain ignorant of the foul impurities which taint the moral atmosphere of thousands among her fellow creatures, even of her own sex and tender years.[1]

Far from any attack upon the sexual division of labour which characterised the Victorian bourgeois home, this is rather a *celebration* of it. Women should be educated in order that they might indeed become Angels in the House.

This kind of argument recurs time and again in the writings of all those who sought reforms: Women needed education not for revolutionary ends, but in order to fit them to become better wives and mothers, better companions for men. It was of course a politic argument, as many of its proponents must have been well aware — it certainly appealed to many cautious conservative elements, and particularly to men. Sir Alexander Grant, Principal of the University of Edinburgh, delivered a speech to the local Ladies' Educational Association in 1872 entitled 'Happiness and Utility as Promoted by the Higher Education of Women'. He rejoiced in the fact that women were seeking more than 'mere accomplishments' in the curriculum, he declared, because he was convinced that reformers were bent on preserving the 'feminine ideal'. Waxing rhetorical, he pleaded,

> Let no one think scorn of the feminine ideal. It is the ideal of a life and character, strong in its weakness, exalted in its lowliness, powerful over others by its abnegation of self; quick, and bright and penetrating, not by means of acquired learning, but through intuitive perceptions sharpened by the exigencies of life and made watchful by affection, full of grace, and graciousness, and sympathy, and good counsel, it is the mainstay of families and commands the worship of the world.[2]

Not surprisingly, Sir Alexander ended his oration on this occasion by quoting Tennyson's lines from *The Princess*,

to live and learn and be
All that not harms distinctive womanhood.[3]

One does not have to dig deep into the archives of the history of women's education in this period to realise that nine out of ten eminent men discoursing on the theme of women's education chose to quote these — or the even better known lines,

For woman is not undevelopt man,
But diverse:

— from the same poem.[4]

Sara Delamont's distinction between the 'separatists' and the 'uncompromising' groups working for reform in women's education in the second half of the nineteenth century has been referred to earlier in this volume.[5] The 'separatists' were prepared to countenance any change which they regarded as an improvement in the existing provision for women and girls. The 'uncompromising' group, led by Emily Davies, demanded access to the same curricula and examinations currently taken by men. 'Separatists' were on the whole more likely to adopt the kind of argument put forward by Emily Shirreff than were their less compromising counterparts. The former rather than the latter were more often found quoting Tennyson approvingly, asserting that masculine and feminine roles as they were currently defined were natural and complementary, that men and women were equal but different, and that educated women made ideal wives and mothers.

This position contrasted strongly with that taken up from time to time by less compromising feminists. Isabella Tod, for instance, contended adamantly that 'there is but one true theory of education for men and women alike'. She could be sharply critical of the existing sexual division of labour, which she argued condemned middle-class women to economic dependence and permanent leisure, turning them into articles of conspicuous consumption, showcases for their husbands' wealth: 'Why,' she demanded angrily 'should the enforced idleness of girls be thought necessary to keep up the status of the rest?'[6] Similarly, ten years earlier, Sophia Jex-Blake had demanded that any education deemed best for one sex must be best for the other too, 'for a common humanity lies deeper . . . and is more essential in each than any differences'.[7]

It is tempting, perhaps, to dismiss what we might dub the 'Tennysonian' group, or the 'separatist' party as not properly 'feminist' at all.

141

This temptation becomes stronger when one examines the ideas of those who in some respects inherited their position. In the 1900s, for instance, Sara Burstall, Headmistress of Manchester High School, argued that those feminists who had sought equality of opportunity with men had pushed women's education too far in this direction; that the girls' schools should realise that men and women *were* different, had different roles to play in life, and that women needed an education which would turn them into better wives and mothers.[8] In the 1940s John (later Sir John) Newsom enraged many contemporary feminists by adopting exactly the same position.[9]

But there remains something highly unsatisfactory about any interpretation which would present the Newnham College 'separatists' as non-feminist (let alone as the philosophical predecessors of Sir John Newsom), on the grounds of their failing to challenge the notion of separate spheres. Sara Delamont has attempted to resolve the problem by endorsing the views put forward by Aileen Kraditor, an historian of American feminism, in her volume, *Up from the Pedestal* (1968).[10] Kraditor defines feminism as women seeking autonomy, demanding to be recognised not merely as 'female relatives of people' but as individuals in their own right. She concludes that:

> Such a recognition could be consistent with a distinction between men and women's 'spheres', even with a continued subordination of the feminine 'sphere', as well as with a merging of men's and women's 'spheres'. The essential change demanded has always been that women's 'sphere' must be defined by women.[11]

However, this does not get us very far. What about the kind of position taken by a woman like Sara Burstall? A present-day feminist cannot but find herself more and more aghast as she turns the pages of Burstall's educational writings: 'Mathematics should be kept at a minimum for girls', we read, 'it does not underlie their activities as it does so many of the activities of men.'[12] Or again, 'science . . . is essential for every woman as a preparation for domestic duties and the care of children.'[13] This is a leading woman educationalist, who would certainly have defended women's autonomy, but it is decidedly not feminism.

We cannot argue that if a nineteenth-century writer or thinker failed to make a central attack on the sexual division of labour or failed to reject the notion of 'separate spheres' then she (or he) was not properly a 'feminist'. The implication of such a stance would be that the nineteenth century produced very few feminists at all. History

142

alters political circumstances, and even a position as 'conservative' as that taken by Emily Shirreff in the 1860s and 1870s, given the state of girls' education at that time, certainly had much more 'feminist' implications than would a similar stance taken forty or fifty years later. Further, we must remember that considerations of strategy mingled with questions of principle and long-term goal in the minds of all those who sought improvement in women's education. It has already been suggested that the claim that a better education would more adequately enable women to fulfil their womanly duties was sometimes used because it was an efficient way of disarming the opposition. Even the highly principled and 'uncompromising' Emily Davies resorted to a variety of stratagems and ploys to further her cause – seating the prettiest girl students in front rows at examination times in order to persuade the public that 'femininity' could go hand-in-hand with intellectual force was one of them.[14] It would be ridiculous to fault her feminism on such grounds. It remains incontrovertible that a 'moderate' feminism, no matter whether such moderation stemmed from conservatism or from calculations of political expediency, stood more chance, in the short-term, of securing concessions from the Establishment.

Ultimately, the historian has to abandon the attempt to make black and white distinctions. But if feminism cannot be defined solely or exclusively in terms of an attack on the sexual division of labour or the notion of separate spheres, these issues must still be regarded as central. We can still legitimately judge feminists bent on securing autonomy for women as more or less radical according to the extent to which they perceived this. For until feminists challenged the sexual division of labour middle-class girls, however 'educated', would continue to grow up in the knowledge that they would one day be confronted with what could be a crippling choice between marriage and employment, children or careers; a situation which had important implications for the way in which they themselves and society generally viewed their education. Again, while the sexual division of labour remained uncontested, working-class women with no choice *but* to earn a living would continue to be driven into notoriously underpaid and usually unskilled 'women's trades', compelled to carry the double burden of waged labour and domestic work. The sexual division of labour reduced women to economic dependency. And definitions of gender – notions about what constituted 'masculinity' and 'femininity' – were intimately bound up with this relation of dependency. 'Masculinity' was defined in terms of resourcefulness, the ability to provide, be active, independent and adventurous. 'Femininity', conversely, was seen as passivity, dependency, timidity and self-sacrifice. As we have seen in the first chapter, children learned these qualities in the family and were well-rehearsed in their roles before their formal education began. By themselves, schools could never hope to effect any radical change in the social position of women: family structures also had to change.

Feminism and the Family

Nineteenth-century feminists were eager to defend the right of un-married women to find employment and fought to extend the range of opportunities available to them in their pursuit of economic inde-pendence. They were less concerned (or more evasive) about the issue of women's economic dependence in marriage. Criticism of the notion of 'separate spheres' generally fell short of an attack on the sexual division of labour within the family. This accounts for a certain ambiva-lence in attitudes towards the purpose of girls' schooling even in femin-ist circles. Mid nineteenth-century feminists such as Jessie Boucherett, Adelaide Proctor, Barbara Bodichon and others associated with 'the Langham Place Circle' had from the beginning identified educational reform as crucial in their campaign to widen opportunities for women to earn their living.[15] Equally, women like Frances Buss, Emily Davies and Maria Grey, centrally involved in educational work, argued that girls needed to envisage something more than economic dependence on a husband as a goal in life if they were to take their schooling seriously. Maria Grey, addressing the Social Science Congress in 1871 insisted that:

> So long as marriage is held out as the only aim of a girl's life . . . so long will all attempts at improvement fail . . . marriage should not be the first object of a woman's life, any more than of a man's: girls should be trained from childhood to the idea that they, like their brothers, must take their share of the work of life . . . they should not only be allowed, but induced to work for their own maintenance.[16]

An ex-student at the North London Collegiate School for Girls recalled that Miss Buss, similarly, had been

> very strongly impressed by the absolute necessity for young girls

144

to be trained to some employment by which they might, if necessary, earn a livelihood. For a woman to be dependent on brothers or relations she considered an evil to be avoided at all costs.[17]

But it is important to note that it was only the idea of economic dependence on 'brothers or relatives' that Miss Buss found abhorrent: a woman's total dependence on her *husband* she conceded to be an entirely acceptable state of affairs. And Maria Grey concluded the speech that I have quoted from by assuring her audience that she had no desire whatsoever to propound 'any wild theory of feminine independence'. On the contrary, she considered marriage to be the perfect state of human existence.[18] When she spoke of work for women it was the plight of the *un*married woman she had in mind. Indeed, throughout her life Mrs Grey retained a distaste for the idea of married women undertaking paid employment outside their homes.[19]

Only a few feminists openly broached the question of careers for married women in the late-nineteenth century. Elizabeth Garrett Anderson, who herself managed to combine motherhood with strong professional commitment, was one of these few. 'The woman question will never be solved in any complete way so long as marriage is thought to be incompatible with freedom and an independent career', she insisted in a letter written to her sister to announce her engagement.[20]

By the early years of the present century more women were ready to express similar opinions. Women educated as self-respecting, independent beings could not easily resign themselves to complete economic, social and psychological dependence in marriage. Education, in itself, helped to teach women the need for further social change. The publication of Engels' *Origin of the Family, Private Property and the State* and Bebel's *Women in the Past, Present and Future* helped to widen the terms of reference hitherto used in feminist analysis.[21] Mid nineteenth-century feminists had addressed themselves primarily to the plight of the *un*married women: their early twentieth-century successors came increasingly to question what they saw as the 'parasitic' position of women as wives and mothers in the family. The focus of debate shifted accordingly. Discussion took on a much more radical complexion, particularly in socialist-feminist circles, where widespread changes in the family were envisaged as being possible only in connection with a general transformation of society in accordance with socialist principles.[22]

A particularly interesting collection of papers summarising discussions organised by the Fabian Society's Women's Group between 1908 and 1910 on *The Disabilities of Women as Workers* and *The Disabilities of Mothers as Workers* show these women centrally concerned with the ways in which the sexual division of labour and the ideology of family life deprived women of economic independence and both sustained and perpetuated definitions of 'femininity' in terms of physical frailty, intellectual weakness and passivity.[23] There was a strong consensus of opinion amongst the group that women should work for their own living, to establish their status as producers and fully qualified citizens. The physical facts of maternity, submitted Dr Vaughan-Sawyer (a gynaecologist at the London School of Medicine for Women and Senior Physician at the Royal Free Hospital) rendered it difficult for women to be self-supporting for only short periods of time. She would argue that the State should support women for a minimum period of twelve weeks − two months before and one month after the birth of each child, to meet this need.[24]

B.L. Hutchins presented a paper to the group in 1909 summarising the views of the German feminist, Lily Braun, who had emphasised the importance of fighting for a modification in conditions of employment so as to accommodate the needs of women with small children. Feminists, she urged, should press for the shorter hours, maternity insurance and well-ordered crèches which would enable these women to work.[25] Many of the women present at the meeting expressed their conviction that children from all social classes would have much to gain from attendance at well-equipped nurseries and crèches, where they could associate freely with children of the same age. Mrs Stanbury submitted that the full-time mother, òften leading a confined and unvaried existence, was all too likely to transmit her boredom to her children:

> The 'good mother' at home, leading a life quite incredibly bare and monotonous, day by day, year after year, with not a penny of her own, becomes extraordinarily like a fixture in her 'model' dwelling; and as a developing agent for her little child appears to have no value at all. To the superficial observer stagnation may easily be mistaken for serenity, inertia for nervous strength. In many cases her function degenerates into nagging the man for money, and fidgetting her child to keep quiet and 'clean'.[26]

There was a strong measure of agreement here. Several members of the group thought that fathers should be induced to play a more important role in childcare. Dr Marion Phillips, for instance, inquired whether

> many fathers were not far too little with their children, whilst many mothers were with them too much? The working father scarcely saw his children from Sunday night to Saturday afternoon. Economic arrangements keeping the mother always in and the father always out were hard on both and on their children.[27]

B.L. Hutchins thought similarly that the time had come to try to teach *both* parents to regard parenthood in the light of social duty,[28] and if neither parent was to be trapped in the home, domestic organisation had to be made more efficient. Mrs Bernard Shaw, summarising the group's discussions for the benefit of members unable to attend, emphasised the necessity for the 'primitively chaotic economy of the home' to be rationally organised in a way that would fully exploit the potential of all the labour-saving and waste-saving devices that technology could provide.[29]

Other writings by feminists in this period which showed a clear realisation of the need to challenge the sexual division of labour, or at least the economic dependence of women in the family, included works by Olive Schreiner, B.L. Hutchins and Clementina Black.[30] Amongst these, Olive Schreiner's *Woman and Labour* (1911) probably achieved the widest publicity. In the first part of the book, entitled 'parasitism', Schreiner contended that history had robbed middle-class women of social usefulness. Technology had removed many kinds of industry from the home. The state was assuming increasing responsibility for the education of the young. Women were having fewer children, so that

> child bearing and suckling, instead of filling the entire circle of human life from the first appearance of puberty to the end of middle age, becomes an episodal occupation, employing from three or four to ten or twenty of the threescore-and-ten years which are allotted to human life.[31]

These changes had reduced the wives of middle-class men to parasitism. Working-class women, with no choice but to work, were confined to the lowest-paid forms of drudgery. As standards of living in the community rose, Schreiner predicted, 'female parasitism' would percolate down the social scale. Hence the key demand of the Woman's Movement must be the right of all women, whether married or not, to work.

Education should address itself to this need.

B.L. Hutchins' short essay on *Conflicting Ideals of Woman's Work* (1915) was a particularly lucid analysis of contemporary controversies over the structure of the family and woman's position. The 'Modern Patriarchal Ideal' of family life (husband as provider, wife as dependent) was, she contended, a middle-class ideal of recent historical origin. Women had reacted bitterly against it for a number of reasons. Marriage had become a passport to subsistence. The unmarried were reduced to a particularly unenviable material position. Married women, on the other hand, were reduced to parasitism, to a position of galling inferiority which a substantial number found intolerable. Hence the demand of the feminists for education and economic independence.

However, the 'individualistic' ideal of family life espoused by many feminists, Hutchins conceded, came up against two major stumbling blocks given existing social conditions. Firstly, the 'episodal nature' of women's work: many women wanted to discontinue work for a period while their children were very young. Secondly, she contended that middle-class feminists had to realise that under existing social conditions many working-class women, lacking any access to self-fulfilling jobs, were quite content to abandon the labour market, given sufficient economic security, on marriage. If these women had no desire to go on working, she thought it better for them to stay at home.

Women should be allowed to choose. But Hutchins was vehement in her defence of the married woman's right to go on working should she opt to do so. Existing conditions made this very difficult for her:

> At present very nearly all the organised forces of society are against her. Many education authorities require women teachers to retire on marriage; in various branches of the Civil Service the same injunction is enforced. In industry some employers will not engage a married woman. Over and above direct compulsion, there is the pressure of social opinion and social sanctions, almost unitedly tending towards the same end. We even hear from time to time rumours of legal enactment to prohibit married women's work.[32]

These sanctions against married women's work Hutchins judged wholly iniquitous. Maternity insurance; some form of state endowment for motherhood; widening social provision for the care and education of very young children (possibly in accordance with Montessorian principles) — all these were desirable and urgently necessary if women were to be free to choose independent existences.[33] And given more appropriate training which would allow them access to more skilled and fulfilling jobs, Hutchins believed that more women would opt to stay in the labour market. At present the education meted out to girls had a confused purpose:

> Girls are alternately told that they must become trained, and skilled, and organised for industrial efficiency, and, on the other hand, that they should devote their youth to domestic arts and preparation for motherhood.[34]

Both education and, even more importantly, social conditions had to change if women were to be allowed to combine motherhood with work of their choice.

Clementina Black, who worked closely with B.L. Hutchins in a survey of married-women's work undertaken under the auspices of the Women's Industrial Council of 1909-10, similarly put forward very strong defence of a woman's right to combine motherhood with paid employment if she so wished.[35] Like Hutchins, she was well aware of the fact that a large proportion of working-class mothers who stayed in the labour market did so either out of necessity or because they chose to work in order to earn a better standard of living for their children; and not, as the opponents of married-women's work so frequently (and, she considered, impertinently) alleged, because they were negligent mothers. In her experience, many of the women who could have managed on their husbands' wages but opted to work in order to provide holidays or other small luxuries were often

> conspicuously competent, and marked by an independence of mind which I believe to be derived from the consciousness of their power of self-support. Almost invariably their houses are well-kept and the family accommodation adequate.[36]

Again, Clementina Black followed Hutchins in the conviction that working conditions and social arrangements would have to be modified to accommodate the needs of mothers as workers. 'It is possible', she suggested,

> that society is evolving in the direction of a family supported financially by the earnings of both parents, the children being cared for meanwhile and the work of the house being performed by trained experts. To me personally that solution seems more in harmony with the general lines of our social development than does any which

would relegate all women to the care of children combined with the care of households.[37]

Three years later, in a book entitled *A New Way of Housekeeping* (1918) she developed some of her ideas on the reorganisation of domestic life further.[38] Existing forms of household organisation were, she contended, labour-intensive and wasteful. Working-class women no longer wanted to work as domestic servants. Many middle-class women, trapped in the home, were bored and found domestic work equally uncongenial. Why could not homes be organised in 'domestic federations', with many more communal facilities for the purchase and preparation of food and for the care of small children? Domestic work could be rationalised and professionalised. Women could then choose their work according to inclination and be properly remunerated for whatever services they performed in the community.

The views outlined above were the views of a minority and made little impact on British society at the time. The first world war only temporarily increased women's participation in industry, and was followed by a period of intensified social opposition to the employment of married women in industry and in professional life. During the 1920s and 1930s feminists like Vera Brittain, Winifred Holtby and others associated with the Six-Point Group fought a defensive battle against restrictions which were being applied by local authorities and the government on the employment of married women in teaching and in the Civil Service. Even so, the ideas discussed by the Fabian Women's Group, and the writings of Schreiner, Hutchins and Black show that 'feminist theory' had advanced considerably over the previous twenty-five years and that feminists had begun to look upon the problems associated with the sexual division of labour and economic dependency as central to questions of women's autonomy. They were beginning to realise that providing girls with 'educational opportunities' could do little by itself to increase the participation and raise the status of adult women in industrial, professional and political life. It was of small avail for women educators to encourage their pupils to develop the vocational goals which would increase their incentive to study seriously when those girls were being taught through almost every other agency that a married woman's place was in the home. Academic and vocational ambitions would never appeal to more than a tiny minority of girls so long as they were offered only as an *alternative* to marriage and parenthood. The compulsion to make a choice was in itself unacceptable.

Feminism and 'Femininity'

I want now to consider the equally important and related question of the extent to which feminists managed to challenge concepts of 'femininity' over the period 1870-1920. The problem is complex and can be broached on several levels. There is first the question of individual psychology. As was argued in the first chapter of this book, women's learning about femininity was inextricably bound up with their earliest forms of learning, their experiences of family life. Concepts of femininity were generally deeply internalised: a girl would grow up with a sense of self shaped in the knowledge that she was female. She could not escape being defined by others and seeing herself as more or less 'feminine'. Women able to reject some aspects of contemporary social definitions of femininity on an intellectual level were still likely to feel uneasy, or to experience some kind of guilt or shame about behaving in a way others would judge 'unfeminine.' In school and college female students gravitated towards history, language and literature rather than pure science. As graduates the large majority drifted into social work and teaching, the traditionally 'feminine' occupations. Educated women often sought men they regarded as more intelligent than themselves because in some way they needed to 'look up to' the men they married: after marriage, more often than not, they sacrificed their own studies in support of their husbands' careers and felt guilty if they were not altogether happy in doing so. Some of these patterns of behaviour have been highlighted earlier in this book. At this point I want first to look at feminist attitudes to concepts of femininity at the more rational, conscious level.

Again, however, it has to be admitted that there are a number of dimensions to the problem. One might, for instance, try to focus on the level of popular attitudes and stereotypes. Merely by way of their serious involvement with education and political issues the feminists may be held to have challenged a widespread conception of woman as a pusillanimous creature, obsessed with the trivial concerns of drawing room and boudoir. The academic distinctions won in the older universities by women such as Agnata Ramsay, Philippa Fawcett and other pioneers further undermined that equation of femininity with intellectual deficiency so generally accepted in mid nineteenth-century Britain. However, this hardly revolutionised the attitudes of the general public. After all, if one started with the assumption that it was feminine to be stupid, then it was quite logical to argue that clever women were simply unfeminine. The popular stereotype of the intelligent, educated woman as eccentric, unfeminine and a 'bluestocking' persisted well into the present century: indeed, it still has currency today. It seems likely that the academic achievements and distinctions won by nineteenth-century feminists were of more importance as a point of reference for or inspiration to the women who followed them than they were in altering the attitudes of the general public: a theme which will be taken up again later in this chapter.

Here I want to consider some of the 'scientific' definitions of femininity elaborated by social-evolutionary thinkers, some biologists, medical authorities and eugenist writers in late-nineteenth-century England; and to comment on the feminist response to them. The justification for linking together what might at first sight appear such a diverse group comes from the fact that those writers and thinkers considered here shared a common concern with, and many common perspectives on the social position of women in their day. In the first instance they defined the subject itself as problematic and saw in feminism a threat to social well-being. They responded by constructing models of femininity which they claimed to have 'scientific' validity — or they attempted to define a 'natural' femininity which was essentially prescriptive. That is, they argued that in a 'healthy' society women's behaviour would accord with their model. Feminism, which from their viewpoint repudiated femininity, was defined as pathological.

Jill Conway and Lorna Duffin have commented in some detail on stereotypes of femininity in social-evolutionary thought and I shall attempt but a brief summary of the main points here.[39] The works of Herbert Spencer, widely read on both sides of the Atlantic in the last quarter of the century, formed an essential point of reference for most writers in this group. Spencer's views on the social position of women were most fully developed in *The Principles of Sociology* (1876), an important section of which focused on the question of the family in Western Industrial Society and attempted an over-view of general human progress. Essentially he believed that the monogamous, nuclear family depending economically on the husband as breadwinner and with the wife 'protected' from the labour market represented the most 'progressive' and efficient stage of human organisation.[40] He perceived what the feminists were increasingly coming to define as an unhappy *restriction* in the social role of women as a *rise in status* for them. Consequently he confessed himself puzzled by feminist demands for access to the professions or business outside the home, and tried to attribute these demands to the 'abnormal' imbalance of the sexes in mid-Victorian society, that 'surplus' of women in the population which condemned many to spinsterdom. To mitigate the sufferings arising from this temporary imbalance he was prepared to countenance social reforms which would enable these celibate women to earn their living, but insisted that this should be seen as a short-term expedient, contending emphatically that:

> no considerable alteration in the careers of women in general can be, or should be, produced, *and further*, that any extensive change in the education of women, made with the view of fitting them for business or professions would be mischievous. If women comprehended all that is contained in the domestic sphere, they would ask no other.[41]

Spencer's 'biological' explanation of sex differences was premised on the assumption that human physiology was governed by a 'fixed fund' of energy: what the body 'spent' on one kind of activity had to be 'saved' somewhere else. Women had to spend a major part of their energy in reproducing the species and this lessened their capacity for psychic or intellectual growth. Women who claimed educational opportunities equal to men would 'overtax' their brains and this would diminish their ability to bear children: women's potential for individual development and for self-fulfillment had therefore to be 'taxed' in the interest of the race.[42]

Patrick Geddes and J. Arthur Thomson took this 'biological' analysis of sex-differentiation and the social order further in their widely read treatise on *The Evolution of Sex*, first published in 1889.[43] This elaborated a theory of sexual dimorphism based on cell-metabolism, which the authors claimed to be an immutable law governing reproduction. Male cells were *katabolic*; characterised by a tendency to be always active, dissipating energy. Female cells were *anabolic*; passive, energy-conserving and stable. Definitions of gender, of sexual differences in temperament, were held to be governed by this distinction. Men were rational, eager, passionate people, keen to take the initiative in things. Women were intuitive, restrained, altruistic: content to nurture and succour others.

These 'biological' definitions of femininity accorded very closely indeed with the cultural prescriptions or ideals of femininity cherished by mid Victorian society. 'Science' could hence be enlisted in support of existing social values. The self-sacrifice commended by Sarah Ellis,

153

Ruskin, Coventry Patmore and the rest as quintessentially womanly could now be held to have a biological, functional basis: women sacrificed themselves, and it was essential that they *should* sacrifice themselves, in the interests of social evolution and 'the progress of the race'. This theme recurs time and time again in the works of the many writers influenced by Herbert Spencer, Geddes and Thomson. I have already commented (in Chapter 3) on the energy with which social-Darwinist and eugenist writers debated 'the Woman Question' during this period. Benjamin Kidd, Karl Pearson, C.W. Saleeby and the Whethams believed that falling birth rates among educated middle-class women supplied conclusive evidence for their contention that such women were receiving the kind of education which debarred them or disinclined them from motherhood.[44] Feminism, they maintained, was 'dysgenic': a threat to social efficiency and racial progress. These ideas bred a markedly authoritarian stance; many writers arguing that it was no use conceding to educated women any right of choice in the matter. England needed its most intelligent women to breed in order to raise the quality of the national stock. The eminent physician, Sir T.S. Clouston, for instance, insisted that

> The ideals which would exalt culture above motherhood are suicidal and should be abandoned. It will not do to say that women should have a choice either to take up culture and intellectual work, whether it has a lessened capacity for motherhood or not, or to select domestic life. Mothers of high brain power are as much needed for an advancing race as fathers — rather more so, in fact.[45]

Spencer's suggestion that too much intellectual work could result in sterility, or at least interfere with female physiology in such a fashion as to render it impossible for an educated woman to breastfeed her progeny in the normal fashion, was echoed by a number of medical authorities on both sides of the Atlantic in the last quarter of the century.[46] The belief that 'intellectual strain' during puberty especially, would militate against the normal establishment of menstruation and the reproductive system has been referred to in the previous chapter. In England this view was given currency by Dr Henry Maudsley, of University College London.[47] A number of specialists in gynaecology and obstetrics, including John Thorburn (Professor of Obstetrics at Owen's College Manchester) and Robert Lawson Tait (sometime President of the British Gynaecological Society), echoed and developed the case against 'overtaxing' female physiology with too much education further.[48]

These views seem to have circulated widely in the 1880s and a good deal of scaremongering followed. John Thorburn occupied the Chair in Obstetrics at Owen's College, Manchester, at a time when women were first being admitted as students (1883). In lectures published in 1884 under the title *Female Education from a Physiological Point of View* he maintained that girls who began studying for a degree were taking a serious risk to their health.[49] When one of the first female students to register in Manchester, Annie Eastwood, died tragically of tuberculosis before completing her studies Thorburn contended publicly that her death was connected with 'over-education'.[50] The alarmism seems to have reached those concerned with the secondary education of girls. Thorburn alleged that he himself had seen 'a very large number of cases where schoolgirls had been permanently injured by schoolwork during menstruation'.[51] Similarly, Lord Hatherley, presiding over the opening of the new Leeds High School for Girls as early as 1876 warned his audience cryptically that there was

> one thing against which he was cautioned by a gentleman who had taken part in the management of the establishment at Girton. There was one point in which the instruction of women ought to be regarded seriously as contrasted with the amount of work put on boys. He did not wish to say anything offensive, but medical men said there was not the same physical power and strength in the fibres of the brain as would enable the majority of girls to compete with each other in the high branches of mathematics and other subjects of that kind requiring great mental power and attention. There were cases of persons having become seriously unwell in consequence of having their studies pushed too far in that direction.[52]

Clearly women educators had little choice other than to try to defend themselves against charges that they were wrecking the health of their pupils, and they responded in a number of ways. As mentioned in the previous chapter, many headmistresses of the newer types of large girls' school set out to defend themselves against allegations of negligence by developing school medical services and carefully supervised programmes of physical education whilst paying meticulous attention to the health of their pupils.[53] At the same time, 'biological' definitions of femininity which emphasised the frailty and vulnerability of female physiology were contested by feminists and women doctors at a more theoretical or 'scientific' level.

The publication of an article in the *Fortnightly Review* in 1874 entitled *Sex In Mind and Education*, by Dr Henry Maudsley had aroused considerable concern in feminist circles.[54] Maudsley's article had drawn attention generally to medical anxieties about the effects of 'over-educating' women and particularly to the work of Edward Clarke in America on this subject. Emily Davies, Barbara Bodichon, Louisa Lumsden and others appear to have discussed the substance of the article in some detail. Prompted by Emily Davies and Frances Buss, Elizabeth Garrett Anderson set out to reply to Maudsley in an article which was published in the next issue of the same journal.

Dr Garrett Anderson confessed herself surprised, in the first instance, that Dr Maudsley and other medical men should be so convinced of the need to pay such 'exceptional attention' to the female reproductive organs. On the whole, when people were well, she suggested, their physiological processes went on more smoothly without special attention being paid to any particular set of organs than with it.[55] Further,

> When we are told that in the labour of life women cannot disregard their special physiological functions without danger to health, it is difficult to understand what is meant, considering that in adult life healthy women do as a rule disregard them almost completely.[56]

It was, she contended, 'a great exaggeration to imply that women of average health are periodically incapacitated from serious work by the facts of their organisation.'[57]

Carefully scrutinising Maudsley's case point by point, Garrett Anderson concluded that it rested on very little evidence. Many of his arguments, she remarked, would already be familiar to all

> who are interested in noticing what can be said in support of the policy of restriction, whether as applied to negroes, agricultural labourers, or women. They remind us more of an Ashantee fight than of a philosophical essay; so abundant is the powder used in their discharge, and so miscellaneous and obsolete are the projectiles.[58]

Scathingly she highlighted the irony of Maudsley being so obsessed with the damage that girls would 'do to themselves' if they were allowed to compete in the educational stakes 'on the same terms' as men:

> Hitherto most of the women who have 'contended with men for the goals of man's ambition' have had no chance of being any the worse for being allowed to do so on equal terms. They have had all the benefit of being heavily handicapped. Over and above their assumed

physical and mental inferiority, they have had to start in the race without a great part of the training men have enjoyed, or they have gained what training they have been able to gain in an atmosphere of hostility, to remain in which has taxed their strength and endurance far more than any amount of mental work could tax it.[59]

The women students who had determined to study medicine in Edinburgh would have found their task immeasurably lightened, Dr Garrett Anderson observed, had they been allowed to contend on the same terms as men:

The intellectual work required from other medical students is nothing compared with what it has been made to them by obliging them to spend time and energy in contesting every step of their course and yet in spite of this heavy additional burden they have not at present shown any signs of enfeebled health or of inadequate mental power.[60]

In her conclusion, Elizabeth Garrett Anderson urged all those who would give a fair hearing to the case for or against the advantages of higher education for women not to be swayed by any loose reliance on the opinions of medical men: they should examine the evidence for themselves.

During the 1880s two surveys were undertaken in this country by women who set out to do exactly what Elizabeth Garrett Anderson had recommended, and to look closely into the question of whether or not higher education had any significantly damaging effects on women's health. Both of these surveys were inspired to some extent by a study which had been carried out in America, by the Committee of Health Statistics in Boston, into the 'reproductive potential' of college-educated women. Reporting in 1885, Annie Howes, chairman of the Committee, claimed that the majority of graduates in her sample had been able to mother children perfectly successfully.[61]

In England, this inspired a group of women academics under the secretaryship of Mrs Sidgwick, in Cambridge, to mount a systematic inquiry into the health of women who had studied in Oxford and Cambridge.[62] Detailed questionnaires were circulated to ex-students of the women's colleges asking for information about the health of the recipient and also that of any sisters or cousins close in age who had not attended college: these were to act as a 'control group' and to make it possible for comparisons to be made. Around the same time

Emily Pfeiffer also set out, more informally, to collect information and opinions on the question of women's health and education from a number of women educators, heads of colleges and suchlike. Pfeiffer's conclusions were published in her essay on *Women and Work*, in 1888.[63] Mrs Sidgwick published the full Report of the Oxford and Cambridge Committee (which analysed schedules returned by 482 ex-students of Newnham, Girton, Lady Margaret Hall and Somerville) in 1890.

Neither Pfeiffer nor Mrs Sidgwick could find any evidence to suggest that higher education might carry any special dangers for women's health or for their reproductive capacity. Pfeiffer emphasised the testimonies of many women educationalists who maintained that the idle vacuous life led at home by so many middle-class girls constituted a much more insidious threat to their health and nervous stability than did the salutary regimes of school or college life.[64] Mrs Sidgwick was characteristically more cautious. Some girls did notice a very slight falling-off in health whilst at college, she conceded; but this was by no means general, nor anything very serious. If sensible hygienic precautions were taken it could easily be avoided.[65]

Both Mrs Sidgwick and Emily Pfeiffer set out specifically to reply to the accusations of social-evolutionary thinkers and social-Darwinists, who denounced higher education for women as 'damaging to the race'. Mrs Sidgwick addressed herself to recent polemic writings by Grant Allen on this theme. There was no evidence whatsoever, she contended, for the case that girls were being educated 'at the expense of their reserve fund of energy'; there was nothing to suggest that educated women would develop into unsatisfactory or 'physically inefficient' mothers.[66] Emily Pfeiffer's criticism of the 'biological' concepts of femininity espoused by Herbert Spencer and other evolutionary theorists went further. She attacked Spencer's initial assumption that women's health could be measured in terms of any 'high reproductive capacity'. Women's health, she pointed out, was often irreparably *damaged* through bearing too many children.[67] Women should not accept that nature was their destiny. Nor should they allow eugenist thinkers to try and saddle them with the whole burden of 'duty to the race.'[68]

However, demonstrating that college-educated women who married had every chance of mothering healthy children was not enough to placate those who were determined to indict higher education for women as 'damaging to the race'. Social-Darwinist and eugenist thinkers merely switched the emphasis of their argument. Even if academic pursuits did not actually render women infertile, writers such as Grant Allen, Karl Pearson, Mr and Mrs Whetham and Dr Lionel Tayler were at the ready to insist that women who had been educated at college were *less inclined* towards marriage and motherhood. Education, it was claimed, rendered women selfish, encouraging them to consider their individual advantage before the 'biological good' of the species.[69]

Women educationalists tended to be embarrassed by discussions of the marriage rate amongst their students. Mrs Sidgwick, for instance, was defensive about the fact that the data she collected on the subsequent histories of ex-students from Oxford and Cambridge colleges revealed that only about 10 per cent of these women had married. Amongst their sisters and cousins 19 per cent had married. It would be too hasty to infer that 'there was something in having been at college which tended to prevent marriage', she insisted.[70] Students were already a selected group in that they were unmarried when they came up, and women students in residence were not able to marry. In any case, most of the women who had been students were still young and might well marry in the future.[71]

B.L. Hutchins, defending higher education for women against the continuing attacks of eugenists and social-Darwinists some twenty years later, re-examined Mrs Sidgwick's data.[72] The marriage rate of college women might indeed appear very low, she conceded, but it was crucial to remember that the low rate was characteristic not merely of girls who had received a higher education, but of the daughters of middle-class and professional families generally. She re-emphasised Mrs Sidgwick's conviction that a college education might delay a girl's chances of finding a husband, but would make little difference to her overall chances of marriage.[73]

In all, however, the careful calculations and measured reassurances of Mrs Sidgwick or B.L. Hutchins failed to disturb the widespread conviction that a college education diminished a girl's chances of marriage. Alice Gordon, writing in *The Nineteenth Century* on 'The After-Careers of University Educated Women', in 1895, reported that her study of the histories of 1,486 ex-students of various women's colleges showed a total of 680 currently engaged in teaching, whilst only 208 of the sample had married. 'According to the law of averages,' she concluded, 'if a mother sends her daughter to one of the universities she is more likely to become a teacher than a wife.'[74] Such observations reinforced popular sentiment. 'How can you send your daughter

to college, Mrs Brittain? . . . Don't you want her ever to get *married*?',
Vera Brittain remembered her mother's friends asking in consternation
whilst she struggled to qualify for Oxford entrance examinations on the
eve of the first world war.[75] Similarly, Katharine Chorley recalled that in
her home suburb of Alderley Edge, near Manchester, earlier this century,

> Even those who had heard of Girton and Newnham thought them
> infected resorts whose products must emerge pitted for life by the
> intellectual smallpox they would be bound to contract, a disfigure-
> ment that would unfit them for the marriage market.[76]

The widespread assumption persisted that 'bookishness' or intellectual
confidence diminished a girl's sexual attractiveness: learning destroyed
femininity.

The decision whether or not to marry remained acutely problematic
for educated women in a society which insisted on their making a
choice between many forms of individual or professional fulfillment
and married life. Celibacy, as was pointed out in Chapter 2, remained
an important political option for late-Victorian women who cherished
their autonomy or a sense of self which clashed with the conventions
of 'femininity'. But on the whole few feminists set out, during this
period, openly to confront and analyse the frictions and problems of
sexual self-identity that so many strong-minded intelligent women
must have experienced acutely during their lives, and which must have
significantly influenced both their attitudes to the opposite sex and any
decision whether or not to marry. Ruth First and Anne Scott's recently
published biography of Olive Schreiner has reminded us that even in
the comparatively liberated and 'advanced' intellectual circles frequented
by their subject in the 1880s and 1890s, the discussion of female
sexuality remained hedged around by limitations and inhibitions.[77]
Olive Schreiner's own problems of sexual identity are a major theme
of the book: problems which seem to have derived in part from the
difficulties she experienced in trying to reconcile strong sexual drives
and feelings with deeply internalised prescriptions about 'feminine'
sexual and social behaviour. Social inhibitions shape language, and
late-Victorian culture did not readily supply women with the language which would have facilitated an analysis of their own repression,
particularly in this area where gender prescriptions govern the expression of sexuality.

Women's novels supply us with some of the sharpest insights into
the problems women experienced in coming to terms with themselves

and their relationships in a society which rigidly differentiated between 'masculine' and 'feminine' forms of behaviour and desire. Schreiner's own fiction and allegories can be used in this way. Both Rosamond Lehmann's *Dusty Answer* (1927) and Clemence Dane's *Regiment of Women* (1917) represent novels which explore complex relationships between women in an educational milieu.[78] Lehmann takes a women's college in Cambridge, Clemence Dane a girl's school for her setting. Both novels attempt to explore the nature of sexual and intellectual attraction between women as well as in heterosexual relationships. This pushes both writers towards treating 'femininity' and female sexual identity as problematic; as socially constructed, to some extent, rather than 'given' (even if Dane's novel, in contrast with Lehmann's, resolves its tensions in an utterly predictable and conventional way).

Late nineteenth-century feminists challenged 'biological' definitions of femininity which emphasised the physiological instability of the female organism and its constitutional liability to 'overstrain'. They rejected the contentions of evolutionary and eugenist thinkers who insisted that 'nature' was and ought to be women's 'destiny'. Many feminists refused to accept that there existed any innate differences in intellect between men and women. They rejected both the 'early arrest' model of femininity propounded by Herbert Spencer and the complementary anabolistic/katabolistic theories of Geddes and Thomson. The fifth chapter of Olive Schreiner's *Woman and Labour* expounded a fully environmental theory of the psychology of sex differences which Cyril Burt and Robert Moore considered to represent 'the clearest and most uncompromising' formulation of this viewpoint since John Stuart Mill.[79] But in spite of all this it is important to realise that feminists were constantly being forced into a defensive position. The traditionally 'whiggish' interpretations of feminist history, which present us with an image of pioneering women mapping their routes up mountains and steadily conquering summit after summit simply do not stand up to scrutiny. Considered from a feminist viewpoint today the history of the women's movement since the late-nineteenth century serves in many ways to demonstrate the resilience and ideological resourcefulness of a society or culture threatened by feminism: there is no simple tale of steady progress. The history of women's education, in particular, furnishes many examples of the kind of defensive battles which feminists continually had to fight, and I shall illustrate this here with reference to curriculum.

161

Feminism and the 'Feminine Curriculum'

Schools established by the Girls' Public Day School Company — indeed perhaps the majority of girls' high schools founded in the last quarter of the nineteenth century — had set out determined to contest any idea that girls were incapable of serious academic study. The founders of these schools were in the main convinced that girls would profit from a solid intellectual training in subjects such as classics, mathematics and later science: subjects conventionally defined as inappropriate for the 'feminine mind'. The schools were keen to provide what they defined as 'a sound, liberal education.' This usually implied the rejection of the notion that there might be any need for technical or vocational subjects in the curriculum. Emily Shirreff's attitude had been typical here: 'The school educates . . .', she declared, 'the technical school instructs.'[80] Professional training or technical instruction might *follow*, but should in no circumstances be allowed to *replace* a general education.

Very few of the late-nineteenth-century high schools for girls would have acknowledged any responsibility for providing domestic training — aside perhaps from a small amount of needlework — for their pupils. It was assumed that any domestic skills the girls might require to fit them as future mistresses of households would be learned from their mothers in the home. Headmistresses claimed that the tradition of morning school only had been evolved specifically with the idea of leaving girls free in the afternoons to help their mothers with domestic and social concerns.[81]

However, in the atmosphere of alarm over 'physical deterioration' and obsessions with 'national fitness' which gradually suffused this country around the turn of the century, it was inevitable that the 'academic bias' of the girls' high schools would come under attack.[82] It was partly in response to increasing public pressure that the Association of Headmistresses set up a Special Committee to consider the role of domestic studies in the curriculum in the 1890s.[83] Not surprisingly, members of the Association were deeply divided on the issue. Some headmistresses adhered staunchly to the conviction that their mission was to provide girls with as nearly as possible the same opportunities as boys for intellectual work: domestic training, they insisted, was none of their business. However one group within the Association keenly identified itself with the campaign to restore to the next generation of women a proper appreciation of their feminine duties. Sara

Burstall, Headmistress of Manchester High School, was particularly vocal in this context. Schooling too often presented intelligent girls with 'unnatural goals' in life, she suggested:

> A girl's teacher is, in general, a student and a spinster — not a woman leading the normal ordinary woman's life; a woman who too often is not living in a home at all, even as sister or daughter. This tends to distort the girl's ideas, and makes her think that she, too would be a teacher, and live this abnormal life.[84]

Margaret Gilliland, Headmistress of Haberdashers' Aske's, confessed herself wholly out of sympathy with professional colleagues who saw no place for domestic arts in the curriculum. She had been scandalised by the admission of one such colleague who, on being questioned about whether or not such subjects were taught in her school, had admitted off-handedly that 'a few girls who were backward in intellectual work learned cookery.'[85] Scholarship was all very well, Margaret Gilliland observed, but schools with a purely academic bias were doing nothing for the nation:

> The old 'blue-stocking' type, who prided herself on not knowing how to sew and mend, and who thought cooking menial and beneath her, no longer appeals to anyone.[86]

An interesting feature of the vocabulary used by the advocates of domestic training is that girls, particularly 'the more intellectual type' of girls, are constantly described as 'shirking' or 'dodging' their 'duties to the nation'. This is noticeable in Margaret Gilliland and Sara Burstall's writings, and also that of Burstall's close friend Alice Ravenhill, the compiler of the Reports on *School Training for the Home Duties of Women* addressed to the Board of Education which were described in Chapter 3.[87] A strong implication in the writings of these three and countless others of similar persuasion is that too much liking for intellectual work is selfish in women, and unacceptably so. The stance has markedly authoritarian undertones. Sara Burstall, for instance, drew attention to the ways in which Darwinistic and 'evolutionary ideas' had demonstrated the necessity of women fulfilling their obligation to the race, judging that this must inevitably modify the goals of educators. She held that the advance of 'the New Collectivism' entailed a belief in the importance of the State, legitimating its claims upon the individual. It was now imperative that women should learn to subordinate private interests to those of National Welfare.[88]

163

Courses in 'housewifery' were introduced into Manchester High School by Sara Burstall as early as 1900. She considered these courses a particular boon for those 'to whom ordinary school studies do not appeal'.[89] However, the clear impression of her educational philosophy derived from a reading of *English High Schools for Girls*, published in 1907, makes it apparent that Burstall favoured a general 'feminization' of the curriculum for all girls in secondary education, irrespective of educational ability or social class. In Burstall's view, all the separate subjects of the curriculum should be taught with the girls' future as wives and mothers in mind. English and history were particularly important, for the mothers of the future would need to inspire their children with ideas of culture and citizenship. As we have already seen, she believed that mathematics could be 'kept at a minimum for girls because it did not underlie their industries as it does so many of the activities of men.' Science was deemed important 'as a preparation for domestic duties and the care of children.' Biology and 'nature study' mattered. Physics and chemistry Burstall regarded as more dispensable, unless they could be taught with a domestic bias and application.[90]

Some of the headmistresses of GPDS Company schools similarly set out to make space for the inclusion of domestic subjects in the curriculum around this time. At Clapham High School, for instance, Mrs Woodhouse introduced a 'Brides-to-be' course and awarded 'Housewives Certificates' to those who successfully completed it.[91] The 'non-college' girls who followed 'home-life' courses were allowed to drop mathematics, science and classics. Blackheath and Streatham High Schools made similar experiments in this area.[92]

However, this enthusiasm for domestic subjects was by no means universal. Inspectors from the Board of Education, visiting high schools in the early 1900s were evidently disturbed to find that only a minority of them made provision for domestic training, and even in some of these the provision was limited to a few token lessons in needlework. In 1906, the year in which the GPDS Company was converted into a Trust, the Board of Education increased its pressure on the Trust's Council to introduce a more substantial element of training in housewifery into the timetable. The Council refused. Such courses, they pointed out, 'would make a serious alteration in the aim and the work of the schools.' They were prepared to go so far as to dispense with government grants, increase the fees, and declare independence rather than to implement the curriculum changes suggested by the Board.[93]

The advocates of domestic training for women considered it lamentable that domestic subjects were seen as 'the Cinderella of the educational family', generally shunned by academic high-fliers and considered particularly appropriate for the 'less able girls.'[94] They unanimously agreed on the necessity for raising the status of the domestic arts. Two avenues seemed particularly promising. The first involved emphasising the 'scientific' nature and possibilities of domestic work, elevating housework to the level of an 'applied science'. The second route led through instituting courses in 'Household Science' in the Universities.

The question of whether it was feasible — or desirable — to teach domestic subjects as an 'applied science' in girls' schools prompted vigorous debate in educational circles between 1900 and 1914. One leading advocate of the need to restructure the scientific curriculum in girls' schools was Professor A. Smithells, who presented his ideas in a paper entitled *School Training for the Home Duties of Women*, presented to the York meeting of The British Association for the Advancement of Science in 1906.[95] Smithells suggested that much time was being wasted trying to teach pure physics and chemistry to schoolgirls, since these subjects usually failed to 'appeal to any logical faculty' or 'feminine interest'. Why could the schools not capitalise on the girls' interests in domesticity and daily life, build 'kitchen laboratories' and provide courses in the 'Applied Science of the Household?'

As discussed in Chapter 3, the Board of Education became increasingly preoccupied with the importance of domestic subjects in elementary schools around this time. There was also a growing concern to see the same subjects taught at the secondary level. From 1905 higher elementary and secondary schools were required to differentiate the girls' curriculum from that offered to boys by providing 'a practical training in home duties applicable to the circumstances of their own homes' for the former.[96] In 1908 the Board stated that it was prepared to countenance schools allowing girls over the age of fifteen to drop science in favour of an approved course in domestic subjects.[97] The *Regulations for Secondary Schools* published in 1909 extended this provision even further, suggesting that girls over fifteen might substitute domestic subjects either 'partially or wholly for science and for mathematics other than arithmetic.'[98] At the same time, the Board expressed its own interest in experiments taking place in schools which were trying to evolve a 'scientific' or theoretical approach to domestic training — an approach which it considered much more appropriate at the secondary rather than the elementary level.

Between 1909 and 1913 the Board of Education referred the subject of domestic teaching in the secondary schools to two separate committees: a Select Committee which presented an Interim Report on Housecraft in Girls' Secondary Schools in 1911, and a Consultative Committee (chaired by Acland) on Practical Work in Secondary Schools which reported two years later.[99] Both of these Committees paid particular attention to contemporary experiments in relating science and housecraft.

A good deal of controversy had been generated by these experiments and the conclusions reached in the Reports of both Committees were rather mixed. Both emphasised that given existing conditions of teacher training, women qualified to teach both 'pure' science and domestic subjects were in very scarce supply. Whilst domestic economy teachers might be enthusiastic over the possibilities of teaching their subject more 'scientifically', Acland's Committee found the majority of science teachers obdurately opposed to restructuring their subject in order to give it a 'domestic' basis. Teachers of chemistry pointed out that any knowledge of their subject imparted largely through lessons in practical cookery could only be of the most fragmentary and disconnected kind. Many of the most simple culinary processes, on the other hand required a highly sophisticated knowledge of organic chemistry if they were to be understood in 'scientific' terms.[100] Ida Freund, a Lecturer in Natural Sciences at Newnham College, Cambridge, argued strongly that the attempt to teach science through housework was an educational mistake. She had no objection to the inclusion of domestic crafts in the curriculum, but every objection to the attempt to bastardize science. Echoing the arguments she had put forward in a lengthy paper entitled 'Domestic Science – A Protest', published in *The Englishwoman* in 1911, she submitted that the very use of the term 'domestic science' was pretentiously incorrect.[101] Girls arriving at the universities to study science were already in the main less well equipped than their male counterparts. The majority of girls' schools made inadequate provision for the teaching of physics and chemistry, preferring to concentrate on botany as the main science subject – even this being regarded in the light of a 'feminine accomplishment' rather than an intellectually demanding subject. The present vogue for 'domestic science', Ida Freund feared, could only have the consequence of lowering still further what was already too often a deplorable level of teaching in girls' schools.[102]

The conclusions reached by Acland's Committee, after taking

evidence from a variety of women educationalists (including Sara Burstall, Margaret Gilliland, L.M. Faithfull and Jane Frances Dove) were ambivalent in tone. The Report emphasised a strong conviction that girls in all types of secondary school should be required to reach at least 'an indispensable minimum of attainment in Domestic Subjects'. At the same time the Committee members agreed with the majority of their witnesses who thought that the teaching of cookery, laundry-work and housewifery should be preceded by at least two years of teaching in pure science, at least where the girls were likely to remain at school until the age of seventeen. (It is worth remembering that the minority of girls from poorer homes who managed to get to secondary school at all usually left before this.) However, the Committee expressed themselves in sympathy with Professor Smithells and others who maintained that science teaching in girls' schools was often 'too academic in character, too remote from the interests of the girls, and taught without reference to the Domestic Subjects'. They felt it too early to pronounce definitely 'as to how far the teaching of elementary physics and chemistry may be modified to form the basis for the scientific study of cookery and other domestic arts', but believed that 'some fruitful experiments were taking place.'[103]

Those convinced of the need to raise the status of domestic subjects in the curriculum pinned a good deal of their hopes on the possibility of establishing courses in 'household science' at the university level. Both Sara Burstall and Alice Ravenhill reported enthusiastically upon the enterprise of American universities such as Columbia which offered undergraduate and even postgraduate courses in household economy.[104] Why, they demanded, was England so far behind?

Around 1906, 'The Ladies' Department' of King's College London began to make plans for a new course in 'home science', aiming to devise a syllabus for 'the higher education of women in the principles underlying the proper management of the home and young children, and in the hygienic and business-like conduct of institutional life.' It was suggested that the scheme might be expected to appeal both to women wanting to follow careers as lecturers in domestic science or hygiene, and to those who anticipated spending their lives in their own homes. There would be a strong emphasis on the application of science to household work.[105]

Lilian Faithfull (who had held the post of Vice-Principal of the Ladies' Department in Kensington before being appointed Headmistress of Cheltenham Ladies' College) commented later that the scheme had 'appealed to many who had had some doubt about the wisdom of University education for women in classics or mathematics.'[106] It attracted Royal Patronage and lavish endowments – donations poured in and rapidly reached the target requirement of £100,000 envisaged by the founders.

King's College for Women introduced its three-year course in 'Home Science and Economics' in 1908. Hilda Oakeley, the Warden of the College, described the aims and objects of the course to Acland's Committee on Practical Work in Secondary Schools in 1912. 'Briefly', she explained, 'the aim of the course was the using of the educational forces at our disposal to combat the depreciation of the activities related to household work due to both social and industrial courses.'[107] At the same time, she pointed out hastily, those responsible for the course were convinced 'that the mental discipline belonging to the subjects concerned could form a real education.' Students did cookery, laundry work and economics. 'Experimental work' in the 'kitchen laboratory' was intended to encourage a scientific attitude in dealing with the problems of everyday household life. For instance, work was done on 'the preparation of floor polishes' 'the use and mixing of dried milk', and 'the necessity or otherwise of soda in cooking greens.' Professor Smithells acted as Honorary Adviser to the Board of Studies in these matters.[108]

There were howls of rage and derision from feminists. Articles in the *Freewoman* described the course as 'a despicable prostitution of educational opportunities', 'a travesty of science', 'a degradation of university standards and an insult to women.'[109] The founders of 'such a retrograde scheme' merely aimed 'at perpetuating woman's inferiority by perfecting her in the one role which puts the greatest difficulties in the way of her development,' suggested one writer. All over the country there were gifted girls 'crushing their rage in the folds of dish-cloths' to whom £100,000 'expended in ordinary educational scholarships would have opened out a new world.' 'There are no reasonable grounds for raising the estimation in which housework is held socially,' inveighed this same writer, 'This estimation is far too high already, and housework absorbs the energies of many intelligent women who, but for the social status which it is unfairly accorded, would be honestly ashamed of not attempting something better.'[110]

The debate grew still more acrid when Rona Robinson, who had been awarded a Gilchrist Postgraduate Scholarship to study Home Science and Economics at King's College for Women decided to resign her fellowship in disgust over what she deemed to be the pitifully low academic standards enshrined in the course. She had been both insulted and angry to find that

> The precious years at a university possible to but a few of us, and bought at a high price by most of those few, (were) to be spent in cleaning pan lids, scrubbing in the old old way, washing dishes and soiled garments and in cooking the ordinary family dishes that have been cooked for many centuries.[111]

It was both in the interests of the integrity of science teaching and also the sensible teaching and practice of domestic crafts, Robinson urged, that such lunatic experiments in scrambling the girls' curriculum should be brought to a halt. In spite of the patronage of Queen Mary, and in spite of its university backing, she was prepared roundly and vehemently to denounce the King's College course as the most 'impudent piece of charlatanry' ever 'perpetrated . . . in the history of education.'[112]

Feminist opposition, however, could not injure a scheme which was welcomed so enthusiastically by wealthy donors and conservative sections of the general public. Stimulated by the growing demand for teachers of domestic science and hygiene in the schools, the courses at King's College for Women continued to flourish. The University of London formally recognised the three-year course in 1920, whereafter those students successfully completing their studies were awarded the degree of BSc in Household and Social Science.[113]

Attempts on the one hand, to raise the status of housework by teaching it 'scientifically' and awarding it examination status; on the other to 'domesticise' science for female consumption continued to be made sporadically over the next fifty years. Sir John Newsom's enthusiastic proposals for 'kitchen laboratories' and an applied household science focusing on such subjects as the chemistry of detergents and polishes were strongly reminiscent of schemes propounded by Professor Smithells in the 1900s.[114] Equally, Newsom's attack upon past generations of feminists, whom he accused of having perverted the course of women's education and having distorted the curriculum with an academic bias he deemed unsuitable for the majority of girls, provoked a debate uncannily similar to that of the period 1905-14.[115] Feminists have constantly found themselves fighting a defensive battle against such attempts to 'feminise' the curriculum — a battle which it seems has never yet been finally won.

Feminism and Women's Education 1870-1920

What, finally, should be said about the relationship between changing provision for girls' education between 1870 and 1920 and feminism? One of the main aims of this book has been to emphasise that the relationship was a complex one, by no means so simple as historians of both women's education and feminism have in the past sometimes assumed.

Feminism had little influence on the changing shape of the curriculum in state elementary schools through the period. This does not mean one cannot point to examples of middle-class feminists who were seriously concerned by, and angrily protested against the growing emphasis on domestic subjects in the schooling of working-class girls. Christina Bremner, whose account of *The Education of Girls and Women in Great Britain* has already been referred to in Chapter 3, was sharply critical of the insistence on teaching needlework, housewifery and laundry to girls in the Board Schools of the 1890s.[116] Mrs Marvin, a former Inspector, giving evidence to the Board of Education's Consultative Committee on Continuation Schools in 1909, registered a strong protest against the growing enthusiasm for domestic instruction in a girl's final years at elementary school.[117] If the interests of working-class mothers were often pitifully narrow, she contended it was because they led dull lives as 'family drudges'. If the schools insisted on teaching girls yet more and more domestic subjects they would merely succeed in turning out 'better drudges'. 'You have not made a satisfactory mother', she observed, 'when you have taught a woman to sew on her children's buttons and make a pudding.' It was much more important to provide a liberal education, 'to raise the woman's status, to elevate her character, and to widen her intellectual outlook.' In any case, she ventured, standards of domesticity might well be much improved if *boys*, as well as girls, were trained to appreciate their responsibilities in the home.[118] Still further expressions of protest were generated by the Board of Education's new enthusiasm for teaching girls infant care in elementary schools. In 1918, Rebecca West gave vent to the bitter resentment she felt over Sir George Newman's attempt to saddle working-class mothers with the blame for high infant mortality figures. In urging the schools to spend more and more time on 'mothercraft' and domestic subjects, she contended, Newman was effectively trying to rob the majority of working-class girls of what small chance they had of securing a general education.[119]

But these somewhat isolated expressions of protest had little effect at the time. And many middle-class feminists undoubtedly found themselves in something of a dilemma when — indeed if — they considered the subject of the education of working-class girls at all. Some adopted what from a present day value-stance can only be described as a frankly elitist position. It comes as something as a shock for a modern feminist — however familiar with the extent of class differences in the nineteenth century — to read the *Memorandum on the Education of Working Class Girls* which Clara Collet addressed to the Bryce Commission on Secondary Education in 1894.[120] Collet staunchly maintained that any secondary education provided for working-class girls should be strongly differentiated in aims and content from the forms currently available for their middle-class counterparts. Working-class girls, she contended, should be trained for the responsibilities of married life. Any occupations they might enter into would be likely to be unskilled and temporary as well as of a 'domestic' nature (such as household service or dressmaking) and therefore technical education would be of little use to them. However, their ignorance of domestic management was likely to be extreme. Collet was strongly opposed to schemes which would encourage too many girls from working-class homes to pursue an 'academic' education, by means of scholarships, in high schools. Unless a girl's mental capacity was 'considerably higher than the high school average', or unless she was determined to become an elementary school teacher, Collet was convinced that scholarships did more harm than good. Her seven years' experience as a high school teacher had led her to believe that such privileges unrealistically raised a girl's aspirations, 'reducing the chances of the exhibitioner's happiness in after life,' where she might well have to content herself with a job as post-office clerk or shop assistant.[121]

Collet herself cannot easily be classed as a feminist. But she was a well-educated woman, and, as Labour Correspondent for the Board of Trade, she had been successful in terms of the male-dominated career structure of the day. Her views would have carried weight and were no doubt indicative of very widely held opinion at the time.

Barriers of social class and outlook rendered any easy sharing of experience of immediate identification of common interests between middle-class feminists and working-class girls difficult. Margaret McMillan's account of her efforts to teach factory girls in Whitechapel during 1888-9 — the girls locked into pitying or resentful incomprehension of her values and motives — reminds us of some of these difficulties.[122] It should be remembered also that many middle-class feminists were themselves in a very defensive position, struggling uncertainly to resolve tensions generated by their feminism in their own lives. They were often understandably uneasy, both about relationships with others of the same social class and about their own political values. As Sara Delamont has reminded us, the majority of middle-class feminists were simply not ready or secure enough in themselves to plan schemes or strategies for the education of working-class girls.[123] Socialist feminists, strengthened by their political faith, may have nurtured a more confident vision. But on the whole, Socialist feminists, who were deeply concerned with the future of working-class girls, saw more scope in trade-union organisation and political education outside school than they did in the possibilities of state schooling as a means of effecting long-term social change.

Let us return to the relationship between the formal education of middle-class girls and feminism. One of the arguments put forward in the second chapter of this book was that in some ways the new high schools and colleges functioned as conservative institutions, fostering conventional values and ideals about femininity and feminine service. Many, indeed perhaps most, of the women who pressed for educational reforms in the second half of the nineteenth century accepted the main features of the sexual division of labour as somehow right and inevitable. We should remember further that many of the new educational institutions for girls owed their foundation as much to the enlightened — often paternalistic — benevolence of the male middle-class intelligentsia, professional men and businessmen who sponsored and supported with endowments as to the crusading zeal of women.

The new schools and colleges for women were not 'feminist' institutions. At the same time, they had a crucial role to play in the history of the feminist movement. In the first place, *any* formal schooling or college education must be seen as having loosened the hold of the family upon female socialisation. However 'homely', 'family-like' or closely protective the social milieu of some of the new educational foundations might have been, however much the girl students or pupils might have complained about petty restrictions on individual freedom, most contemporary observers recognised this degree of freedom from family demands which formal education afforded. As pupil or student a girl had space to consider herself as an individual, not merely as dutiful daughter or mother's helper in the family.

The reminiscences of perhaps the majority of women who studied at one of the women's colleges in Oxford or Cambridge in the period refer to the sense of intoxication or sudden thrill they recalled as having been provoked by the realisation that time was their own. In 1897 the *Cambridge University Reporter* recorded Dr Verrall speaking on the benefits of the new women's colleges: he had stressed 'the joy and pleasure and energy of self-development which come to women from being put in a position to be themselves for a short time.' Verrall judged this a privilege of particular importance to the female sex, 'because society presses upon women more hardly than it does upon men, and leaves them in ordinary circumstances less leisure and liberty to be themselves.'[124] Lilian Faithfull, remembering her days at Oxford, commented:

> To women, more than to men, the delight of having three years in
> which it was right to be selfishly absorbed in intellectual pursuits
> was unspeakable, for claims small and great are apt to beset women
> in life at a very early age.[125]

The wording here is significant: at home, earnest application to studies on the part of a girl was apt to be seen as selfishness. In the environment of school or college, studiousness meant diligence and was even rewarded. Of course, not all girls could so easily free themselves from a feeling of guilty self-indulgence when they opened a book; but the licence was there.

Further, the school or college environment gave women access to their peers; for many, an entirely new reference group. The college allowed women to 'choose their associates and mutually to educate one another', Verrall had remarked in the speech already quoted. Accentuated by the feeling that they were pioneers, a very strong sense of camaraderie seems to have prevailed amongst the first groups of women students in the Universities. More enduringly, in the colleges and also in the schools, experiences could be shared and compared. The realisation that one might not be alone in one's discontents and pleasures could undoubtedly become an important source of inner strength. Here and there the historian catches glimpses of what this might have meant, of the excitement which could be generated by the discovery of angers shared and commitment to a common cause. A pupil of Cheltenham Ladies' College late last century recalled that when a friend in her boarding house 'smuggled in *The Story of an African Farm*, just out, the whole sky seemed aflame, and many of us became violent feminists.'[126] Maybe this went some way, at least, towards

173

mitigating the impact of Miss Soulsby's famous lectures on 'The Virtuous Woman' (emphasising the indispensibility of housekeeping skills and of wives knowing enough of public affairs to be able to discuss them with their menfolk), which were delivered around the same time.[127]

Widening reference groups also meant that girls who went to schools and colleges were supplied with new role models. They might, like the young Vera Brittain at St Monica's, have come into contact with teachers of decidedly feminist convictions. Miss Heath Jones, whom Vera Brittain described as 'an ardent though always discreet feminist', lent her students books on the Woman's Movement and even took a handful of her senior pupils along to a constitutional suffrage meeting in Tadworth Village in 1911.[128] Intelligent, well-qualified and economically independent teachers demonstrated a new kind of lifestyle, even if the general association with celibacy limited its appeal for the majority of girls. The lifestyles of intelligent, well-qualified and *married* women in academic life were a constant focus of interest for younger women in their circles, as pointed out earlier in this volume. Women such as the young Mrs Pattison and the young Mrs Marshall were much admired, even venerated by some students; the details of their dress, demeanour and attitudes were carefully observed. Even if the relationships and many of the features of the lifestyle of married women in academic circles were wholly traditional, these women still provided a much more positive model of womanhood than did the average provincial middle-class wife and mother, comparatively insulated from public and intellectual concerns.

Finally on this theme of role-models, the new schools and colleges produced their honours lists. Their most distinguished pupils and students achieved a good deal of publicity. Few historians of women's education fail to mention *Punch*'s tribute to Agnata Ramsay's outstanding first in Cambridge's classical tripos in 1887. No man had achieved higher than the second class that year and the *Punch* cartoon depicted a woman being shown into a first-class railway carriage marked 'Ladies Only'.[129] Philippa Fawcett's brilliant success in the mathematical tripos (she was placed above the senior wrangler) in 1890 attracted an equal amount of public notice.[130] Thus the educational movement produced its heroines: the names of these women and many others became enshrined in feminist literature, providing a source of reference and inspiration to future generations of women scholars.

The new girls' high schools and the university colleges for women founded in the second half of the nineteenth century provided at least a small number of middle-class girls with the best academic education available for women at that time. Dora Russell, a particularly sensitive critic of educational practice, recalling her own schooldays at the Girls' Public Day School foundation in Sutton, Surrey, remembered that she had received 'an academic, intellectual and literary education with, as was rare in girls' curricula, quite good science.'[131] The regime had in her view been over-regulated and unnecessarily competitive, but on the whole she judged the education the school had provided to have been 'excellent'. Compared with the girls who had attended a 'School for the Daughters of Gentlemen' immediately over the road from Sutton High School, Dora Russell remembered, she and her fellow pupils had enjoyed a relative freedom from petty restrictions on 'ladylike' dress and behaviour. 'Not to wear gloves', she added, 'became for me almost a principle that has lasted all my life.'[132]

Formal education did not and could not free women from the constraints of socially-defined concepts of 'femininity' and feminine behaviour. The new schools and colleges in some ways even reinforced these concepts and helped to reproduce the very same ideas and forms of behaviour which girls had learned from childhood onwards in the family. But at the same time these institutions furnished space for self-development, affording some relief from the constrictions of family life. Further, they gave women access to their peers and to new reference groups, and hence constituted environments in which feminist ideas might be articulated and shared. Finally, and crucially, of course, the new schools and colleges guided an albeit small section of women, each generation, towards high status areas of knowledge and expertise, and hence, indirectly, towards power. Formal education and academic achievement gave women the confidence and the competence to challenge the orthodoxies of the time. The new schools and colleges for women were not 'feminist' institutions, but they were still institutions wherein the feminist tradition — with all its class limitations — was nurtured and kept alive.

Notes

Chapter 1 First lessons in femininity: the experience of family life

1 K. Chorley, *Manchester Made Them*, London, Faber & Faber, 1950, p. 149.
2 *1901 Census of England and Wales*, Summary Tables, Parliamentary Papers (hereafter P.P.) 1903, LXXXIV, pp. 230-1.
3 The unreliability of Census returns on the extent of married women's work has been discussed, *inter alia* by B.L. Hutchins, 'Statistics of Women's Life and Employment', in *Journal of the Royal Statistical Society*, June 1909, pp. 215-16; by S. Alexander, 'Women's Work in Nineteenth Century London; A Study of the years 1820-50', in J. Mitchell and A. Oakley (eds), *The Rights and Wrongs of Women*, Harmondsworth, Penguin, 1976; and by E. Roberts, 'Working Class Standards of Living in Barrow and Lancaster, 1890-1914', in *Economic History Review*, Second Series, 1977, vol. XXX, no. 2, pp. 306ff.
4 D.C. Marsh, *The Changing Social Structure of England and Wales, 1871-1961*, London, Routledge & Kegan Paul, 1965, p. 128.
5 P.N. Stearns, 'Working Class Women in Britain, 1890-1914', in M. Vicinus (ed.), *Suffer and Be Still: Women In The Victorian Age*, Bloomington and London, Indiana University Press, 1972.
6 Chorley, *op. cit.*, p. 150.
7 Ministry of Reconstruction, *Report of the Women's Employment Committee*, P.P. 1918, XIV, p. 853.
8 G. Partington, *Women Teachers In the Twentieth Century*, Windsor, National Foundation for Educational Research Publishing Company, 1976, pp. 33-4.
9 C.L. Mowat, *Britain Between the Wars 1918-1940*, London, Methuen, 1955, p. 23.

176

10 D.C. Marsh, *op. cit.*, p. 128.

11 Chorley, *op cit.*, p. 149.

12 *Ibid.*, p. 150.

13 *Ibid.*, p. 149.

14 F. Nightingale, *Cassandra*, published as an appendix to R. Strachey, *The Cause: A Short History of The Women's Movement in Great Britain*, Bath, Cedric Chivers, 1974, p. 402.

15 B. Webb, *My Apprenticeship*, Cambridge University Press, 1979, pp. 49, 116-18.

16 F. Thompson, *Lark Rise to Candleford*, London, Oxford University Press, 1954, pp. 15-16.

17 *Ibid.*, p. 163.

18 M.K. Ashby, *Joseph Ashby of Tysoe, 1859-1919: A Study of English Village Life*, London, The Merlin Press, 1974, pp. 215ff.

19 *Ibid.*, p. 218.

20 G. Mitchell (ed.), *The Hard Way Up: The Autobiography of Hannah Mitchell, Suffragette and Rebel*, London, Virago, 1977, pp. 42-3.

21 *Ibid.*, p. 43.

22 M. Chamberlain, *Fenwomen: A Portrait of Women in an English Village*, London, Virago, 1975, pp. 33-4.

23 M. Llewelyn Davies (ed.), *Life as We Have Known It, by Co-operative Working Women*, London, Virago, 1977, p. 4.

24 *Ibid.*, pp. 8-9.

25 J. Rennie, *Every Other Sunday: The Autobiography of a Kitchen Maid*, London, Arthur Barker, 1955, gives many examples from first-hand experience.

26 E. Raikes, *Dorothea Beale of Cheltenham*, London, Constable, 1908, p. 16.

27 The 'improving' literature directed by the middle classes at children further down the social scale in the late-nineteenth century tended to emphasise the need for small girls to help their mothers with even smaller younger siblings as a prime moral duty. See, for instance, stories entitled 'Minding the Baby' and 'Tired of Baby', in *Our Darlings: The Children's Treasury*, edited by T.J. Barnardo, London, 1881ff., nos 1074 (p. 288) and 1078 (p. 316) respectively.

28 L.M. Faithfull, *In the House of My Pilgrimage*, London, Chatto & Windus, 1925, pp. 43-7.

29 *Ibid.*, p. 45.

30 C.M. Yonge, *The Daisy Chain, or Aspirations*, London, Cassell, 1914.

31 M. Cadogan and P. Craig, *You're A Brick, Angela!: A New Look at Girls' Fiction from 1840-1975*, London, Gollancz, 1977, p. 76.

32 M.V. Hughes, *A London Child of the 1870s*, Oxford University Press, 1977.

33 *Ibid.*, p. 7.
34 *Ibid.*, p. 127.
35 *Ibid.*, p. 129.
36 *Ibid.*
37 *Ibid.*, p. 57.
38 V. Brittain, *Testament of Youth: An Autobiographical Study of the Years 1900-1925*, London, Gollancz, 1933, pp. 86-91.
39 E. Sidgwick, *Mrs Henry Sidgwick: A Memoir, By Her Niece*, London, Sidgwick & Jackson, 1938, p. 21.
40 Raikes, *op. cit.*, pp. 15-16.
41 M.V. Hughes, *A London Girl of the 1880s*, Oxford University Press, 1978, p. 226.
42 *Ibid.*, pp. 80-4.
43 Mitchell, *op. cit.*, p. 44.
44 *Ibid.*, pp. 52, 56-7 and *passim*.
45 *Ibid.*, p. 39.
46 *Ibid.*
47 *Ibid.*, p. 57.
48 F. Thompson, *op. cit.*, pp. 175-6.
49 J. McCrindle and S. Rowbotham (eds), *Dutiful Daughters: Women Talk About Their Lives*, Harmondsworth, Allen & Lane, 1977, p. p. 217.
50 W. Foley, *A Child In The Forest*, London, Futura Publications, 1977, pp. 133-6.
51 M.L. Davies (ed.), *Maternity: Letters from Working Women Collected by the Women's Co-operative Guild*, 1915; reprinted London, Virago, 1978; M. Spring-Rice, *Working Class Wives: Their Health and Conditions*, Harmondsworth, Penguin, 1939.
52 McCrindle and Rowbotham, *op. cit.*, p. 122.
53 B.A. Clough, *A Memoir of Anne Jemima Clough*, London, Edward Arnold, 1897; Sidgwick, *op. cit.*; C.B. Firth, *Constance Louisa Maynard: Mistress of Westfield College, A Family Portrait*, London, Allen & Unwin, 1949.
54 W. Holtby, *Women and a Changing Civilization*, 1935; reprinted Chicago, Academy Press, 1978, pp. 101-2.
55 R. Hall (ed.), *Dear Dr Stopes: Sex In the 1920s*, London, Deutsch, 1978.
56 McCrindle and Rowbotham, *op. cit.*, p. 119.
57 *Ibid.*, pp. 218-19.
58 N. Mitchison, *All Change Here*, London, Bodley Head, 1975, pp. 11-12.
59 U. Bloom, *Sixty Years of Home*, London, Hurst & Blackett, 1960, pp. 96-102.
60 *Ibid.*, p. 97, and Mitchison, *op. cit.*, pp. 15-16.

61 Bloom, *op. cit.*, pp. 97-8.
62 K. Fitzpatrick, *Lady Henry Somerset*, London, Cape, 1923, p. 83.
63 S. Keppel, *Edwardian Daughter*, London, Hamilton, 1958, pp. 4, 13-17.
64 L. Davidoff, *The Best Circles: Society, Etiquette and The Season*, London, Croom Helm, 1973, pp. 51-2.
65 *Ibid.*, pp. 52-5.
66 Bloom, *op. cit.*, p. 110.
67 Chorley, *op. cit.*, p. 153.
68 *Ibid.*, pp. 151-2.
69 *A Conversation with some Home Daughters on the question 'Wherein does a Girl's Usefulness Really Lie?'* By the Author of 'What Do You Consider The Most Beautiful Thing on Earth?', Walsall, W. Henry Robinson, 1881.
70 *Ibid.*, p. 21.
71 A. Barnard, *A Girl's Book About Herself*, London, Cassell, 1912.
72 *Ibid.*, pp. 124-5.
73 Webb, *op. cit.*, p. 116.
74 S. Ellis, *Daughters of England: Their Position in Society, Character and Responsibilities*, London, Fisher, 1842.
75 Bloom, *op. cit.*, p. 116.
76 *Ibid.*
77 E. Eiloart, *The Laws Relating To Women*, London, Waterlow, 1878, pp. 39ff.
78 Clough, *op. cit.*; Webb *op. cit.*; M. McMillan, *The Life of Rachel McMillan*, London, Dent, 1927.
79 C. Hall, 'The Early Formation of Victorian Domestic Ideology', in S. Burman (ed.), *Fit Work for Women*, London, Croom Helm, 1979.
80 H. More, *Strictures on The Modern System of Female Education*, London, Bohn, 1853, p. 81 (first published 1799).
81 *Ibid.*
82 Sidgwick, *op. cit.*, p. 11.
83 More, *op. cit.*, p. 82.
84 Fitzpatrick, *op. cit.*, p. 69.
85 Firth, *op. cit.*, *passim*.
86 *Ibid.*, p. 60.
87 *Ibid.*
88 *Ibid.*, p. 53.
89 Nightingale, *op. cit.*, p. 404.
90 *Ibid.*, p. 406.
91 P. Willmott and M. Young, *Family and Kinship in East London*, London, Routledge & Kegan Paul, 1957.
92 C. Woodham-Smith, *Florence Nightingale, 1820-1910*, London,

179

The Reprint Society, 1952.
93 V. Glendinning, *A Suppressed Cry: Life and Death of a Quaker Daughter*, London, Routledge & Kegan Paul, 1969.
94 Brittain, *op. cit.*, p. 59.
95 Hughes, *A London Girl. op. cit.*, pp. 7-9.
96 *Ibid.*, p. 241.
97 M.V. Hughes, *A London Home in the 1890s*, Oxford University Press, 1978.
98 *Ibid.*, pp. 138, 144ff.
99 *Ibid.*, p. 150.
100 J. Courtney, *The Women of My Time*, London, Lovat Dickson, 1934, pp. 146-7.
101 E. Sidgwick, *op. cit.*
102 *Ibid.*, pp. 66-7.
103 *Ibid.*, p. 21.
104 B.A. Clough, *op. cit.*, pp. 22ff.
105 *Ibid.*, pp. 195ff.; pp. 232-4, 240.
106 Firth, *op. cit.*, *passim*.
107 V. Woolf, 'Professions for Women', in L. Woolf (ed.), *Collected Essays*, vol. II, London, Chatto & Windus, 1967, p. 285.
108 Holtby, *op. cit.*, pp. 104-5.
109 *Ibid.*, p. 104.
110 W. Holtby, *South Riding: An English Landscape*, London, Collins, 1936.
111 *Ibid.*, p. 144.
112 *Ibid.*, pp. 422ff.
113 V. Woolf, *To The Lighthouse*, 1927; reprinted London, Dent, 1938.

Chapter 2 Schooling, college and femininity: some experiences of middle-class girls

1 Frances Power Cobbe described the Ladies' Academy she attended in Brighton in the first volume of her Autobiography, *The Life of Frances Power Cobbe*, Boston, Houghton Mifflin, 1894. There is a description of Heathfield in the Duchess of Westminster's *Grace and Favour: Memories of Loelia, Duchess of Westminster*, London, Weidenfeld & Nicolson, 1961, pp. 70ff.
2 Report of Schools Inquiry Commission (hereafter SIC), P.P. 1867-8, vol. XXVIII, ch. VI, p. 558.
3 N. Mitchison, *All Change Here*, London, Bodley Head, 1975, pp. 11-12.
4 Loelia, Duchess of Westminster, *op. cit.*, p. 70.
5 SIC, P.P. 1867-8, vol. IX, ch. VIII, pp. 823-6.
6 *Ibid.*, p. 826.

7 K. Chorley, *Manchester Made Them*, London, Faber & Faber, 1950, p. 197.

8 V. Brittain, *Testament of Youth: An Autobiographical Study of the Years 1900-1925*, London, Gollancz, 1933, pp. 28-32.

9 SIC, P.P. 1867-8, vol. IX, ch. VIII, p. 791.

10 *Ibid.*, p. 826.

11 *Ibid.*

12 SIC, P.P. 1867-8, vol. XXVIII, ch. VI, p. 547.

13 *Ibid.*

14 *Ibid.*, p. 559.

15 SIC, P.P. 1867-8, vol. IX, ch. VIII, p. 793.

16 M.V. Hughes, *A London Child of the 1870s*, Oxford University Press, 1977, pp. 41-58.

17 *Ibid.*, pp. 58-60.

18 M. Wilkinson, unpublished MS on life of Sophie Bryant.

19 E. Shirreff and G.C.T. Bartley (eds), *Journal of Women's Education Union*, vols 1-9, 1873-81.

20 See (*inter alia*), M.J. Peterson, 'The Victorian Governess: Status Incongruence in Family and Society', in M. Vicinus (ed.), *Suffer and Be Still: Women In The Victorian Age*, Bloomington and London, Indiana University Press, 1972.

21 D. Beale, MS Autobiography quoted by E. Raikes, *Dorothea Beale of Cheltenham*, London, Constable, 1908, pp. 8-9.

22 J. Rosenberg, *Dorothy Richardson: The Genius They Forgot*, London, Duckworth, 1973, p. 7.

23 Loelia, Duchess of Westminster, *op. cit.*

24 Chorley, *op. cit.*, pp. 186-96.

25 Brittain, *op. cit.*

26 B. Webb, *My Apprenticeship*, Cambridge University Press, 1979; E. Sidgwick, *Mrs Henry Sidgwick: A Memoir*, London, Sidgwick & Jackson, 1938; N. Mitchison, *All Change Here*, London, Bodley Head, 1975.

27 SIC, P.P. 1867-8, vol. IX, ch. VIII, p. 794.

28 *Ibid.*, p. 795.

29 SIC, P.P. 1867-8, vol. XXVIII, ch. VI, p. 560.

30 SIC, P.P. 1867-8, vol. IX, ch. VIII, p. 817.

31 M.E. James, *Alice Ottley, First Headmistress of the Worcester High School for Girls, 1883-1912*, London, Longmans, 1914.

32 *Ibid.*, pp. 19ff.

33 J.B.S. Pedersen, 'The Reform of Women's Secondary and Higher Education in 19th-Century England: A Study In Elite Groups' (University of California, (Berkeley), D.Phil. thesis, 1974). See also an article by the same author, 'Schoolmistresses and Headmistresses: Elites and Education in 19th-Century England' in

Journal of British Studies, Autumn 1975.

34 Pedersen, *Reform of Women's Secondary and Higher Education* ... p. 186.

35 *Ibid.*, pp. 188-193.

36 A.M. Stoddart, *The Life and Letters of Hannah E. Pipe*, Edinburgh, Blackwood, 1908.

37 *Ibid.*, p. 253.

38 *Ibid.*, p. 237.

39 *Ibid.*, p. 236-7.

40 James, *op. cit.*, pp. 19-32.

41 *Ibid.*, p. 36.

42 *Ibid.*, p. 21.

43 *Ibid.*

44 *Ibid.*, pp. 23-4.

45 *Ibid.*, p. 25.

46 A. Zimmern, *The Renaissance of Girls' Education in England*, London, A.D. Innes, 1898, p. 167.

47 C.S. Bremner, *The Education of Girls and Women in Great Britain*, London, Swann Sonnenschein, 1897, p. 112.

48 Royal Commission on Secondary Education (Bryce Commission), P.P. 1895, vols XLIII-XLIX.

49 Bryce Commission, P.P. 1895, vol. XLVIII, p. 97.

50 *Ibid.*, pp. 94-5.

51 *Ibid.*, pp. 265-68.

52 SIC, P.P. 1867-8, vol. IX, ch. VIII, p. 826.

53 Bryce Commission, P.P. 1895, vol. XLVIII, p. 96.

54 *Ibid.*, p. 95.

55 See (*inter alia*) Loelia, Duchess of Westminster, *op. cit.*, pp. 70-1; M. Asquith, *Autobiography of Margot Asquith*, vol. I, London, Thornton Butterworth, 1920, pp. 72-7, for examples.

56 Bryce Commission, P.P. 1895, vol. XLVIII, pp. 88ff.

57 *Ibid.*, p. 95.

58 *Ibid.*

59 W. Peck, *A Little Learning, or A Victorian Childhood*, London, Faber & Faber, 1952, pp. 59ff.

60 *Ibid.*, pp. 62-3.

61 *Ibid.*, p. 69.

62 *Ibid.*, p. 75.

63 *Ibid.*, pp. 75-7.

64 Chorley, *op. cit.*, pp. 199ff.

65 *Ibid.*, p. 204.

66 *Ibid.*, p. 203.

67 *Ibid.*, p. 205.

68 Brittain, *op. cit.*, p. 39.

69 Chorley, *op. cit.*, p. 202.
70 *Ibid.*, pp. 201-2.
71 *Ibid.*, p. 201.
72 *Ibid.*, p. 202.
73 *Ibid.*, p. 203.
74 These reforms have been documented in some detail by J. Kamm, in *Hope Deferred: Girls' Education in English History*, London, Methuen, 1965. See also B. Turner, *Equality for Some*, London, Ward Lock, 1974.
75 E. Kaye, *A History of Queen's College, London, 1848-1972*, London, Chatto & Windus, 1972.
76 M. Tuke, *A History of Bedford College for Women, 1849-1937*, Oxford University Press, 1939.
77 A.K. Clarke, *A History of the Cheltenham Ladies' College, 1853-1953*, London, Faber, 1953.
78 A.E. Ridley, *Frances Mary Buss and her Work for Education*, London, Longmans, 1895. See also R.M. Scrimgeour (ed.), *The North London Collegiate School, 1850-1950*, Oxford University Press, 1950.
79 J. Kamm, *Indicative Past: 100 Years of The Girls' Public Day School Trust*, London, Allen & Unwin, 1971; L. Magnus, *The Jubilee Book of the Girls' Public Day School Trust, 1873-1923*, Cambridge University Press, 1923; E. Moberly Bell, *A History of the Church Schools Company, 1883-1958*, London, SPCK, 1958.
80 Bremner, *op. cit.*, pp. 119-21.
81 Kamm, *Hope Deferred*, pp. 219-20.
82 M.E. James, *op. cit.*
83 Zimmern noted of Cheltenham Ladies' College in the 1890s that 'it does not receive all comers, but is distinctly intended for "the daughters of gentlemen", and references in regard to social standing are required before admission.' *The Renaissance*, p. 38.
84 Pedersen, *The Reform of Women's Secondary and Higher Education*... ch. 1. S. Delamont, 'The Domestic Ideology and Women's Education' in S. Delamont and L. Duffin (eds), *The Nineteenth Century Woman: Her Cultural and Physical World*, London, Croom Helm, 1978.
85 *Ibid.*, See also the same author's 'Schoolmistresses and Headmistresses: Elites and Education in 19th-Century England' in *Journal of British Studies*, Autumn 1975; 'The Reform of Women's Secondary and Higher Education: Institutional Change and Social Values in Mid and Late Victorian England', in *History of Education Quarterly*, Spring 1979.
86 Pedersen, *The Reform of Women's Secondary and Higher Education*..., ch. 1.

87   A. Percival, *The English Miss Today and Yesterday*, London, Harrap, 1939, p. 206.

88   Pedersen, *The Reform of Women's Secondary and Higher Education . . .*, p. 125.

89   S. Delamont, 'The Contradictions in Ladies' Education', and 'The Domestic Ideology and Women's Education', in Delamont and Duffin, *op. cit.*

90   *Ibid.*, p. 184.

91   *Ibid.*, pp. 154ff.

92   Kaye, *op. cit.*, p. 73.

93   *Ibid.*, p. 88.

94   *Ibid.*, p. 39.

95   *Ibid.*, p. 59.

96   *Ibid.*, pp. 73-7. See also E. Raikes, *Dorothea Beale of Cheltenham*, London, Constable, 1908, pp. 33-5.

97   Bremner, *op. cit.*, p. 147.

98   Tuke, *op. cit.*, pp. 21-2.

99   *Ibid.*

100 *Ibid.*

101 *Ibid.*, p. 13.

102 *Ibid.*, pp. 29-31.

103 *Ibid.*

104 *Ibid.*, p. 32.

105 *Ibid.*, p. 99.

106 SIC, P.P. 1867-8, vol. XXVIII, p. 251.

107 *Ibid.*

108 *Journal of Women's Education Union*, 15 April 1876, p. 53.

109 *Ibid.*, pp. 107-9.

110 These were the Rev. H. Walford Bellairs, the Rev. W. Dobson, the Rev. H.A. Holden and Dr S.E. Comyn. (F. Cecily Steadman, *In The Days of Miss Beale*, London, Burrow, 1930, p. 6.)

111 Mary James, *Alice Ottley . . .*, pp. 42-4.

112 Pedersen, *The Reform of Women's Secondary and Higher Education . . .*, pp. 114-5.

113 E. Moberly Bell, *op. cit.*

114 Magnus, *op. cit.*, pp. 14ff.

115 J. Kamm, *Indicative Past*, p. 42.

116 *Ibid.*, pp. 204-5.

117 Magnus, *op. cit.*, p. viii.

118 Peck, *op. cit.*, pp. 170-1.

119 M.V. Hughes, *A London Home in the 1890s*, Oxford University Press, 1978, p. 22.

120 *Ibid.*

121 M. Murray, *My First Hundred Years*, London, William Kimber,

1963, pp. 159-60.

122 *Ibid.*

123 *Ibid.*, pp. 160-1.

124 *Ibid.*

125 Delamont and Duffin, *op. cit.*, p. 145.

126 A. Huth Jackson, *A Victorian Childhood*, London, Methuen, 1932, p. 146.

127 M. James, *Alice Ottley* . . . ., pp. 98-9.

128 See (*inter alia*) Peck, *op. cit.*, p. 113. Cf. also ch. 5.

129 B.A. Clough, *A Memoir of Anne Jemima Clough*, London, Edward Arnold, 1897, p. 240, Pedersen, *The Reform of Women's Secondary and Higher Education* . . . , p. 366.

130 Clough, *op. cit.*, pp. 212ff. and *passim*.

131 M.P. Marshall, *What I Remember*, Cambridge University Press, 1947, p. 11.

132 *Ibid.*

133 Peck, *op. cit.*, p. 175.

134 F. Widdowson, 'Elementary Teacher Training and the Middle-Class Girl c. 1846-1914', unpublished MA dissertation, University of Essex, 1976, p. 37.

135 *Ibid.*, p. 54.

136 E. Cholmondeley, *The Story of Charlotte Mason*, London, Dent, 1960, p. 34.

137 *Ibid.*, pp. 69-70.

138 C.B. Firth, *Constance Louisa Maynard: Mistress of Westfield College, A Family Portrait*, London, Allen & Unwin, 1949, p. 260.

139 Pedersen, 'Schoolmistresses and Headmistresses . . .'

140 M. James, *Alice Ottley* . . ., p. 26.

141 *Ibid.*, *passim*.

142 Pedersen, *The Reform of Women's Secondary and Higher Education* . . ., p. 450.

143 S.E. Burstall, *English High Schools for Girls: Their Aims, Organisation and Management*, London, Longmans, 1907, p. 196.

144 Duchess of Westminster, *Grace and Favour* . . ., pp. 74-5.

145 J. Kamm, *How Different From Us: A Biography of Miss Buss and Miss Beale*, London, Bodley Head, 1958, p. 41.

146 *Ibid.*, p. 42.

147 For recollections of Miss Buss' regime see (*inter alia*) M.V. Hughes, *A London Girl of the 1880s*, Oxford University Press, 1978, and R.M. Scrimgeour (ed.), *op. cit.*

148 Pedersen, 1975, *op. cit.*

149 Delamont and Duffin, *op. cit.*, p. 178.

150 Magnus, *op. cit.*, pp. 11-12.

151 Percival, *op. cit.*, p. 207.

185

152 Cf. (*inter alia*) Sarah Stickney Ellis, *The Daughters of England: Their Position In Society, Character and Responsibilities*, London, Fisher, 1842.

153 Clough, *op. cit.*, pp. 255-6.

154 Peck, *op. cit.*, p. 173.

155 *Ibid.*, p. 180.

156 *Ibid.*, p. 178.

157 C. Woodham-Smith, *Florence Nightingale, 1820-1910*, London, Constable, 1950.

158 *Ibid.* See also L. Strachey's essay on Florence Nightingale in *Eminent Victorians*, London, The Reprint Society, 1942.

159 C.L. Maynard, *Between College Terms*, London, Nisbet, 1910. The essay is discussed by Firth, *op. cit.*, pp. 300-2.

160 Quoted by Firth, p. 301.

161 Kamm, *How Different From Us . . .*, pp. 120-1.

162 James, *op. cit.*, pp. 32ff.

163 *Ibid.*, pp. 52-3, 97-8.

164 Although it should be pointed out that Miss Beale herself had been very disappointed by the decision taken by the Guild of the Ladies' College in 1888-9 to establish a settlement. She herself had favoured an alternative scheme whereby the Guild would build, organise and control an elementary school. Cf. Kamm, *How Different From Us . . .*, pp. 216-9.

165 F.M. Wilson, *Rebel Daughter of A Country House: The Life of Eglantyne Jebb*, London, Allen & Unwin, 1967.

166 *Ibid.*, p. 104.

167 L. Manning, *A Life for Education: An Autobiography*, London, Gollancz, 1970, pp. 42-8.

168 V. Glendinning, *A Suppressed Cry: Life and Death of a Quaker Daughter*, London, Routledge & Kegan Paul, 1969, p. 73.

169 *Ibid.*, p. 181.

170 *Ibid.*, p. 71.

171 J. Courtney, *The Women of My Time*, London, Lovat Dickson, 1934, p. 149.

172 *Ibid.*, p. 147.

173 G.M. Trevelyan, Introduction to M.P. Marshall, *op. cit.*, p. xi. See also J.M. Keynes, 'Mary Paley Marshall' in Royal Economic Society, *The Collected Writings of John Maynard Keynes*, vol. X, *Essays in Biography*, London, Macmillan, 1972, pp. 232-50.

174 Delamont and Duffin, p. 184.

Chapter 3 Good wives and little mothers: educational provision for working-class girls

1 S. Smiles, quoting a passage from a paper he had written in 1843 in *Character*, London, Murray, 1890, p. 60 (note).
2 *Ibid.*, p. 59.
3 *Ibid.*, p. 58.
4 *Ibid.*, pp. 32, 40.
5 Cf. (*inter alia*), S. Smiles, *Thrift*, London, Murray, 1886, pp. 168-9.
6 Smiles, *Character*, p. 42.
7 *Ibid.*
8 Smiles, *Thrift*, p. 169. See also *Character*, pp. 61ff.
9 Lord Shaftesbury, speaking before the Social Science Congress at Liverpool in 1859. Quoted by J. Kamm in *Hope Deferred: Girls' Education in English History*, London, Methuen, 1965, p. 162.
10 M. Arnold, *Reports on Elementary Schools 1852-1882*, London, HMSO, 1908, pp. 25-6.
11 *Ibid.*, p. 26.
12 T. McBride, ' "As The Twig is Bent", The Victorian Nanny', in A.S. Wohl (ed.), *The Victorian Family: Structure and Stresses*, London, Croom Helm, 1978, p. 53.
13 B.L. Hutchins, introduction to D.J. Collier, *The Girl in Industry*, London, Bell, 1918, pp. ix-x.
14 See for instance, a textbook written by A. Newsholme and M.E. Scott for the use of teachers in elementary schools (*Domestic Economy*, London, Swann Sonnenschein, 1894), p. 202.
15 See M. Headdon, 'Industrial Training for Girls'; Lady Leigh, 'For Lack of Knowledge'; 'R.C.', 'A Plea for Industrial Training for Girls'; F.L. Calder, 'Cookery in Elementary Schools', all in Lord Brabazon (ed.), *Some National and Board School Reforms*, London, Longmans, 1887.
16 *Ibid.*, p. 133.
17 Royal Commission on the Working of the Elementary Education Acts (Cross Commission) P.P. 1887, vol. XXX, pp. 302-4.
18 Mrs Pillow, 'Domestic Economy Teaching in England' (Education Department, *Special Reports on Educational Subjects*, vol. I, London, HMSO, 1896-7), pp. 168-9.
19 Newsholme and Scott, *Domestic Economy*, p. 202.
20 See (*inter alia*), E. Sellers, 'An Antediluvian on the Education of Working-Class Girls', in *The Nineteenth Century and After*, August 1916, pp. 337ff.
21 Ministry of Reconstruction, *Report of Women's Advisory Committee on the Domestic Service Problem*, P.P. 1919, vol. XXIX.

22 *Ibid.*, p. 8.

23 *Ibid.*, p. 11.

24 D. Gardiner, *English Girlhood at School*, Oxford University Press, 1929, p. 480.

25 C.S. Bremner, *The Education of Girls and Women In Great Britain*, London, Swann Sonnenschein, 1897, p. 220.

26 M. Smith, *The Autobiography of Mary Smith, Schoolmistress and Nonconformist, A Fragment of a Life*, London, Bemrose, 1892.

27 *Ibid.*, p. 26.

28 *Ibid.*, p. 30.

29 *Ibid.*, p. 32.

30 M. Arnold, *Reports on Elementary Schools*, p. 25.

31 M.K. Ashby, *Joseph Ashby of Tysoe, 1859-1919, A Study of English Village Life*, London, The Merlin Press, 1974, p. 17.

32 Cf. (for instance) the time spent by girls on needlework and domestic subjects in a rural school in the Fens in the early decades of the present century recalled by one of Mary Chamberlain's respondents, in her *Fenwoman: A Portrait of Women in an English Village*, London, Virago, 1975, p. 58.

33 E.M. Sneyd-Kynnersley, *HMI – Some Passages In The Life of One of HM Inspectors of Schools*, London, Macmillan, 1910, pp. 250-60 provides many examples.

34 *Ibid.*, p. 251.

35 *Ibid.*, p. 252.

36 C.E. Grant, *Farthing Bundles*, London, C.E. Grant, 1931, p. 47.

37 *Ibid.*

38 *Ibid.*, pp. 47-51.

39 Board of Education, *Suggestions for the Consideration of Teachers and Others concerned in the work of the Public Elementary Schools*; Circular 750, London, HMSO, 1909. See 'Suggestions for the Teaching of Needlework', pp. 4-6.

40 E.g. Sneyd-Kynnersley, *op. cit.*

41 E. Shirreff, in *Journal of the Women's Education Union*, 15 May 1974, pp. 72-3.

42 *Ibid.*

43 T.A. Spalding, *The Work of the London School Board, . . . presented at the Paris Exhibition, 1900*, London, King, 1900, p. 237.

44 Board of Education, Circular 750, *op. cit.*, p. 3.

45 *Ibid.*, p. 4.

46 Pillow, *op. cit.*, p. 159.

47 *Ibid.*, p. 167.

48 E. Briggs, section on Cookery in Spalding, *The Work of the London School Board*, p. 226.

49 Spalding, *op. cit.*, p. 228.

50 Pillow, *op. cit.*, p. 159.

51 Spalding, *op. cit.*, pp. 226-7.

52 This chapter includes material which has already appeared in my article, 'Good Wives and Little Mothers: Social Anxieties and the Schoolgirl's Curriculum, 1890-1920' in *Oxford Review of Education*, vol. 3, no. 1, 1977, pp. 21-35.

   See also C. Dyhouse, 'Social Darwinistic Ideas and the Development of Women's Education in England, 1880-1920', in *History of Education*, 1976, vol. 5, no. 1, pp. 41-58, and 'Working-Class Mothers and Infant Mortality in England, 1895-1914', in *Journal of Social History*, vol. 12, 1979. A. Davin, 'Imperialism and the Cult of Motherhood', *History Workshop Journal*, Spring 1978, covers similar ground.

53 For discussion of these ideas see B. Semmel, *Imperialism and Social Reform: English Social Imperialist Thought 1895-1914*, London, Allen & Unwin, 1960, esp. pp. 29-52. Also, *inter alia*, G.R. Searle, *The Quest for National Efficiency: A Study in British Politics and Political Thought, 1899-1914*, Oxford, Blackwell, 1971, (esp. chs 1, 3), and H.C.G. Matthew, *The Liberal Imperialists: The Ideas and Politics of a post- Gladstonian elite*, Oxford University Press, 1973, (esp. ch. 7).

54 See (*inter alia*) K. Pearson, 'Woman and Labour', in *Fortnightly Review*, May 1894, pp. 561-77, and 'The Woman's Question' in *The Ethic of Freethought*, London, Fisher Unwin, 1901; W.C.D. and C.D. Whetham, *Heredity and Society*, London, Longmans, 1912, and *The Family and the Nation*, London, Longmans, 1909. Also C.W. Saleeby, *Parenthood and Race Culture*, London, Cassell, 1906, *Woman and Womanhood*, London, Heinemann, 1912, and *Evolution the Master-key*, London, Harper, 1906. The way in which evolutionary thinkers perceived women's role has recently been discussed by Lorna Duffin in 'Prisoners of Progress: Women and Evolution' in S. Delamont and L. Duffin (eds), *The Nineteenth-Century Woman, Her Cultural and Physical World*, London, Croom Helm, 1978.

55 An idea discussed by (among others) Havelock Ellis, in *The Task of Social Hygiene*, London, Constable, 1912.

56 *Report of Inter-Departmental Committee on Physical Deterioration*, vol. I, P.P. 1904, vol. XXXII, pp. 1ff.

57 *Ibid.*, vol. III, Appendix and Index, P.P. 1904, XXXII, pp. 153-4.

58 *Ibid.*, vol. I, pp. 55-6.

59 *Ibid.*, vol. II, List of Witnesses and Evidence, P.P. 1904, XXXII, paras, 1165-9.

60 *Ibid.*, vol. I, para. 293.

61   *Ibid.*, vol. I, para, 230.

62   Board of Education, *Special Reports on Educational Subjects*, 'School Training for the Home Duties of Women', (Part I) 'The Teaching of Domestic Science in The United States of America (P.P. 1905, XXVI, pp. 783ff.) (Part II) 'Belgium, Sweden, Norway, Denmark, Switzerland and France', (P.P. 1906, XXVIII, pp. 437ff.) (Part III) 'The Domestic Training of Girls in Germany and Austria' (P.P. 1908, XXVII, pp. 1ff.)

63   Cf. (for instance) A. Ravenhill, 'Eugenic Ideals for Motherhood', in *Eugenics Review*, I, 1909-10, pp. 265ff.

64   Board of Education, *Suggestions for The Consideration of Teachers and Others Concerned in the Work of the Public Elementary Schools* (P.P. 1905, LX, pp. 151ff. and esp. p. 78).

65   Board of Education, *Special Report on The Teaching of Cookery to Public Elementary School Children in England and Wales*, by the Chief Woman Inspector of the Board, London, HMSO, 1907.

66   *Ibid.*, p. 3.

67   *Ibid.*, pp. xi and xv.

68   *Ibid.*, pp. xi-xiv.

69   Board of Education, *Suggestions for the Consideration of Teachers*, P.P. 1905, LX, pp. 78-9.

70   G.F. McCleary, *The Maternity and Child Welfare Movement*, London, King, 1935, p. 5.

71   *Supplement to 65th Annual Report of the Registrar General* (P.P. 1905, XVIII, p. cv).

72   See, for instance, G. Newman, *Infant Mortality: A Social Problem*, London, Methuen, 1906, pp. v-vi.

73   *Ibid.*, pp. 257, 221.

74   M. Hewitt, *Wives and Mothers In Victorian Industry*, London, Rockliff 1958; see esp. ch. VIII, 'The Sacrifice of Infants'.

75   *Report of Physical Deterioration Committee*, vol. I, P.P. 1904, XXXII, paras 241, 260.

76   Home Office Correspondence, in Public Record Office. (P.R.O./ H.O. 45 10 335/138532.) See also Circular dated 10 May 1907, (P.R.O./HO 158/13, No 126388/9).

77   Cf. reference in Ministry of Reconstruction, *Report of Women's Employment Committee*, P.P. 1919, XIV, p. 52.

78   City of Birmingham Health Department, *Report on Industrial Employment of Married Women and Infantile Mortality*, Birmingham, 1910. (Birmingham Reference Library.)

79   'The Industrial Employment of Married Women and Infantile Mortality' in *Public Health*, vol. XXIII, April 1910.

80   *39th Annual Report of Local Government Board, 1909-10,*

Supplement to Report of Board's Medical Officer, Containing a Report on Infant and Child Mortality, (P.P. 1910 vol. XXXIX); *42nd Annual Report of Local Government Board, Supplement Containing a Second Report on Infant and Child Mortality*, (P.P. 1913, vol. XXXII); and *43rd Annual Report of Local Government Board, Containing a Third Report on Infant Mortality Dealing with Infant Mortality In Lancashire*, (P.P. 1914, vol. XXXIX).

81 Newsholme, *Third Report on Infant Mortality*, (P.P. 1914 vol. XXXIX, p. 19).

82 Board of Education Circular 940, *Education and Infant Welfare*, London, HMSO, 1916. (Reprint from Report of Chief Medical Officer of Board of Education, 1914, with additional appendix.)

83 Parliamentary Bills, 1910, no. 262. *Elementary Schools/ Instruction in Hygiene* (19 July 1910) (P.B. 1910, vol. 1, p. 627).

84 C. Addison, *Politics from Within, 1911-18*, vol. I, London, Jenkins 1924, pp. 18-19.

85 Board of Education Circular 758, *Memorandum on the Teaching of Infant Care and Management In Public Elementary Schools* (London, HMSO, 1910). Quotations from prefatory note by R. Morant, p. 1.

86 Board of Education Circular 758, *op. cit.*

87 Dyhouse, 'Working Class Mothers and Infant Mortality', pp. 258-9.

88 M.W. Beaver, 'Population, Infant Mortality and Milk', in *Population Studies*, no. 27, 1973.

89 Newsholme, *Report on Infant and Child Mortality* (P.P. 1910 XXXIV, pp. 70-4).

90 F.J.H. Coutts, *Report to Local Government Board on an Inquiry as to Condensed Milks, with Special Reference to their Use as Infants' Foods*, London, HMSO, 1911, pp. 3-7.
   See also Dyhouse, 'Working Class Mothers and Infant Mortality', pp. 255-7.

91 F.J.H. Coutts, *Report Upon an Inquiry as to Dried Milks, With Special Reference to Their Use in Infant Feeding*, Report to Local Government Board on Public Health and Medical Subjects, New Series, no. 116, London, HMSO, 1918, pp. 58ff.

92 *Ibid.*

93 Dyhouse, 'Working Class Mothers and Infant Mortality'.

94 E. Roberts, 'Learning and Living – Socialisation Outside School', in *Oral History*, vol. 3, no. 2, Autumn 1975.

95 R. Johnson, 'Educational Policy and Social Control in early Victorian England' in *Past and Present*, no. 49, 1970, pp. 96ff.

96 M.L. Davies (ed.), *Life As We Have Known It*, by Co-operative Working Women, London, Virago, 1977, p. 4.

97 A. Davin 'Board School Girls' (a paper read to the Feminist History Group in London, June 1974).

98 G.C.T. Bartley, 'Elementary Education' in *Journal of Women's Education Union*, 15 July 1875, p. 98.

99 *Report of Physical Deterioration Committee*, vol. II, List of Witnesses and Evidence, P.P. 1904 XXXII, paras. 2742-5.

100 *Ibid.*, para. 729.

101 *Ibid.*, vol. I, para. 315.

102 Whethams, *Heredity and Society*. See esp. chapters on 'The Position of Women' and 'The Problem of Education'.

103 *Ibid.*, pp. 120-1.

104 *Girls At Home: A Domestic Economy Reader for Use in Schools*, (London, Nelson Royal School Series, 1895).

105 *Life As We Have Known It* . . . p. 20.

106 B.L. Hutchins, introduction to D.J. Collier, *op. cit.*, pp. ix-x.

107 L.H. Montagu, 'The Girl in The Background', in E.J. Urwick (ed.), *Studies of Boy Life in Our Cities*, London, Dent, 1904, p. 246.

108 *Ibid.* See also J. Shelley, 'From Home Life to Industrial Life: with special reference to the Adolescent Girl', in J.J. Findlay (ed.), *The Young Wage Earner*, London, Sidgwick & Jackson, 1918.

109 M. Stanley, *Clubs for Working Girls*, London, Macmillan, 1890, pp. 4-5.

110 Montagu in Urwick, *op. cit.*, p. 251ff.

111 *Ibid.*, p. 251.

112 Cf. (for instance), Shelley, in Findlay, *The Young Wage Earner*.

113 Miss Nunneley, 'Snowdrop Bands', in *Women Workers* (Papers Read at a Conference convened by the Birmingham Ladies' Union of Workers Among Women and Girls in November 1890) Birmingham, 1890, p. 28.

114 Montagu in Urwick, *op. cit.*, p. 238.

115 E. Matthias, 'The Young Factory Girl', in Findlay, *The Young Wage Earner*, *op. cit.*, p. 87.

116 *Report of Physical Deterioration Committee*, vol. I, P.P. 1904, XXXII, p. 55.

117 M. Heath-Stubbs, *Friendship's Highway, Being The History of the Girls' Friendly Society, 1875-1925*, London, GFS, 1926.

118 *Ibid.*, see also B. Harrison, 'For Church, Queen and Family: The Girls' Friendly Society 1874-1920' in *Past and Present*, November 1973, pp. 107-38.

119 Harrison, pp. 116-20.

120 *Ibid.*, p. 117.

121 Heath-Stubbs, pp. 36-7.

122 *Ibid.*, p. 38.
123 *Ibid.*, pp. 40-1.
124 Harrison, p. 118.
125 Nunneley, 'Snowdrop Bands', p. 23.
126 *Ibid.*, pp. 23-4. See also Miss Nunneley's contribution to *The Nation's Morals*: Proceedings of the Public Morals Conference Held in London, July 1910. (London 1910) pp. 98ff.
127 R. Kerr, *Story of the Girl Guides 1908-1938*, London, Girl Guides Association, 1976, p. 13. See also Olave Baden-Powell, *Window on My Heart: the Autobiography of Olave, Lady Baden-Powell, as told to Mary Drewery*, London, Hodder & Stoughton, 1973.
128 Quoted in Kerr, *op. cit.*, pp. 25-6.
129 *Ibid.*
130 *Ibid.*, p. 30.
131 E. Wade, *The World Chief Guide, Olave, Lady Baden-Powell*, London, Hutchinson, 1957, p. 68.
132 *Home Notes*, 25 August 1910.
133 *Home Notes*, 8 December 1910.
134 *Window on My Heart*, pp. 108ff.
135 R. Baden Powell, *Girl Guiding* (official handbook) 1918, p. 178.
136 *Home Notes*, 11 August 1910.
137 J. Shelley, 'From Home Life to Industrial Life, with special Reference to the Adolescent Girl', in Findlay, *op. cit.*
138 Lady Baden-Powell, 'How I Became A Commissioner' in *Training Girls As Guides: Hints to Commissioners and all who Are Interested in the Welfare and Training of Girls*, London, Pearson, 1917, pp. 13ff.
139 *Ibid.*, pp. 15-19.
140 *Ibid.*, pp. 23-5.

Chapter 4 Adolescent girlhood: autonomy versus dependence

1 Cf. (*inter alia*) J. and V. Demos, 'Adolescence in Historical Perspective', in *Journal of Marriage and the Family*, no. 31, 1969, pp. 632-8; J. Kett, 'Adolescence and Youth in 19th Century America', in *Journal of Interdisciplinary History*, no. 2, 1971, pp. 283-99.
2 G. Stanley Hall, *Adolescence: Its Psychology and the Relation to Physiology, Anthropology, Sociology, Sex, Crime, Religion and Education*, New York, Appleton, 1904.
3 It is not possible to give a comprehensive bibliography here. Some examples of the various kinds of approach can be found in W.F. Lestrange, *Wasted Lives*, London, Routledge, 1936;

A.E. Morgan, *The Needs of Youth*, London, King George's Jubilee Trust, 1939; The Carnegie United Kingdom Trust's Survey, *Disinherited Youth*, Dunfermline, 1943; G.W. Jordan and E.M. Fisher, *Self-Portrait of Youth, or the Urban Adolescent*, London, Heinemann, 1955; T. Ferguson and J. Cunnison, *The Young Wage Earner: A Study of Glasgow Boys*, London, Nuffield Foundation/ Oxford University Press, 1951; Staff and Students of Westhill Training College, *Eighty Thousand Adolescents: A Study of Young People in the City of Birmingham*, described by B. Reed, London, Allen & Unwin, 1950. See also P. Jephcott's studies, *Girls Growing Up*, London, Faber, 1942; *Rising Twenty*, London, Faber, 1948; *Some Young People*, London, Allen & Unwin, 1954. There is a useful bibliography relating to works on youth culture in S. Hall and T. Jefferson (eds), *Resistance Through Rituals: Youth Subcultures in Post-War Britain*, London, Hutchinson, 1976.

4   P. Ariès, *Centuries of Childhood*, Paris, Libraire Plon, 1960. English version, London, Jonathan Cape, 1962.

5   I. Pinchbeck and M. Hewitt, *Children In English Society*, London, Routledge & Kegan Paul, vol. I, *From Tudor Times to the Eighteenth Century*, (1969), vol. II, *From the Eighteenth Century to the Children's Act of 1848* (1973).

6   J. Gillis, *Youth and History: Tradition and Change in European Age Relations 1770 to the present*, New York and London, Academy Press, 1974; J. Springhall, *Youth, Empire and Society: British Youth Movements 1883-1940*, London, Croom Helm, 1977; J. Kett, *Rites of Passage: Adolescence in America 1790 to the present*, New York, Basic Books, 1977.

7   A. McRobbie and J. Garber, 'Girls and Subcultures: and exploration', in Hall and Jefferson, *Resistance Through Rituals*, pp.209-22.

8   T.R. Fyvel, *The Insecure Offenders*, London, Chatto & Windus, 1963. Cited by McRobbie and Garber, *op. cit.*, p. 209.

9   L.H. Montagu, 'The Girl in The Background' in E.J. Urwick (ed.), *Studies of Boy Life in Our Cities*, London, Dent, 1904, p. 246 and *passim*.

10   L. Hollingworth, *The Psychology of the Adolescent*, London, King, 1930, p. 244.

11   Hall, *Adolescence*, p. 624.

12   Cf. Doris Lessing, *The Summer Before the Dark*, London, Cape, 1973; P. Mortimer, *The Pumpkin Eater*, London, Hutchinson, 1962.

13   Gillis, *op. cit.*, pp. 105ff. and *passim*.

14   *Ibid.*, pp. 141ff.

15   Cf. ch. 2, *supra*.

16 See J.N. Burstyn, 'Education and Sex: the Medical Case against Higher Education for Women in England 1870-1900', in *Proceedings of The American Philosophical Society*, 117, April 1974, pp. 79-89, and 'Religious Arguments Against Higher Education for Women in England, 1840-1890' in *Women's Studies*, 1(1) 1972, pp. 111-31.

See also C. Dyhouse, 'Towards a "Feminine" Curriculum for English Schoolgirls: the Demands of Ideology, 1870-1963' in *Women's Studies International Quarterly*, vol. I, no. 4, 1978, pp. 297-311.

17 Burstyn, 'Religious Arguments'.

18 Burstyn, 'Education and Sex'.

19 C. Dyhouse, 'Social Darwinistic Ideas and the Development of Women's Education in England, 1880-1920' in *History of Education*, 1976, vol. 5, no. 1, pp. 41-58.

20 Quoted in J. Stacey, S. Béreaud and J. Daniels (eds), *And Jill Came Tumbling After: Sexism in American Education*, New York, Dell, 1974, p. 277.

21 G.S. Hall, 'The Budding Girl' in *Educational Problems*, New York, Appleton, 1911, p. 16.

22 G.S. Hall, *Youth: Its Regimen and Hygiene*, New York, Appleton, 1906, p. 293.

23 E.g. 'I keenly envy my Catholic friends their Maryolatory. . . . The glorified Madonna ideal shows us how much more whole and holy it is to be a woman than to be artist, orator, professor or expert', *Adolescence*, p. 646.

24 Hall, *Educational Problems*, vol. II, p.1.

25 *Ibid.*, p. 2-11.

26 *Ibid.*, pp. 11-15.

27 Burstyn, 'Education and Sex', p. 85. See also Hall, 'Adolescent Girls and Their Education' in *Adolescence*, ch. XVII, pp. 561-647.

28 Hall, *Educational Problems*, vol. II, p. 33.

29 *Ibid.*, p. 34.

30 *Ibid.*, p. 16.

31 Hall, *Youth: Its Regimen and Hygiene*, pp. 284-95.

32 *Ibid.*, pp. 299-301, 304-5.

33 *Ibid.*, p. 303.

34 *Ibid.*, p. 306.

35 *Ibid.*, p. 309.

36 *Ibid.*, p. 314.

37 *Ibid.*, p. 316.

38 *Ibid.*, p. 319.

39 *Ibid.*, pp. 303-4.

40 Cf. Truby King's contribution to discussion following Dr Caroline

Hedger's paper, 'The Relation of the Education of the Girl to Infant Mortality', in *Report on the Proceedings of the First English Speaking Conference on Infant Mortality, held in August 1913*. (Westminster, 1914.)

41 Hall, *Youth: Its Regimen and Hygiene*, pp. 320-1.

42 *Ibid.*, p. 298.

43 D. Ross, *G. Stanley Hall, The Psychologist As Prophet*, University of Chicago Press, 1972.

44 *Ibid.*, p. 9.

45 *Ibid.*, pp. 97-8.

46 *Ibid.*, pp. 261-2. See also A.H. Drummond, *The Ascent of Man*, London, Hodder & Stoughton, 1904, esp. ch. VIII 'The Evolution of a Mother'.

47 Ross, *The Psychologist As Prophet*, p. 339.

48 C. Christ, 'Victorian Masculinity and The Angel in the House', in M. Vicinus (ed.), *A Widening Sphere: Changing Roles of Victorian Women*, Bloomington and London, Indiana University Press, 1977.

49 Cf. Ross, *op. cit.*, p. 266 and *passim*.

50 *Ibid.*, pp. 287ff.

51 See Address in vol. I of *Child Study: The Journal of the Child Study Society*, London, Edward Arnold, 1908.

52 M.E. Findlay, 'The Education of Girls' in *The Paidologist*, vol. VII, 1905-7, pp. 83-93.

53 M. Scharlieb, 'Recreational Activities of Girls During Adolescence' in *Child Study*, vol. 4, 1911; 'Adolescent girls from the viewpoint of the physician', *Child Study*, vol. 4, 1911, and vol. 5, 1912.

54 Scharlieb, 'Recreational Activities of Girls During Adolescence', *Child Study*, vol. 4, 1911, p. 9.

55 T.S. Clouston, *Female Education from A Medical Point of View*, Edinburgh, Macniven & Wallace, 1882.

56 T.S. Clouston, 'Adolescence' in *Child Study*, vol. 5, 1912, and 'Psychological Dangers to Women in Modern Social Developments', in *The Position of Women, Actual and Ideal. A Series of Papers Delivered in Edinburgh, 1911, with A Preface by Sir Oliver Lodge*, London, Nisbet, 1911.

57 Sir James Crichton Browne, 'Sex in Education', in *Educational Review*, 1892, pp. 164ff. See also Clouston's reference to Crichton Browne's views in his 'Psychological Dangers to Women', p. 108.

58 J.W. Slaughter, *The Adolescent*, London, G. Allen, 1911.

59 *Ibid.*, p. 95.

60 P. Blanchard, *The Care of the Adolescent Girl*, London, Kegan Paul, 1921.

61 *Ibid.*, preface by G.S. Hall.
62 *Ibid.*, p. 67.
63 *Ibid.*, p. 47.
64 *Ibid.*, p. 84.
65 E. Saywell, *The Growing Girl*, London, Methuen, 1922.
66 *Ibid.*, pp. 26-8.
67 *Ibid.*, p. 29.
68 Scharlieb, 'Adolescent girls from the viewpoint of the physician'; A.B. Barnard, *The Girl's Book About Herself*, London, Cassell, 1912.
69 Barnard, *op. cit.*, pp. 1-2.
70 *Ibid.*, pp. 21-2.
71 Board of Education, *Report of Consultative Committee on the Differentiation of the Curriculum for Boys and Girls Respectively in Secondary Schools*, London, HMSO, 1923.
72 *Ibid.*, pp. xiii-xiv.
73 *Ibid.*, p. 82.
74 *Ibid.*, p. 86.
75 *Ibid.*, p. 84.
76 *Ibid.*, p. 85.
77 *Ibid.*, p. 119.
78 J.M. Campbell, 'The Effect of Adolescence on the Brain of the Girl', a paper presented to the AUWT meeting in London, 23 May 1908, pp. 5-6.
79 Board of Education Consultative Committee *Report on Differentiation of Curriculum for Boys and Girls*, pp. 138ff.
80 *Ibid.*
81 P. Atkinson, 'Fitness, Feminism and Schooling', in S. Delamont and L. Duffin (eds), *The Nineteenth Century Woman, her Cultural and Physical World*, London, Croom Helm, 1978.
82 *Ibid.*, pp. 107-17.
83 C. Chisholme, *The Medical Inspection of Girls in Secondary Schools*, London, Longmans, 1914.
84 *Ibid.*, pp. 8-9.
85 *Ibid.*, p. 104.
86 A. Burn, 'The Hygiene of the Adolescent Girl' in T.N. Kelynack (ed.), *Youth*, London, Charles Kelly, 1918.
87 A.B. Robertson, 'Children, Teachers and Society: The Over-Pressure Controversy, 1880-6', *British Journal of Educational Studies*, XX, 1972, pp. 315-23.
88 A point made by E. Garrett Anderson in her 'Sex in Mind and Education: A Reply' (to Dr Maudsley) in *Fortnightly Review*, vol. 15, 1874, p. 585.
89 D.J. Collier, *The Girl in Industry*, London, Bell, 1918.

90 E. Sloan Chesser, *From Girlhood to Womanhood*, London, Cassell, 1913; *Physiology and Hygiene for Girls' Schools and Colleges*, London, Bell, 1914; *Woman, Marriage and Motherhood*, London, Cassell, 1913; *Vitality: A Book on the Health of Women and Children*, London, Methuen, 1935.

91 Sloan Chesser, *Physiology and Hygiene for Girls' Schools and Colleges*, p. 79.

92 Sloan Chesser, *Vitality*, p. 3.

93 M. Humphreys, *Personal Hygiene for Girls*, London, Cassell, 1913, p. 54.

94 *Ibid.*, p. 6.

95 See (*inter alia*) Olave, Lady Baden-Powell, *Training Girls as Guides: Hints for Commissioners and all Who Are Interested in the Welfare and Training of Girls*, London, Pearson, 1917.

Chapter 5 Feminist perspectives and responses

1 E. Shirreff, *Intellectual Education and its Influence on the Character and Happiness of Women*, London, 1858, p. 320.

2 Sir A. Grant, *Happiness and Utility As Promoted by the Higher Education of Women . . . A Paper read before the Sixth Session of the Edinburgh Ladies' Educational Association*, 5 November 1872, Edinburgh, 1873, p. 9.

3 *Poems of Alfred Lord Tennyson*, Selected with an Introduction by Stephen Gwynn, London, Oxford University Press, 1972, p. 189.

4 Cf. P. Thomson, *The Victorian Heroine; A Changing Ideal 1837-1873*, London, Oxford University Press, 1956, p. 60.

5 S. Delamont, 'The Contradictions in Ladies' Education', in S. Delamont and L. Duffin (eds), *The Nineteenth Century Woman: Her Cultural and Physical World*, London, Croom Helm, 1978, p. 154. See also ch. 2, *supra*.

6 I. Tod, *On the Education of Girls of the Middle Classes*, London, Ridgeway, 1874, p. 16.

7 S. Jex-Blake, *A Visit to Some American Schools and Colleges*, London, Macmillan, 1867, p. 240.

8 S.A. Burstall, *English High Schools for Girls: Their Aims, Organisation and Management*, London, Longmans, 1907, pp. 12ff, and ch. XIII.

9 J. Newsom, *The Education of Girls*, London, Faber & Faber, 1948.

10 S. Delamont, 'The Domestic Ideology and Women's Education' in Delamont and Duffin (eds), *op. cit.*, p. 177; A.S. Kraditor, *Up From the Pedestal*, New York, Quadrangle, 1968, p. 8.

11 Kraditor, *ibid.*

12 Burstall, *op. cit.*, p. 110.
13 *Ibid.*, p. 111.
14 J. Kamm, *How Different From Us: A Biography of Miss Buss and Miss Beale*, London, Bodley Head, 1958, p. 67.
15 R. Strachey, *The Cause: A Short History of the Women's Movement in Great Britain*, Bath, Cedric Chivers, 1974, pp. 89-99.
16 M. Grey, *On the Special Requirements for Improving the Education of Girls*, Paper read before Social Science Congress, Oct. 1871, London, Ridgeway, 1872, pp. 25-6.
17 A.E. Ridley, *Frances Mary Buss*, London, Longmans, 1895, p. 79. Quoted by J.S. Pedersen, 'The Reform of Women's Secondary and Higher Education in 19th Century England: A Study in Elite Groups', unpublished doctoral thesis, Berkeley, California, 1974, p. 557.
18 M. Grey, *On the Special Requirements . . .* , p. 26.
19 *Ibid.*, See also M. Grey, *Last Words to Girls on Life in School and After School*, London, Rivingtons, 1889, pp. 239-40. Cited by Pedersen, *op. cit.*, p. 557.
20 R. Strachey, *Millicent Garrett Fawcett*, London, J. Murray, 1931, p. 57, quoted by E. Reiss, *The Rights and Duties of Englishwomen: a Study in Law and Public Opinion*, Manchester, Sherraff & Hughes, 1934, p. 255.
21 F. Engels, *Der Ursprung der Familie, des Privateigenthums und des Staats*, Hottingen-Zürich, 1884. (A translation by Ernest Utermann was published by Kerr, Chicago, in 1902.) F.A. Bebel's *Die Frau in der Vergangenheit, Gegenwart und Zukunft*, Zurich, 1884, was translated into English by Dr Harriet B. Adams Walther and published in London by The Modern Press, 1885. Both works were brought to the wider attention of the English public by Eleanor Marx and Edward Aveling in their article 'The Woman Question from a Socialist Point of View' in *Westminster Review*, vol. VI, no. 25, 1885, pp. 207-22.
22 Cf. S. Rowbotham, *Hidden From History: 300 Years of Women's Oppression and the Fight Against It*, London, Pluto Press, 1973, pp. 94ff.
23 Fabian Women's Group, *A Summary of Six Papers and Discussions upon the Disabilities of Women as Workers* (private circulation) 1909, and *Summary of Eight Papers and Discussions upon the Disabilities of Mothers as Workers* (private circulation) 1910.
24 E. Vaughan-Sawyer, 'The Physical Disabilities of Maternity' in Fabian Women's Group, *op. cit.* (1910), pp. 8-10.
25 B.L. Hutchins, 'Motherhood and Work', in Fabian Women's Group, *op. cit.* (1910), pp. 22-4.
26 Mrs Stanbury, 'The Effect upon Little Children of the Mother

Undertaking Work Outside the Home', in Fabian Women's Group, *op. cit.* (1910), p. 19.

27 Fabian Women's Group, *op. cit.* (1910), pp. 21-2.

28 *Ibid.*, p. 18.

29 *Ibid.*, p. 30.

30 O. Schreiner, *Woman and Labour*, London, Fisher Unwin, 1911; (reprinted London, Virago, 1978); B.L. Hutchins, *Conflicting Ideals of Woman's Work*, London, Murby, 1915; Clementina Black (ed.), *Married Women's Work: Being the Report of an Enquiry Undertaken by the Women's Industrial Council*, London, Bell, 1915; *A New Way of Housekeeping*, London, Collins, 1918.

31 Schreiner, *Woman and Labour*, p. 65.

32 Hutchins, *Conflicting Ideals*, p. 71.

33 *Ibid.*, pp. 77ff.

34 *Ibid.*, p. 41.

35 Black, *Married Women's Work*, pp. 1-14.

36 *Ibid.*, p. 7.

37 *Ibid.*, p. 14.

38 Black, *op. cit.*

39 J. Conway, 'Stereotypes of Femininity in a Theory of Sexual Evolution', in M. Vicinus (ed.), *Suffer and Be Still: Women in the Victorian Age*, Bloomington and London, Indiana University Press, 1972; L. Duffin, 'Prisoners of Progress: Women and Evolution', in Delamont and Duffin, *op. cit.* See also the very useful article by F. Alaya, 'Victorian Science and the "Genius" of Woman', in *Journal of the History of Ideas*, vol. XXXVIII, 1977.

40 H. Spencer, *Principles of Sociology*, London, Williams and Norgate, 1876, vol. I. See esp. Part III, 'Domestic Relations'.

41 *Ibid.*, p. 792.

42 Cf. Duffin, *op. cit.*, pp. 61-2.

43 P. Geddes and J.A. Thomson, *The Evolution of Sex*, Contemporary Science Series, London, Walter Scott, 1889.

44 C. Dyhouse, 'Social Darwinistic Ideas and the Development of Women's Education in England, 1880-1920', in *History of Education*, vol. 5, no. 1, 1976, pp. 41-50; A. Davin, 'Imperialism and Motherhood', in *History Workshop Journal*, no. 5, Spring 1978, pp. 9-65; for more specific references see ch. 3, *supra*, n. 54.

45 Sir T.S. Clouston, 'Psychological Dangers to Women in Modern Social Developments', in *The Position of Women, Actual and Ideal. A Series of Papers Delivered in Edinburgh, 1911, with a preface by Sir Oliver Lodge*, London, Nisbet, 1911, pp. 108-11.

46 H. Spencer, *Principles of Biology*, London, Williams & Norgate, 1867, vol. II, pp. 485-6. See also Dyhouse, 'Social Darwinistic

Ideas', pp. 43-6; J.N. Burstyn, 'Education and Sex: the Medical Case Against Higher Education for Women in England, 1870-1900', in *Proceedings of the American Philosophical Society*, 117, April 1974, pp. 79-89.

47 H. Maudsley, 'Sex In Mind and Education', in *Fortnightly Review*, vol. XV, pp. 466-83.

48 J. Thorburn, 'Female Education from a Physiological Point of View', Manchester, 1884, and *A Practical Treatise on the Diseases of Women*, London, Griffin, 1885, pp. 99-103; W. Withers Moore, Presidential Address before the Annual Meeting of the British Medical Association, Brighton, 1886, reported in the *British Medical Journal*, 1886, pp. 338-9 and the *Lancet*, 1886, pp. 314-15. See also J.N. Burstyn, 'Education and Sex'.

49 Thorburn, 'Female Education'.

50 M. Tylecote, *The Education of Women at Manchester University, 1883-1933*, Publications of the University of Manchester, no. 277, 1941, p. 31.

51 Thorburn, 'Female Education', pp. 8-9.

52 Lord Hatherley, speech delivered at opening of Leeds High School for Girls, 1876, quoted in *Journal of Women's Education Union*, 15 April 1876, p. 142.

53 Cf. P. Atkinson, 'Fitness, Feminism and Schooling' in Delamont and Duffin (eds), *op. cit.*

54 Maudsley, *op. cit.*; Strachey, *The Cause*, p. 251; Atkinson, *op. cit.*, pp. 103-7.

55 E. Garrett Anderson, 'Sex In Mind And Education: A Reply' in *Fortnightly Review*, no. 15, 1874, pp. 582-94.

56 *Ibid.*, p. 585.

57 *Ibid.*

58 *Ibid.*, p. 594.

59 *Ibid.*, pp. 588-9.

60 *Ibid.*, p. 589.

61 Cited in E. Pfeiffer, *Women and Work: An Essay*, London, Trübner, 1888, p. 106.

62 Mrs H. Sidgwick, *Health Statistics of Women Students of Cambridge and Oxford and of Their Sisters*, Cambridge University Press, 1890.

63 Pfeiffer, *op. cit.*

64 *Ibid.*, esp. pp. 95-108.

65 Sidgwick, *op. cit.*, pp. 71-91.

66 *Ibid.*, p. 66.

67 Pfeiffer, p. 81.

68 *Ibid.*, pp. 146-7.

69 Grant Allen, 'Plain Words on The Woman Question' in *Fortnightly*

Review, no. 46, 1889, pp. 448-58; W.C.D. and C.D. Whetham, 'The Present Position of Women', in *Heredity and Society*, London, Longmans, 1912; J.L. Tayler, *Aspects of Social Evolution*, London, Smith Elder, 1904; *The Nature of Woman*, London, Fifield, 1912.

70 Sidgwick, *op. cit.*, pp. 57-66.

71 *Ibid*.

72 B.L. Hutchins, 'Higher Education and Marriage' in *The Englishwoman*, vol. XVII, 1913, pp. 257-64.

73 *Ibid.*, p. 262.

74 A. Gordon, 'The After-Careers of University Educated Women' in *The Nineteenth Century*, XXXVII, June 1895, pp. 955-60.

75 V. Brittain, *Testament of Youth: An Autobiographical Study of the Years 1900-1925*, London, Gollancz, 1933, p. 73.

76 K. Chorley, *Manchester Made Them*, London, Faber & Faber, 1950, p. 248.

77 R. First and A. Scott, *Olive Schreiner*, London, Deutsch, 1980.

78 R. Lehmann, *Dusty Answer*, London, Chatto & Windus, 1927, and Clemence Dane (Winifred Ashton) *Regiment of Women*, London, Heinemann, 1917.

79 Schreiner, *op. cit.*; C. Burt and R. Moore, 'The Mental Differences Between the Sexes', *Journal of Experimental Pedagogy*, vol. I, no. 5, December 1912, p. 359.

80 E. Shirreff, *The Work of the National Union*, London, Ridgway, 1872, p. 18.

81 See, for instance, S.A. Burstall, *op. cit.*, p. 196.

82 See ch. 3, *supra*.

83 J. Milburn, 'The Secondary Schoolmistress: A Study of her Professional Views and Their Social Significance In The Educational Developments of the Period 1895-1914', unpublished doctoral thesis, University of London 1969, esp. ch. 9.

84 Burstall, *op. cit.*, p. 197.

85 Margaret Gilliland, 'Home Arts', in S.A. Burstall and M.A. Douglas (eds), *Public Schools for Girls; A Series of Papers on Their History, Aims, and Schemes of Study*, London, Association of Headmistresses, 1911, p. 154.

86 *Ibid.*, p. 155.

87 *Ibid.*, see also Burstall, *English High Schools for Girls*, esp. ch. XIII, and A. Ravenhill 'Eugenic Ideals for Motherhood' in *Eugenics Review*, vol. 1, 1909-10, and 'The Education of Girls and Women in the Functions and Duties of Motherhood', in *Report of Proceedings of Second National Conference on Infantile Mortality held in Caxton Hall, Westminster, 23-25 March 1908*, Westminster, 1908.

88 Burstall, *English High Schools for Girls*, pp. 12-13.
89 *Ibid.*, p. 198.
90 *Ibid.*, pp. 106-11.
91 A.S. Paul, *Some Memories of Mrs Woodhouse, Sheffield High School 1878-1898, Clapham High School 1898-1912*, London, Silas Birch, 1924, pp. 20-1.
92 Burstall, *English High Schools for Girls*, p. 199.
93 J. Kamm, *Indicative Past: A Hundred Years of the Girls' Public Day School Trust*, London, Allen & Unwin, 1971, pp. 144-6.
94 Gilliland, *op. cit.*, p. 154.
95 Prof. A. Smithells, 'School Training for the Home Duties of Women', *Report of Meeting of British Association for Advancement of Science held in York, 1906*, pp. 781-4.
96 Board of Education, *Annual Report 1904-5*, P.P. 1906, XXVIII, pp. 27-8.
97 Board of Education, *Regulations for Secondary Schools*, P.P. 1908, LXXXII, p. 215.
98 Board of Education, *Regulations for Secondary Schools*, P.P. 1909, LXVII, p. 495.
99 Correspondence in the Public Record Office indicates that the appointment of these two Committees with overlapping terms of reference appears to have been the result of oversight at the Board of Education; and the cause of some embarrassment to Sir Robert Morant. Morant tried to cover the mistake by telling Acland that an Interim Report had been necessary before the Consultative Committee had had time to complete its investigation because of matters of administrative urgency and also because the Board had been 'literally bombarded' with inquiries about housecraft teaching in the secondary schools. (Cf. Correspondence in P.R.O. E.D. 24/386.)
100 Board of Education, *Report of Consultative Committee on Practical Work in Secondary Schools* (1913), pp. 46-7, 50-1.
101 I. Freund, 'Domestic Science — A Protest' in *The Englishwoman*, vol. X, 1911, pp. 147-63, 279-96.
102 Board of Education, *Report of Consultative Committee on Practical Work in Secondary Schools*, pp. 312-16.
103 *Ibid.*, pp. 42-52.
104 Cf. A. Ravenhill's Report for the Board of Education on 'The Teaching of Domestic Science in the United States of America', Board of Education, *Special Reports on Educational Subjects*, vol. 15, 1905-8; also the same author's 'Hygiene and Household Economics', in Spenser Wilkinson (ed.), *The Nation's Need: Chapters on Education*, Westminster, Constable, 1903; S.A. Burstall, 'Home Economics', in *Impressions of American Education*

in 1908, London, Longmans, 1909.

105 H. Oakeley (Warden of King's College for Women), evidence submitted to Board of Education's Consultative Committee on Practical Work in Secondary Schools, see *Report, op. cit.,* pp. 329ff.

106 L.M. Faithfull, *In The House of My Pilgrimage*, London, Chatto & Windus, 1925, pp. 121-2.

107 *Report of Board of Education Consultative Committee on Practical Work in Secondary Schools*, pp. 330-3.

108 *Ibid*.

109 'Educationist', 'A University Degree for Housewives?' in *The Freewoman*, 23 November 1911, pp. 16-18; R. Robinson, 'King's College for Women', *The Freewoman*, 15 February 1912, pp. 255-6; 'Home Science', *The Freewoman*, 29 February 1912, pp. 294-6.

110 'Educationist', *op. cit.*

111 R. Robinson, 'King's College for Women', p. 256.

112 *Ibid*.

113 H. Sillitoe, *A History of The Teaching of Domestic Subjects*, London, Methuen, 1933, p. 230.

114 Report of the Central Advisory Council for Education, (Newsom Report) *Half Our Future*, London, HMSO, 1963, pp. 135-7.

115 J. Newsom, *The Education of Girls, op. cit.*

116 C.S. Bremner, *The Education of Girls and Women in Great Britain*, London, Swann Sonnenschein, 1897, pp. 47-8.

117 Board of Education, *Report of Consultative Committee on Attendance, Compulsory or otherwise, at Continuation Schools*, 1909, vol. 2, Summaries and Evidence, pp. 593-5.

118 *Ibid.*, p. 594.

119 R. West, 'Women As Brainworkers', in M. Phillips (ed.), *Women and The Labour Party*, London, Headley, 1918, pp. 61-2.

120 C. Collet, *Memorandum on the Education of Working-Class Girls* presented as evidence to Bryce Commission on Secondary Education (P.P. 1895, XLVII, pp. 380-5).

121 *Ibid*.

122 M. McMillan, *The Life of Rachel McMillan*, London, Dent, 1927, pp. 38-41.

123 Delamont, 'The Domestic Ideology and Women's Education', in Delamont and Duffin (eds), *op. cit.*

124 Dr Verrall, speech on the question of the admission of women to degrees, printed in *Cambridge University Reporter*, 26 March 1897, pp. 786-7, quoted by B. Stephen in *Emily Davies and Girton College*, London, Constable, 1927, pp. 339-40.

125 L. Faithfull, *op. cit.*, p. 61.

126 A. Huth Jackson, *A Victorian Childhood*, London, Methuen, 1932, pp. 160-1.
127 *Ibid.*, pp. 150-1.
128 V. Brittain, *op. cit.*, pp. 38-9.
129 Reproduced in M.C. Bradbrook, *That Infidel Place*, London, Chatto & Windus, 1969.
130 J. Kamm, *Hope Deferred: Girls' Education in English History*, London, Methuen, 1965, p. 261n.
131 D. Russell, *The Tamarisk Tree: My Quest for Liberty and Love*, London, Virago, 1977, p. 23.
132 *Ibid.*, p. 25.

Index

110-11, 112-13, 138
Balfour, Lady Blanche, 28
Balfour, Eleanor M. (Nora) (Mrs
  Henry Sidgwick), 15, 20, 34,
  46, 70, 157-9
Barnard, Amy B., 25, 132
Bartley, G.C.T., 102
Beale, Dorothea, 11, 15, 45, 56,
  58, 61, 67, 72, 74-5, 76, 186
Beaver, M.W., 100
Bebel, F.A., 145
Bedford (Ladies') College,
  London, 33, 56, 61-3, 66
Bedford College Magazine, 61
Bell, Vanessa, 38
Benenden School, 56
Benson, Dr E.W. 64
Bible, 21, 26, 73; *see also* curricu-
  lum (religion)
Birmingham, 5, 56, 97
birth rates, 91, 95, 154
Bishop Otter College, Chichester,
  69
Black, Clementina, 147, 149-50
Blackheath High School, 164
Blakesley, Canon J.W. 64
Blanchard, Phyllis, 130-2
Bloom, Ursula, 22, 24, 27
'Bluestockings', 151-2, 163
Board of Education, 1, 88, 89, 93,
  94, 95, 98, 109, 132-5, 163,
  164, 165-6, 170
Board of Trade, 171
Bodichon, Barbara (née Leigh-
  Smith), 144, 156
Boer War, 91-2
Booth, Charles, 103
botany, *see* curriculum
Boucherett, Jessie, 144
Boy Scouts, 110-11, 120, 138
boys: attitudes to authority, 12,
  119-20; education and schools
  of, 14, 15, 16, 40; employment
  of, 9, 18; entry into a 'man's
  world', 7, 58, 117-18; leisure-
  time of, 10, 11, 12, 106; and
  'manly' virtues, 110, 120, 124,
  127; relations with sisters, 2,

12, 13-14, 54; work of, around
  the house, 10, 11, 102, 170;
  see also adolescence; curriculum; division of labour, sexual;
  education; family; 'masculinity'; mothers; schools; youth
  culture
Boys' Club Movement, 106,
  119-20; *see also* Boy Scouts
Brabazon, Lord (Earl of Meath),
  82
Brabrook, Sir Edward, 129
Braun, Lily, 146
breastfeeding, 96, 100, 154
Bremner, Christina S., 84, 170
Briggs, Emily, 90
British Association for the
  Advancement of Science, 165
British Gynaecological Society,
  154
Brittain, Edward, 15, 42
Brittain, Vera: conflict with
  parents, 32, 33; and marriage,
  159-60; and married women's
  work, 150; schooling, 42, 46,
  54, 174; at Uppingham School,
  15; and Winifred Holtby, 37;
  and Woman's Movement, 174
Brontë, Charlotte, 37
brothers, *see* boys
Browne, Sir James Crichton, 129,
  130
Bryant, Sophie, 45
Bryce, James, 41-4, 46, 47, 51,
  53; *see also* Bryce Commission
  (1894-5); Schools' Inquiry
  Commission (1867-8)
Bryce Commission (1894-5), 50,
  171
Bryn Mawr College (USA), 121
Burgon, J.W., 121
Burn, Alice, 136
Burstall, Sara, 135, 142, 162-3,
  164, 167
Burt, Cyril, 133, 161
Buss, Frances Mary, 15, 33, 45,
  56, 58, 70-1, 72, 144-5, 156
Butler, Rev. Canon H. Douglas, 64

STUDIES IN SOCIAL HISTORY

Editor: HAROLD PERKIN
Professor of Social History, University of Lancaster

Assistant Editor: ERIC J. EVANS
Lecturer in History, University of Lancaster